Preface

My interest in the subject of this book is rooted in long theoretical and practical involvement with the problems of the operation of a socialist economy. In the course of this work and as a result of various discussions, I have come to feel that there is an urgent need for reviewing these problems generally. Because the general difficulties in this field have been poorly formulated, basic misunderstandings have emerged and been fostered, and thus proper solutions to both specific and general problems of operating a socialist economy have been hampered.

This book attempts to present the problems of operating such an economy in a broad framework. It is intentionally general and not devoted to a theory of prices, the construction of a system of incentives, individual institutional factors, or to many other problems which it touches in passing. It deals with general principles and under a simplified assumption that there is only one form of ownership of the means of production (non-labour inputs)—state ownership. So defined, the subject itself establishes the role of particular problems within the work as a whole and the way in which they are treated. The relatively prominent position accorded to the operation of the law of value is explained by the author's conviction that it is in this sphere that the theoretical misunderstandings are greatest and most important.

Obviously, it is not for me to judge either the validity of my organizational framework or the conclusions which I reach. But I ease my conscience in the knowledge that I have obeyed the maxim that a writer should reach for his pen only when he is certain that he is unable not to. If for no other reason, I was unable not to write this book because of the need to specify and sometimes correct a great number of my own theoretical opinions voiced in earlier publications. In the more important instances I allude to this in the text; in less important cases no mention is made.

I am grateful to Zofia Morecka and Kazimierz Laski for their criticisms of a large section of the book.

1 The model of the functioning of a socialist economy and socialist production relations

Because of the unique situation in Poland, problems of the functioning of a socialist economy have become matters of common interest and attracted universal attention. The upshot of this has been to create advantages and disadvantages whose net results were hard to judge. As is often the case, a spontaneous wave of public interest was accompanied by a flood of misunderstanding and oversimplification which in turn hindered dispassionate consideration of the problem. Furthermore, the entire situation was aggravated by an overreadiness to interpret it politically both at home and abroad.

The possibility of such complications makes it unusually necessary to introduce and describe the level at which our considerations are to take place.

Definition of the concept 'model of the functioning of a socialist economy'

The concept 'model' in economic theory is defined by Jan Drewnowski in the *Short Economic Dictionary* as:[1]

> In the science of political economy, 'model' means a mental construction which, in a simplified form, represents the operation or the growth of a national economy or a part of it . . .
>
> In constructing a model it is necessary to omit less important elements of the economy in order to set off basic elements more clearly. According to the 'level of abstraction' . . . it will reflect the reality to a greater or lesser degree.

How does this concept relate to the well-known expression, 'the Polish economic model'?

According to the author just cited—there is no relation.

But the writer adds that the economic model of a country can also mean 'the basic principles of the organization of a nation's economy within a given economic system'. Drewnowski formulates two meanings in order to focus attention on the model 'whose contents

[1] J. Drewnowski, *Mały Słownik Ekonomiczny* (*A Short Economic Dictionary*), Warsaw, 1958, pp. 406-7.

are numerically quantifiable' for purposes of proving their assertions.

This separation of the concept of 'economic model' from that of the 'model' of economic theory hardly seems justified. Likewise making the possibility of accountification the criterion of differentiation is not convincing.

In the conventional sense, of course, abstractions may be applied to numerical problems but no less so to the varied field of structural questions and the problems of politico-economic organization. This is so unless we assume that every economic issue can be expressed in the formalized shape of functional relations, because structural and organizational questions are generally qualitative rather than quantitative.

Disallowing this assumption gives scope to Oscar Lange's definition,[1] he defines the model so that the definition is not so limited, it is qualitative as well as quantitative.

Economic theories specify the conditions in which abstract laws are true and connected in a definitive way. The conditions specified in an economic construct are called its *assumptions* and a set of such assumptions has recently come to be called a *theoretical economic model*. Thus we refer to a model of freely competitive capitalism. Alternatively we speak of a model of the process of reproduction (generally—growth) in which, let us say, all the means of production (roughly—non-labour inputs in western terminology) are used up in the same period of time or of a model of the accumulation (roughly—saving which in society where it is forced, is invested by the organ which extracts it).

In this sense, using the term 'model' to mean a picture of the functioning of an economic mechanism seems to be justified, provided that it gives an abstract picture of the main principles of the functioning of an economy, free from complicating details. 'Economic model' must not be confused with a concrete system of the functioning of an economy.[2]

The model and the socialist system

At a later point we will deal with the criteria for differentiating various models of the functioning of a socialist economy. For the

[1] O. Lange, *Political Economy*, vol. 1 (Warsaw, 1963), p. 106.

[2] Thus it is difficult to agree with Czesław Bobrowski's definition, according to which the model is 'a set of methods for the organization of management, planning or economic policy applied in a particular country at a particular time'. ('Models of the socialist economy' in *Zagadnienia ekonomii politycznej* (*Problems of the Political Economy of Socialism*), Warsaw, 1960, p. 238).

moment, however, let us consider the relationship of the concept 'economic model' to the concept 'socio-economic system'.

The phrase 'socialist economic models' makes quite clear that we are not concerned with various *kinds* of socio-economic systems but with *variants* of the principles of the functioning of a socialist type of economy. In the past it has not been possible to differentiate between the type of production relations and the type of mechanism of the functioning of the economy. Those were the times when the principles developed in the Soviet Union and in the People's Democracies were considered the only possible ones for a socialist economic model. As the possibility and the usefulness of various solutions were realized, and especially after their adoption in all socialist countries, the need for such a differentiation became obvious. This problem, then, is of great significance to the development of Marxist economic theory.

Strictly speaking, *every* form of the economic organization of society should be included in the production relations (social relations among those engaged in economic activity). However, in order to differentiate socio-economic systems we need not analyse all of the extremely complicated forms in which production relations are manifested. According to Stalin's definition, with which I generally concur, there are three criteria for differentiating basic production relations:[1] a, the forms of ownership of the means of production; b, the status of various social groups in production deriving from a; and c, the principles of distribution of products determined by a. An economy is, thus, socialist in character if the basic means of production are owned socially and not privately. It is socialist if the relations between people in the economic process are based on co-operation in the use of society's means of production and not on the exploitation of direct producers. It is socialist if the share of units or groups in the income produced is determined by labour input or by general social criteria and not by private control of production.

It is obvious that the nature of production relations *themselves* determines certain basic elements in the mechanism of the functioning of an economy. Thus, a socialist economy is one in which direct economic activity is public and in which the general control of the means of production is vested in the state authorities.[2] To achieve this it must have a planning-cum-management centre making, at least, the chief economic decisions and co-ordinating economic life as a whole. However, there is nothing to prevent the application of different types of economic mechanisms on the basis of a given type of production relations, in this case on the basis of socialist produc-

[1] J. Stalin, *Economic Problems of Socialism in the USSR* (Moscow, 1952), p. 81.

[2] J. Schumpeter, *Capitalism, Socialism, and Democracy* (London, 1957), p. 167.

tion relations. There may be differences in organization of the social ownership of the means of production, fields for centralized and decentralized decisions, forms and degrees of participation by employees in management of enterprises and forms of incentives. Moreover, in the framework of socialist production relations, experience shows that the application of different kinds of model is not only possible but necessary. A new social system, so radically different from previous ones does not and cannot find ready-made adequate forms of economic organization. Freedom to choose forms which will ensure the optimum use of material means in given conditions is one of the most important factors in the march of socialism. At the same time, such freedom best stimulates social activity and educates people in the new principles of mutual interrelations; thereby revealing one of the most important manifestations of the fact that by destroying capitalism, humanity wins the opportunity consciously to shape its own history.

I do not intend to undermine the premises of the socialist system by framing the question of the economic model in this way. What was meant was to break away from the narrow conception of the socialist form of economic management which has long been so all-encompassing. This means breaking away from the inconsistent or, at least, insufficiently consistent application of the dialectic to the section of historical development which begins after the victory of the socialist revolution.

The problems of the model in the light of the economic contradictions of socialism

Scientific socialism was based on an analysis of the contradictions of capitalism. The main Marxist conclusion, corroborated by history, is that capitalism contains many contradictions and creates barriers to the development of productive forces. These contradictions can be disposed of only by revolutionary replacement of capitalist by socialist production relations. For understandable reasons, for some time it was not possible to complain that Marxist economics yielded no solutions to the problems of economic development under socialism. Unrestrained discussions among socialists about the details of the functioning of the future socialist system sometimes resulted in Utopian reveries. These predictions strike the reader today as being naïve not only in comparison with present criteria but in relation to those of their own day. However, particularly with reference to the essence of dispute—the direction in which history is moving—it was the naïve socialist and not the sober bourgeois scholars who were right.

Though it can be explained by a special combination of socio-political circumstances, it is difficult to justify latter attempts to discard the dialectic when Marxist social science, and especially political economy, were faced with the problem of discovering the 'laws of motion' of a socialist society. For some time almost the only kind of contradiction acknowledged by official teaching was that between the socialist economic base and the remnants of the old capitalist system. These contradictions were manifested in the transitional vestiges of private ownership of capital and the 'remnants of capitalism in people's consciousness'. Socialist production relations themselves were presented as basically free of conflict and described as the infallible motive force driving the development of productive forces. From the end of the 1920s until Stalin's unexpected pronouncement in *Economic Problems of Socialism in the USSR* the conception of 'the complete conformity of socialist production relations with the productive forces' prevailed universally. Paradoxically it was Stalin himself who, having brought to perfection the system of refusing to see the conflicts which appeared in reality, disturbed the blissful calm of the theory of 'complete conformity'.[1] This was a real step forward, especially in view of the political changes which shortly followed. By definition socialist relations of production ceased, once and for all, to fulfil the needs of the productive forces. It was possible for them to 'age' and transform themselves from a motive force into a brake on development. Political economy now had the opportunity to analyse the real conflicts; after twenty years it was faced with problems of the model. (Stalin did not, however, point in the right direction for solutions but, on the contrary, in the opposite direction.)

What then is the real meaning of the thesis that socialist production relations may, to some degree, cease to meet the needs of the development of productive forces? It does not mean that in every case the basic elements of these relations would have to be transformed. It is mainly a problem of the secondary elements; those which, if not decisive in the determination of the nature of a system, are connected with one aspect or another of the organization of economic processes in this system. Therefore, it is not strange that in this period, through the veneer of dogmatic formulae, discussions about the mechanism of the functioning of an economy began to make their appearance.

---

[1] 'The words "complete conformity" must not be understood in the absolute sense. They must not be understood as meaning that there is no lagging of the relations of production behind the growth of the productive forces under socialism. The productive forces are the most mobile and revolutionary forces of production. They undeniably move in advance of the relations of production even under socialism. Only after a certain lapse of time do the relations of production change into line with the character of the productive forces' (J. Stalin, *op. cit.*, p. 57).

Their focal point was the problem of commodity production and the operation of the law of value.

But the concept found in *Economic Problems of Socialism in the USSR* was limited in at least two basic points which even later were never given a sufficiently thorough examination. The first is the question of the social conditions necessary for the resolution of conflicts; and the second is the question of the degree to which the dynamics of socialism is relative to each given period and not just a result of their 'ageing'.

The limited applicability of the first point is seen in the well-known thesis that a socialist system can avoid conflict or contradiction between the productive forces and the production relations. The thesis holds that without social classes, which would oppose necessary changes in defence of their own interests, no contradictions can exist—even though certain conservative groups may, through *inertia*, offer resistance to progress. Although fundamentally different from conditions operating under capitalism, the period immediately after 1953 proves that, none the less, serious upheavals are by no means out of the question in the socialist socio-political and economic organization. One of the most important problems in the study of the mechanism by which contradictions in the socialist system are resolved is that of the mergence of specific 'groups or interests'. These may emerge on the basis of a very close connection, almost a symbiosis, of the political authorities with both the management of the economy and with the ineluctable establishment of a hierarchical apparatus. This question is the subject of study of a number of the other social sciences as well and can only be touched upon lightly here.

On the other hand, there is a second problem directly connected with our subject. Again, *prima facie* it may seem to be merely a question of redistributing the stress, but the problem has basic significance. Though it is undoubtedly fair to say that the transformation from capitalist into socialist production relations changes these relations from a brake into the chief motive force, this thesis cannot be accepted as an absolute. Furthermore, it is not enough to treat the thesis so that with the passage of time, the actual forms in which the socialist relations of production are manifested must be transformed as they become inadequate for the needs of the development of productive forces. The point at issue is that socialist production relations contain not only positive elements but at every stage also contain certain elements negatively affecting the productive forces. Thus, in this as in every other connection, there are no absolute solutions which are perfect in all respects. The solutions of one set of conflicts—capitalist, gives rise to other sets—socialist. It is true that the latter are no greater than those which have been already resolved, but they are sufficiently important to merit closer examinations especially since the new contradictions often become involved with what we call the 'remnants of the old system'.

Some examples of the emergence of new problems with the removal of older ones are appended here.

A chief feature of the socialist economy is its planned distribution of labour on a social scale; an incalculably valuable factor in eliminating the competition between enterprises and branches of production which is typical of capitalism. At the same time, however, the elimination of competition gives rise to adverse conditions in the structure of incentives to improve production and all kinds of innovation—especially in matters of quality.

Another feature is the ability, especially of small countries, to specialize production in line with the dictates of rationality and to concentrate the production of one good in one or, at the most, a few enterprises. Along with the positive economic effects, however, arises the danger of the creation of a monopoly. Although its significance is altogether different from the similar situation under capitalism, it is by no means without importance to consumers.

The superiority of the socialist economic system over capitalism expresses itself, among other things, in its ability to make full use of productive capacity. This again is an undoubtedly positive phenomenon in which the thesis that socialism is not only a more just but also an economically more efficient system finds confirmation. This positive phenomenon of justice and economic efficiency may result in too little flexibility in the adaptation of the structure of supply to the structure of demand. The problem can be taken one step further by connecting the continual increase of purchasing power of the population with a growth of the ability to underwrite the increased flow of money with an increased supply of goods and services. It is untrue to call the reining in of supply in the face of demand an economic law of socialism; this is simply an upsetting of general market equilibrium. However, it is fair to say that socialism does away with the structural causes of the overproduction of goods and services, making possible the adjustment of the level of incomes to the actual ability to satisfy needs. Yet such a situation impedes the creation and maintenance of a 'consumers' market' and may give rise to the much proclaimed producer's 'terrorization' of the consumer. Furthermore general market equilibrium by relatively close 'buttoning up' of both sides of the balance-supply of goods and purchasing power—which is characteristic of socialism—quite often creates danger of partial equilibria in the markets for particular goods which in turn has an adverse effect on the general situation.

Regarding the personal factor in the productive process, though radically changed by socialism, it is not free from contradictory effects. Full utilization of productive capacity applies not only to material factors of production but also to labour by the elimination of structural unemployment. The value of this achievement cannot be underrated. But, even this has deleterious effects on work discipline, with an increase in the instability of the labour force, etc. While we must be on guard against the exaggerated reaction that some small percentage of employment is necessary, nevertheless the problem does exist and it is no great comfort to say that it is the result of an inadequate consciousness of the masses.

There is also the question of the distribution of income which is also connected with the attitude of the individual in the production process. Socialization of the means of production undoubtedly increases egalitarian tendencies in the distribution of that part of national income destined for consumption. Such tendencies which conform to a particular set of objective conditions and even more to the subjective ideas about socialism, nevertheless conflict with the need for incentives to be founded on the principle of payment according to productivity.

Another group of problems is caused by such negative aspects of the socialization of the means of production as bureaucracy and what we enigmatically describe as 'an unsocialist attitude to society's property'. Likewise problems arise in connection with weighing centralized management against the maximum development of the initiative of all the economic branches and the active participation of the masses in management.[1]

Trends towards centralization in the control of economic processes derive from the development of the productive forces themselves. The progressive socialization of production which finds expression both in the concentration of manufacturing in larger and larger factories and in the development of the social distribution of labour, and hence in the establishment of a complex network of economic interrelations—local, national and international—demands an ever-increasing degree of unity of direction, the co-ordination of different centres and the application of extensive criteria of rationality. Two symptoms of this process, the concentration of production into larger and larger units and the evolution of the distribution of society's labour (process of reallocation of labour according to structural changes in the

---

[1] There is a very interesting discussion of this problem by an eminent Soviet economist of the old generation, V. Novozhilov, in an article entitled 'Voprosy demokraticheskogo centralizma v upravlenii sotsialisticheskim khozyaistvom', *Trudy Leningradskogo Inzhenernoekonomicheskogo Instittuta Kafedry Obshchestvennykh Nauk*, Vypusk 24 (Leningrad, 1959).

economy), manifest themselves in capitalism through concentration of capital, through cartelization, and through increasing state intervention and attempts at international integration. Capitalist production relations (again--social relations among those engaged in economic activity) in spite of their evolution do not satisfy the needs for a centralized planned management requisite to the modern development of productive forces (technological advances). Here is one of the places where the retarding effects of capitalist relations of production on the development of productive forces can be seen.

Socialism shows itself in agreement with the laws of development in that it provides everything necessary to satisfy the needs of a centralized, planned management of the economy. Thereby it is able to tap the gushing sources of economic progress.

At the same time there can be no doubt as to the part played in development by initiative, enterprise and the active attitude of those of all levels who participate in productive activity. By eliminating exploitation and shaping new social relations, socialism makes it possible also in this to remove difficulties in the path of the development of productive forces. We are convinced of this and realize that a failure to utilize it means the waste of a mighty force for progress. It is emphatically true that the creation of the conditions for realizing this potential force are as indispensable to the development of productive forces as centralization.

By treating the socialist system as an expression of the laws of socio-economic development, we mean it to fulfil both requirements: a centralized planned economic management and the blossoming of the creative activity of the masses. Based on objective assumptions either of these two expectations is completely justified; yet there is a basic contradiction in that both of these requirements spring from the same root and must be satisfied jointly. At a deeper level, mere execution of economic tasks to promote active participation in production requires a system of management based on a thorough-going economic democracy. This democracy should guarantee each economic branch a wide area of independence in its own sphere of operations and also a real influence on general matters. Centralization, on the other hand, means something else; the concentration of decision-making at the centre to the detriment of the lower levels.

The reason for our long exegesis on the problems of centralization versus democracy in the management of the economy is that they are connected with the basic subject of this book. Furthermore, they present a particularly good picture of the problems of contradictions within the socialist system. Far from making a balance sheet of the virtues and failings of the socialist economic system, these examples were meant to illustrate that the resolution of the contradictions of

B

capitalism does not mean the elimination of contradictions in general. Moreover, the contradictions met in the socialist system are not caused by external factors only, but arise, at least partially, from the socialist relations of production.

It would be difficult to treat the contradictions referred to above as belonging to any basic category specific to the system itself and threatening the very nature of the production relations with inevitable alterations. These are rather the side products of a system which in the present epoch is basically a progressive one. They should not, however, threaten serious upheavals or, at any rate, slow down the rate of the development normally associated with socialism.

To propound the method for resolving the economic contradictions of socialism is not to forecast their complete and irrevocable elimination. The problem is rather of capitalizing on the positive aspects of socialist production relations and reducing to the minimum their negative aspects. This is accomplished by exploiting to the full the motive progressive forces innate in the socialist system. One aspect of the fulfilment of this task is the application of the proper principles of the functioning of a socialist economy.

It is no accident but a phenomenon to be expected that solutions to the problems of models have had overwhelming success. The analysis of models of the functioning of the economy (models being only the more concrete manifestations of basic production relations) is one of political economy's most important tasks. This analysis must not be seen as a once for all attempt to eradicate the overgrowth of centralization but as a continual problem of comparing the accepted principles of the functioning of an economy with the requirements of its development. Thus, it is a problem of the continual construction of new solutions to the model. At the present time interest is focused on these problems because it is realized that there is a connection between the principles of the functioning of an economy and the rate of growth.

The rate of growth depends, generally, on two factors: 1. on the magnitude of the means which an economy is able to devote to extended reproduction; and 2. the efficiency with which these means and the whole of the productive resources are employed. Certainly a planned socialist economy is able to guarantee the means necessary for the realization of the first factor. However, the efficiency of investment and the efficiency with which existing productive resources are employed has not reached a satisfactory level even when certain unfavourable circumstances for growth are taken into account. Obviously, there are many elements involved here; among them some which can rightly be termed subjective. But subjective elements do not account for everything and they are themselves to some extent a result of the institutional conditions of the functioning of the economy. The attempt to optimize these conditions, which is the chief point in the endeavour to change the model, is thus by no means the expression of some new dogmatism. Instead it is a reflection of the pressing necessity of economic advance in socialism.

2   A survey of the history of the problem

It seems necessary to make a brief survey of the treatment of the principles of the functioning of a socialist economy, not only to avoid the rediscovery of old truths but also because an objective recapitulation of the achievements of the last decade is a basic factor in the elimination of Marxist economic science from the solecism of dogmatism.

For a number of years the application of the history of Marxist economic thought to actual political needs was either through a peculiar interpretation of the Marxists' writings or by simply removing names and works which were regarded as politically compromising from the history of science, the bookshelves and the card catalogues. As a result, Marxist political economy, especially the political economy of socialism, was rather like the hero of Chamisso's classic Peter Schlemihl—a man without a shadow. If we discount the small number of official pronouncements and documents (which even then were generally interpreted in isolation from the actual circumstances in which they arose) it was a science without a history.

Similarly Marxists frequently ignored non-Marxist or unofficial Marxist writings devoted to the problems of the functioning of a socialist economy. This constituted yet another factor in the impoverishment of our own scientific achievements in the field.

Thus there is sufficient reason to justify devoting some space to an excursion into the past. However it will be nothing more than a foray and not an attempt to present a systematic history of the problem. (The latter task is currently being attempted by several young Polish economists.) From the vantage point of the problems being discussed at the present time I shall be concerned with some aspects of the work of three groups of writers, who have from time to time pronounced on the subject of the principles of the functioning of a socialist economy. The first group is Marx and his followers, up to the period immediately after the October Revolution; the second comprises those who took part in the discussion on economic calculation in socialism during the interwar period, and the third comprises

Soviet economists who made commentaries during the 1920s.[1]

Marx and the Marxists in the pre-revolutionary period (including the later works of Lenin)

One of the chief differences between the Marxists and the Utopian socialists is the former's extreme caution in describing the future socialist society. This fact derived from a feature which marked the vision of the creators of the modern socialist idea—an approach which was both scientific and revolutionary. Scholars, and at the same time revolutionaries, they devoted their whole attention to an analysis of the laws of capitalist development. They sought thereby to be armed with a correct understanding of historical processes, through which old orders were replaced by new ones. The construction of castles in the air was not only at odds with science but also with the tasks of revolutionaries. As August Blanque wrote: 'Are we in possession of the plans and materials, do we have all the elements necessary for this precious construction (socialism)? The sectarians say "yes". The revolutionaries say "no", since they know much better the nature of the future which belongs to socialism.'[2]

This is not to imply that there was nothing of interest in pictures of the future society painted by the Utopian socialist; special significance exists for socialism in countries that were backward in economic development. Nor were Marx and the Marxists free from the influences of these Utopian ideas in the period before the Revolution. However, they did realize that they lacked a sufficient basis for scientifically demonstrating actual forms in the future socialist economy. Furthermore they were aware of the inherent dangers of scholasticism for practical revolutionary activity. For these reasons they not only restrained themselves from such discussions but also tried to discourage others.[3]

[1] It is something of a problem to establish the order in which the various views dealing with the principles of a socialist economy should be discussed. The order which I have adopted is not perfect. I have, for example, separated party programme documents and the works of Lenin written in the period immediately after the October Revolution from the views put forward by Soviet economists in the 1920s. Nevertheless my solution does have its own logic. We start with hypotheses about the future socialist economy (the works of Lenin open a new stage, but they are closely connected with the writings of the previous period) and go on through theoretical discussions largely detached from actual practice to attempts directed towards a generalization of the actual operation of a socialist economy.

[2] *Critique Sociale*, vol. 2, p. 194, cited by E. Preobrazhenski in his 'Sotsyalisticheskiye i kommunisticheskiye predstavleniya o sotsializmie', *Vestnik Kommunisticheskoi Akademii*, no. 12, 1925.

[3] See, for example, the ironic remarks about Wilhelm Liebknecht in the correspondence of Marx and Engels in 1876.

If I call attention again to these well-known points it is because one can still encounter attempts to discover in Marx answers to specific problems on the functioning of a socialist economy. Concomitantly such attempts carry various efforts to condemn various opinions because of their supposed lack of agreement with Marx.

It is true that there are a few statements by Marx and Engels on the principles of the functioning of the future socialist economy; they are of very general character and are little more than leading ideas which arose in two contexts:

1. In connection with the analysis of the capitalistic pattern of development, most frequently in order to emphasize the transitory nature of the capitalist mode of production. A number of such remarks in *Capital* were meant to fulfil the same function that is served by the anatomy of man when considered as a key to the anatomy of the ape.

2. As a result of the practical needs of the ideological struggle, especially when it was necessary to oppose false theses in political programmes. Among other things this is the source of the comments on socialism in *Critique of the Gotha Programme* and in the third part of *Anti-Dühring*.

The question of the programme to be followed by the future socialist government immediately after the Revolution must be handled separately.

Lenin, like Marx, avoided the building of a Utopian vision, although problems of the transitional period from capitalism to socialism are discussed by him in greater detail, especially in the period shortly before the Revolution.

The paucity of systematized and developed analysis of the functioning of a socialist economy does not necessarily mean that no conclusions can be divined from the work of Marx and Engels. Such conclusions, or—perhaps better—suggestions, are undoubtedly there, though they are not always explicit.

Most of the material concerned with the functioning of a socialist economy is found in conjunction with criticism by Marx (and Engels) of the role of the law of value as a regulator of capitalist production.[1]

Marx begins by demonstrating the spontaneous and, from the macro-economic point of view, expensive process whereby the distribution of society's labour (satisfaction of the various sectoral and industry-wide labour markets) is achieved by the law of value. In so doing, and while showing how, spontaneously acting and wasteful from the global point of view, the law brings individual inputs per unit of output into socially necessary dimensions, he contrasts this form of regulation *ex post* with the conscious regulation *ex ante* in an

[1] For interpretation of the law of value, see chapter 4.

economy based on the social ownership of the means of production.

In this connection, Marx stresses the similarity between a conscious regulation of the division of labour on the social (macro-) scale and the regulation of the division of labour within an enterprise.[1]

The *a priori* system on which the division of labour, within the workshop, is regularly carried out, becomes in the division of labour within the society, an *a posteriori*, nature-imposed necessity, controlling the lawless caprice of the producers, and perceptible in the barometrical fluctuations of the market prices. Division of labour within the workshop implies the undisputed authority of the capitalist over men, who are but parts of a mechanism that belongs to him. The division of labour within the society brings into contact independent commodity producers, who acknowledge no other authority but that of competition, of the coercion exerted by the pressure of their mutual interests; just as in the animal kingdom, the *bellum omnium contra omnes* more or less preserves the conditions of the existence of every species. The same bourgeois mind which praises division of labour in the workshop . . . denounces with equal vigour every conscious attempt to control socially and regulates the process of production . . . It is very characteristic that the enthusiastic apologists of the factory system have nothing more damning to urge against a general organization of the labour society into one immense factory.

Marx does not find the latter prospect at all disturbing. On the contrary, the very nature of the division of labour, consciously directed from a central point of control and not by means of market mechanism of signals and incentives is basic to Marx. This is a basic feature of 'a community of free individuals, carrying on their work, with the means of production in common, in which the labour power of all the different individuals is consciously applied as the combined labour power of the community.'[2]

This applies equally to the division of the whole of society's labour between the output of consumer goods and the means of production and also to the division among different areas within each of these groups.

It is here, in my opinion, that the *first*, and very essential suggestion for the organization of a planned socialist economy is to be found in the Marxist analysis of capitalism. All the other ones are, in fact, contained in it.

Marx's *second* very essential suggestion for organizing a planned socialist economy is closely connected with the first. From the

[1] K. Marx, *Capital* (Moscow, 1954), vol. 1, p. 356.
[2] *Capital*, vol. 2, p. 78.

beginning, a society which divides labour in a direct way among various uses must also define in advance the amount of that labour necessary per unit of output (labour input coefficient).[1]

From the moment when society enters into possession of the means of production and uses them in direct association for production, the labour of each individual, however varied its specifically useful character may be, becomes at the start and directly social labour. The quantity of social labour contained in a product need not then be established in a roundabout way; daily experience shows in a direct way how much of it is required on the average. Society can simply calculate how many hours of labour are contained in a steam engine, a bushel of wheat of the last harvest, or a hundred square yards of cloth of a certain quality. It could, therefore, never occur to it to express the quantities of labour put into the products, quantities which it will then know directly and in their absolute amounts . . . in a measure which . . . is . . . relative . . . rather than in their natural, adequate and absolute measure, time . . . Hence, on the assumptions we made above, society will not assign values to products. It will not express the simple fact that the hundred square yards of cloth have required for their production, say, a thousand hours of labour in the oblique and meaningless way, stating that they have the value of a thousand hours of labour . . . People will be able to manage everything very simply without the intervention of much vaunted 'value'.

Consequently, the direct division of labour and the direct determination of the necessary input per unit of output requires in a socialist society calculation in physical terms.[2] The conversion of economic calculation to physical terms presupposes a new role to be played by use-value in an economy where the main concern is to satisfy social needs.[3] Apart from these factors the importance of calculation in physical units has its roots in the macro-economic nature of the problem facing a socialist economy. This difficulty

[1] F. Engels, *Anti-Dühring* (Moscow, 1954), pp. 429–30.

[2] It is difficult to answer definitely how Marx and Engels imagined the calculation of inputs and results in physical units. One must suppose that what they had in mind was the expression of outlays in units of labour time while results were expressed in the physical units most suitable for the individual products (of volume, weight, energy, etc.).

[3] Edward Lipiński noted this point as early as 1948 in 'Wartość użytkowa w ekonomii socjalizmu' ('Use-value in the economy of socialism') *Ekonomista*, no. 4, 1948. There are some interesting comments on the subject of use-value in Marx's theory contained in an article by Roman Rozdolski, 'Der Gebrauchswert bei Karl Marx', *Kyklos*, 1959, vol. 12, part 1. The author is a Marxist of Polish descent.

which Marx never explicitly linked with the socialist economy, derives from the mode in which he conceives the reproduction of 'the whole of society's capital'. Whenever the question of reproduction on the macro-scale arises, it is insufficient merely to consider its proportions from the point of view of value; it is absolutely necessary to consider its proportions in physical terms, too. Marx clarifies the question and makes his famous division of society's product into two departments (means of production and means of consumption):[1]

> So long as we looked upon the production of value and the value of the product of capital individually, the bodily form of the commodities produced was wholly immaterial for the analysis, whether it was machines, for instance, corn or looking glasses . . . So far as the reproduction of capital was concerned, it was sufficient to assume that the portion of the product in commodities which represents capital value finds an opportunity in the sphere of circulation to reconvert itself into its elements of production and thus into its form of productive capital; just as it sufficed to assume that both the labourer and the capitalist find in the market those commodities on which they spend their wages and the surplus value (that part of the total product which remains after payments to labour variable inputs and capital replacement). This purely formal manner of presentation is no longer adequate in the study of the total social capital and of the value of its products. The reconversion of one portion of the value of the product into capital and the passing of another portion into the individual consumption of the capitalist as well as the working class form a movement within the value of the produce itself in which the result of the aggregate capital finds expression, and this movement is not only a replacement of value, but also a replacement in material and is therefore as much bound up with the relative proportions of the value components of the total social product as with their use-value, their material shape.

The notion treated here on the role of physically expressed proportions in the macro-growth process is gaining ever more attention in the bourgeois theory of growth. Economists who handle the problem of growth realistically and are genuinely concerned with finding a solution are no longer satisfied with aggregate analyses. More and more they study key proportions in physical terms and search for ways of overcoming the problem of bottle-necks. The socialist economy which develops by the full (or nearly so) utilization of productive capacity and available labour force makes this question its

[1] *Capital*, vol. 2, p. 394.

special concern. Planning and physical calculation in these circumstances are indispensable; and as such constitute the *third* essential guide for the study of a socialist economy implied in the work of Marx and Engels.

The *fourth* problem is that of the allocation of the accumulated capital in a socialist system. It was Engels who elaborated this point in a criticism of Dühring. The latter had proposed a division of the whole of the social product (sum of the gross outputs of all the sectors) among the individual members of society. Among other things this would mean that the individual would be entrusted with dividing income between consumption and saving (accumulation).[1]

> The worker should receive the 'full proceeds of labour'; not only the labour product, but labour itself should be directly exchangeable for products; one hour's labour for the product of another hour's labour. This, however, gives rise at once to a serious hitch. The *whole product is distributed.* The most important progressive function of society, accumulation (saving), is taken from society and placed at the arbitrary discretion of individuals. The individuals can do what they like with their 'proceeds', but society, at best, remains as rich or as poor as it was. The means of production accumulated in the past have, therefore, been centralized in the hands of society only in order that all means of production accumulated in the future may once again be dispersed in the hands of individuals. One knocks to pieces one's own premises; one has arrived at a pure absurdity.

It follows unequivocally from this assertion that the main part of the accumulated capital should be gathered in the hands of society as a logical consequence of the socialization of the means of production.

Closely related to this point is the *fifth* essential element in which the views of Marx and Engels have meaning for the functioning of a socialist economy. This problem, the criteria for the division of national income among individuals, is initiated in the *Critique of the Gotha Programme* and further elaborated by Lenin in chapter 5 of *State and Revolution.* The principle of income distribution according to labour in the socialist stage of development is generally accepted by Marxists and does not need further explanation.

Instead let us attempt a summary of this point and some general conclusions. The socialist economy should have the following features:

1. direct, *ex ante*, regulation of the social distribution of labour;
2. direct determination of labour input coefficients, for both living

[1] F. Engels, *op. cit.*, pp. 432–3.

and embodied labour (a crystallization of labour time found in capital goods);

3. equilibrium of supply and demand in physical units;

4. the distribution of social product in accordance with the satisfaction of general needs, and at the same time the allocation of the fund intended for individual consumption according to the amount of labour contributed;

5. centralization of the saving and investment decisions.

Admittedly these five points do not present a full picture especially since they are not formulated directly but in contrast to capitalism. However, they do give a rough outline. To the creators of scientific socialism there was to be, in contrast to capitalism, a centrally planned economy, one in which the main elements of social reproduction were not subject to the uncontrolled operation of the law of value (Maurice Dobb calls this 'economic law'; *Soviet Economic Development since 1917*, New York, 1948, p. 325). All of Marx's writings on political economy emphasize his opposition to the capitalist situation in this regard, and, therefore, to look among them for a theory of the operation of the law of value in socialism is futile. Even when he uses the term 'value' with regard to a socialist society[1] he means neither value as the feature of a *commodity* nor the law of value as the law of *commodity production*. He refers to the direct calculation of social labour.

How, then, are we to assess the conclusions to be drawn from the work of Marx and Engels? If these few points are taken as general assumptions, as the broadest of outlines to the functioning of a socialist economy, then they are remarkable for their accuracy and are entirely borne out by practical experience and later theoretical elaboration. Understandably they do not exhaust the problem but only provide its skeleton. The discovery of the 'laws of motion' of the capitalist mode of production provided *a contrario* data for a rough sketch of a socialist economy: they could not and did not, however, make the construction of an advanced model possible.

In spite of this, both the rank-and-file socialists and intellectuals (including theoretical economists) came to believe that a direct system of physical-term distribution which controlled the factors of production and production itself would correspond most literally to the reality of the socialist economy.

Did this view correspond with the intentions of Marx and Engels? If we ignore their reluctance to scientifically describe the future socialist economy and draw conclusions from scattered incomplete statements, the answer would be 'yes'. At any rate in their work it is

[1] See e.g. *Capital*, vol. 3, pt. 2, p. 826; *Critique of the Gotha Programme* (*Marx and Engels Selected Works* (Moscow, 1950), vol. 2, p. 13).

comparatively easy to find corroborating formulations and hard to find contradictory statements—for instance, one's foreseeing the introductions of market forms. Moreover, from the point of view of the creation of ideology and its influence on practice, the ultimate important fact is what the socialist movement *understood* Marx to have said. And of this there is no doubt.

Everywhere, in scientific monographs, the socialist party programmes and brochures and propaganda articles, are found discussions of a production process in which all the elements, down to the smallest detail, are determined *ex ante*, by a central planning body. We can see there also an economy without exchange prices and money and of gigantic warehouses and stores distributing products on the basis of work coupons, etc.

Obviously, this situation was not merely the result of a certain interpretation of the view of Marx and Engels. A number of factors are involved: a. Utopian influence which was criticized primarily for its false concept of the way in which a transition to socialism would be made rather than for its view of the future society; b. the conviction that in every element socialism would be the opposite of capitalism (especially regarding the market mechanism which was treated not as a form able to absorb a new socio-economic content but simply as a feature of exploitation); c. an overvaluation of apparent tendencies toward concentration in capitalism (according to some Marxists, especially Hilferding, in *Das Finanzkapital*, this was supposed to lead rapidly to the concentration of the whole of production into a few trusts and of the whole credit system into a few giant banks). Lenin cautioned against such an interpretation of capitalism's monopoly stage ('imperialism and finance capitalism are a superstructure on old capitalism').[1] But at least, to the time when it was possible to draw conclusions from the first experience of the Revolution, he did not draw conclusions from it which were applicable to the functioning of a socialist economy.

Apart from the works of Wilhelm Liebknecht, mentioned in chapter 1, it must be conceded that even the most important pre-revolutionary attempt to outline the mechanism of the future socialist economy, Kautsky's *Die soziale Revolution*[2] (especially the second part), is lacking in realism. He is vaguely aware of the 'technical' difficulties in achieving a system of in-kind distribution, but he did not consider them of any great importance. The difficulties inherent in the management of production from a single centre could be removed by eliminating the numerous small-scale enterprises and

[1] V. I. Lenin, 'Speech on the Party Programme at the 8th Congress of the Russian Communist Party (b)', *Works* (in Polish), vol. 29, pp. 156, 506.
[2] K. Kautsky, *Die soziale Revolution* (Berlin, 1902).

concentrating production into a few larger ones. He also considered that income equalization would eliminate or minimize the difficulties arising from the varied structure of demand. Even in Kautsky's work the germs of differentiation between the law of value and the money–commodity forms in socialism can be clearly seen. For example, he allows money to be used as a technical means, while expressing the general belief that the ground for the operation of the law of value will disappear with the socialization of the means of production.[1]

The need to regulate production by the exchange of various values (barter) will cease to exist. At the same time the need for money to act as a measure of value and as a representation of the substance of value (*Wertgegenstand*) is also removed ... The prices of products can now be established independently of value although the labour time which is embodied in them still has a major significance in the determination of these prices ...

In his work, Kautsky indicated that the theses contained in it should not be taken axiomatically. He vigorously opposed all claims that only one system of the functioning of a socialist economy could be constructed. Special attention was paid to the mutual relationships of different forms of ownership and methods of democratizing economic management: 'Nothing could be more mistaken than to imagine the socialist society in the shape of a uniform, rigid mechanism, the wheels of which, once set in motion, continually revolve in the same unchanging fashion.'[2]

Some years later, in the face of imminent socialization of Germany, Kautsky and other social democrats (among them Otto Bauer) began to abandon their previous position and to oppose the primitive supporters of an economy based on in-kind distribution (Ballod, Neurath, etc.). This turnabout was inspired partly by their experience of the German war economy. Kautsky's later book, *The Proletarian Revolution and its Programme*, contains a number of novel views among which is his attitude toward the problem of commodity production in socialism. This development was partly influenced by his critical opinion of 'war communism' in the USSR.

Still later, in the interwar period, different views were held by social democratic theorists on the question of the mechanism of a socialist economy, many favouring the idea of a 'competitive socialism'.[3] A Polish example was the left-wing youth group of the Polish Socialist Party, *Płomienie*, which formulated principles of a socialist

[1] *Ibid.*, p. 19.
[2] *Ibid.*, pp. 36–7.
[3] See *infra* pp. 22–4.

economy based on the 'competitive solution' of H. D. Dickinson.[1]

However, the stand taken by communists, and especially the Russian Communists, on the question of the socialist economic mechanism, has far more adherents for obvious reasons. The reality of practice, in general, kept the basic point of view close to that described above. With this in mind, the main effort of theoretical economists was aimed at explaining why it was not yet possible to establish an economic system founded on distribution in physical terms. The theory was that a completely centralized, moneyless economy should be introduced as quickly and consistently as was possible. Not only Bukharin and Preobrazhenski in the *ABC of Communism* and the former alone in the *Economics of the Transitional Period*, but also Lenin in his own writing in the period of 'war communism' and in the transition to NEP promoted this type of view.[2]

More clearly than other leaders, Lenin realized the need both to preserve and to normalize money–(for)–commodity relations (the use of money in purchasing rather than other goods in barter) immediately after seizing power. This was evidenced in, among other things, the role he attributed to the currency reform preparations for which were nearly complete.[3] The attainment of these aims was frustrated by the outbreak of Civil War and the necessity to introduce the system of 'war communism'. It is evident that Lenin clearly understood the nature of the causes which underlay this necessity and realized the abnormality of the situation. Nevertheless it occurred to him that such a peculiar situation might be more than a mere episode. He realized that *faits accomplis* influenced by the necessity of total mobilization in defence of the revolution, might become irrevocable, so that what seemed impossible in the light of the cold analysis of all economic assumptions, might become a reality. It might be possible to jump directly to a 'purely communist' organization of production and distribution. Doubtless in this interpretation of the circumstances is concealed the basic feeling that money–commodity relations are a necessary evil to be eliminated at the first opportunity. 'War communism' provided the opportunity and it had to be utilized. Lenin made no secret of this attitude when

---

[1] Cf. *Gospodarka-polityka-taktyka-organizacja socializmu* (*The Economy-Politics-Tactics-Organization of Socialism*), Warsaw, 1934.

[2] Lenin's views are discussed here and not in the section on the 1920s since they, together with the views of Marx and Engels, constituted the starting point for the theoretical discussion referred to above.

[3] V. I. Lenin, *Collected Works*, London, n.d., vol. 23, pp. 32–5, Speech at the Congress of Representatives of Finance Departments of Local Soviets, May 18, 1918.

he said later: 'We calculated—or perhaps more accurately, we supposed without any grounds for doing so—that we would be able, in a land of small peasant holdings, to organize state production and state distribution of products according to communist principles. Time has shown our mistake.'[1]

Even exposing this error did not remove the pressure of the conviction that an economic system of physical-term distribution was the only form which corresponded to the dictatorship of the proletariat. No alternative conception could easily replace it. Lenin stated, 'there was a change in our economic policy; instead of a requisition, a tax was introduced. This was not conceived full-blown but was pieced together over several months. Over a period of months in the Bolshevik press, you can find a whole series of propositions, but nobody could find a project which really guaranteed success.'[2]

'NEP, a project really promising success' came to life shortly, undoubtedly as a result of enormous personal effort on Lenin's part. However, it is interesting that even in NEP there were attempts to preserve commodity forms of exchange in the countryside, by direct exchange of products in local trade. These attempts to avoid the intermediary of money were unsuccessful:[3]

A series of decrees and decisions, a mass of articles, wholesale propaganda, large scale legislation—beginning in the spring of 1921—was aimed at the increase of commodity exchange [i.e., the direct exchange of products] ... And what happened? It turned out ... that nothing came of the commodity exchange: nothing came of it in the sense that it assumed the form of buying and selling. And we must now realize this if we do not want to hide our heads in the sand, if we do not wish to act the part of people who cannot see when they are beaten, if we are not afraid to face the danger.

From the situation Lenin was able to fathom a number of profound practical lessons as well as a series of theoretical conclusions. He perceived that market links with the countryside, especially when socialist industry was weak and burdened by a large sector of small-scale producers, menaced planning with inundation by a tide of market spontaneity. His response to the danger was not by paralysing the money–commodity relations but by mastering and transforming them into an instrument of socialism. During the inauguration of the NEP Lenin returned to certain ideas outlined in 1918 in

[1] V. I. Lenin, *Works*, vol. 30, p. 42 (Polish edition).
[2] 'On the Tactics of the Russian Communist Party at the Second Congress of the Communist International', V. I. Lenin, *Works*, vol. 30, p. 517.
[3] *Ibid.*, vol. 23, p. 84.

Left-Wing Communism: an Infantile Disorder. In connection with the NEP he developed the idea of using money–commodity forms in the socialist state during the transition to communism.

Important to this conception was the assertion that these money–commodity forms in NEP could not be limited to links between town and countryside; they must include the socialist sector.[1]

> The adoption of so-called *khozraschot* [see p. 44] in state enterprises is by force of circumstances very closely connected with the New Economic Policy, and in the near future this type of undertaking will undoubtedly predominate—if it is not the only type. When free trade is allowed and develops, this in fact means the adoption by state enterprises of commercial principles to a large extent.

In this situation it was clearly necessary to base the criteria of the efficiency of state industry on profitability thereby involving broad areas of autonomy for enterprises or their associations (trusts). Lenin realized that the use of market forms in the mechanism of the functioning of state enterprises did not necessarily mean the abandonment of central planning. If the basic decisions belong to the state and its institutions and where there is still the possibility of state intervention in the activity of an enterprise, planning exists. Succinctly stated the formula is this: 'The new economic policy *does not change* the unified state economic plan and *does not go beyond* its framework, but it alters the *means* by which it is realized.'[2]

Without a doubt Lenin's pronouncements in the years 1921–2 constitute a basic step forward in understanding the relation of the plan to the market and the role of money and commodity exchange. (Later we shall see that they had an important influence on Soviet economic science.) Equally there can be no doubt that Lenin referred directly to the mixed economy of the transitional period when he considered the question of applying market forms. Further he saw the necessity of them as a result of factors external to socialism—the large small-scale peasant sector and the low level of industrialization.

Thus it is impossible to conclude from Lenin's work that the system of 'war communism' is basically erroneous. The mistake is not in the premises of the system themselves, but in the fact that it was introduced prematurely before the conditions were ripe. We see that for the planned socialist economy in the strict sense (i.e. the situation when all the means of production are socialized) it remains true that the only suitable system is one which is highly centralized and in which production and distribution are controlled in physical terms.

[1] *Ibid.*, pp. 185–6.
[2] *Ibid.*, vol. 33, p. 84.

As suitable conditions arise this system ought to be brought into existence.

Two documents of major ideological importance support this interpretation—the programme of the Russian Communist Party of 1919 (8th Congress) and the programme of the Communist International of 1928 (6th Congress).

In the programme of the Russian Communist Party, point 3 of the chapter devoted to general economic problems reads:[1]

> The decay of the imperialist economy bequeathed to the first period of Soviet construction a largely chaotic organization of production and management. As one of the basic tasks there is all the greater need to achieve the maximum unification of the whole of the country's economic life by means of a state plan. Further, there is the necessity of achieving the maximum centralization of production in three senses: a. merging of production by branches and groups of branches, b. a concentration of production in the best possible productive units, c. an acceleration of the realization of economic tasks.

In distribution (point 13):

> In the field of distribution the task of the Soviet authorities at present still consists of replacing trade as quickly as possible by the planned state-wide distribution of products. The aim is to organize the entire population into a uniform network of consumer communes which will be able to conduct the distribution of indispensable products rapidly, economically, in a planned way and by a strict centralization of the entire distributive apparatus.

In the money and banking systems (point 15):

> In the first phase of the transition from capitalism to communism, so long as the communistic production and distribution of products has not been fully organized, the abolition of money is impossible ... Basing its policy on the nationalization of the banks, the Russian Communist Party intends to realize a number of measures expanding the sphere of accounting without money and preparing for the abolition of money: the obligatory depositing of money in bank accounts, the introduction of budget books, the replacement of money by cheques, short-term coupons entitling the holder to products, etc.

The same pattern—a merely temporary tolerance of money—commodity trade and the intent to introduce direct methods of

---

[1] All the quotations are from the *KPSS v Rezolutskiyakh i Resheniyakh Syezdov, Konferentsii i Plenumov CK* (Moscow, 1953), Part 1, pp. 421, 425–6, 427.

C

in-kind distribution as quickly as possible—appears in the programme of the Communist International. The significance of this document is enhanced by the fact that it does not limit itself to the analysis of conditions existing in any one country. Not only does it deal with problems generally but, it will be remembered, the document was binding on all parties by virtue of the organizational principles of the International. For these reasons the theoretical parts of the programme were formulated with comparative care and expressed the views generally accepted in the communist movement. Hence added import must be attached to the pertinent sections. For example the sections describing the origins of the use of money in trade and the relation between plan and market (chapter 4 of the Programme):[1]

> Owing to the prevalence of a large number of small units of production . . . in colonies, semi-colonies and economically backward countries . . . and even in centres of capitalist world industry . . . it is necessary, in the first stage of [socialist] development to preserve to some extent, market forms of economic contacts, the money systems, etc. . . . Hence, the greater the importance of scattered, small peasant labour in the economy of the country, the greater will be the volume of market relations, the smaller will be the significance of directly planned management, and the greater will be the degree to which the economic plan will depend upon the forecasting of spontaneously developing economic relations. On the other hand, the smaller the share of small-scale production . . . the smaller will be the volume of market relations, the greater will be the importance of plan as distinct from spontaneity and the greater and more universal will be the role played by the methods of direct planned management in the sphere of production distribution . . . Provided the Soviet state carries out a correct policy, the process of development of market relations under the proletarian dictatorship will lead to its own destruction . . . thus they help to destroy market relations altogether.

These extracts can be seen to reiterate at least two basic points:

1. Money-commodity trade relationships are treated as external to the socialist economy; they derive from the existence of non-socialist sectors and their extent and importance depend almost entirely on the extent and part played by small peasant holdings (in applying this criterion the programme names the countries in which commodity relations will for a certain period have a broad, medium and narrow compass).

2. Money-commodity trade relationships, the market, are economic phenomena at variance with a planned economy—the

[1] *Programme of the Communist International* (London, 1929), pp. 31-3.

Contents

First published in 1972
by Routledge & Kegan Paul Ltd
Broadway House, 68-74 Carter Lane,
London EC4V 5EL and
9 Park Street,
Boston, Mass. 02108, U.S.A.
Translated from the Polish
Ogolne problemy funkcjonowania
gospodarki socjalistycznej
(P.W.N. 1964)
by Angus Walker
and revised by the author

Printed in Great Britain by
C. Tinling & Co. Ltd, London and Prescot
© Włodzimierz Brus 1972
No part of this book may be reproduced in
any form without permission from the
publisher, except for the quotation of brief
passages in criticism

ISBN 0 7100 7276 7

The market in a socialist economy

Włodzimierz Brus

Routledge & Kegan Paul
London and Boston

CALVIN T. RYAN LIBRARY
KEARNEY STATE COLLEGE
KEARNEY, NEBRASKA

embodiment of the uncontrollable. According to the programme the scope and effectiveness of planning in the strict sense are inversely proportional to the extent of, and part played by, money-commodity trade relationships.

It is worth noting the date when the document was drafted. These are no longer the years immediately following the October Revolution; this is the beginning of the second decade after the Revolution —the period when the five-year plan offensive was opened and the collectivization of agriculture was started. It is indisputable that formulations contained in the programme of the International had more than a theoretical significance.

This brings us to the termination of the first part of our historical survey. The most important conclusion is that in the theoretical and ideological outlook of the revolutionary movement was rooted the conviction that the socialist economy is centrally planned not only generally but in all its elements. Furthermore, the market mechanism forms a foreign body in the socialist system which must be tolerated for a period but which should at all cost be eliminated as soon as feasible.

In the practical application of the principles of the functioning of a socialist economy this doctrinal standpoint has had an important influence. We cannot explain the history of the formation of the 'model' unless we take into account this factor, even if that history has, to some extent, been independent of strictly economic conditions and needs.

The Western inter-war discussion of the problem of economic calculation in socialism

It may be that the above heading does not give an accurate description of the period within which the well-known discussion about economic calculation in socialism took place. Actually it began in the latter half of the nineteenth century or at any rate in the first years of this century. Moreover, the discussions were not terminated in the inter-war period but extended into the period after World War II. (Immediately after the war interesting attempts were made to synthesize the results to that time, but they went so far as to become new contributions to the discussions.) Despite this the limitation found in the heading can be justified since it was then that the debate developed on a large scale. In the earlier period individual contributions rarely met with a direct reaction, and in the later period the level of the disputes underwent an important modification.

As I have already made clear I do not intend to write a history of the problem. Nor do I intend to give a full account of the discussion

of economic calculation in socialism (especially since there are many serious attempts at a synthesis, with Abram Bergson's being distinguished by its precision and breadth of vision).[1] Rather I want to assess those aspects of the discussion which are important for the problems of the mechanism of the functioning of a socialist economy at the present time. Therefore, what is of interest is not the discussion as to whether socialism can be rational but the discussion as to the suitability of the various solutions which were considered. And I shall touch upon the general problems only in so far as it is necessary to make the main theme clear.

Oskar Lange begins his famous work on the economic theory of socialism[2] with an ironic passage in praise of Ludwig von Mises for the services which the latter rendered by drawing attention to the problem of economic rationality in socialism. As is evident from even our short foray into the views of Marx, the question of economic calculation (*in its most general sense as the criteria and methods for choosing between different uses of the available means (resources) for the achievement of optimum economic results*) was never, or hardly ever, the subject of consideration. Schaeffle, in *Die Quintessenz des Socialismus*, and others (among them Kautsky's adversary, the Dutchman, N. G. Pierson), have drawn attention to this point. Pareto, and especially Barone,[3] even attempted to produce their own theoretical solution of the problem. The particular importance of Mises,[4] however, lies in the fact that, on the basis of the arguments already put forward, he attempted to form a coherent theory. In it he asserted that rational economic calculation in a socialist economy was impossible. We must remember that unlike previous works which dealt with the problems of the socialist economy in the pre-revolutionary period, Mises's article appeared at a time when socialism had ceased to be a theoretical problem. The 'social need', so to speak, for this kind of study was thus much greater and Mises's article subsequently, if not immediately, became very well known.

[1] A. Bergson, 'Socialist Economics' in a *Survey of Contemporary Economics*, vol. 1, published by the American Economic Association and edited by Howard S. Ellis in 1949 (repeatedly republished).

[2] O. Lange and F. Taylor, *On the Economic Theory of Socialism* (Minneapolis, 1938).

[3] E. Barone, *Il Ministerio della Produzione nella Stato collectivista*, English translation in *Collectivist Economic Planning*, edited by F. A. Hayek (London, 1935).

[4] L. von Mises, 'Die Wirtschaftsrechnung im sozialistischen Gemeinwesen' (*Archiv fuer Sozialwissenschaften*, April, 1920). His article is expanded in his book *Die Gemeinwirtschaft*, 1st ed. 1922, 2nd 1932. English translation, *Socialism*, 1936.

Like other bourgeois critics of socialism, Mises took advantage of the paucity of socialist literature, seizing upon a highly centralized model based on physical allocation and which was seemingly confirmed in practice by 'war communism'. Although it is true that he allowed for the appearance of a market for consumer goods in socialism, he felt that the inevitable consequence of the socialization of the means of production would be the stifling of a market for capital goods, thus precluding the possibility of a rational control of the economy.[1]

Because no production good will ever become the object of exchange, it will be impossible to determine its monetary value. Money could never fill in a socialist state the role it fills in a competitive society in determining the value of production goods. Calculation in terms of money will be impossible.

From this Mises concluded that it would be impossible in a socialist economy to determine the economic efficiency of production or investment decisions. Thus the only form of rational economy—despite socialist accusations that it is anarchic—is one based on private ownership of the means of production and, hence, on universal exchange relations: 'As soon as one gives up the conception of a freely-established money price for goods of a higher order rational production becomes completely impossible. Every step that takes us away from the private ownership of the means of production and from the use of money also takes us away from rational economics.'[2] Apart from criticisms of both the lack of value criteria and of the impossibility of establishing incentives for management personnel, this is Mises's main argument. Today its primitive nature is evident, not only in the light of socialist experience but also in the light of the development of state capitalism. Nevertheless since then a considerable number of bourgeois economists have followed Mises's arguments (even the reasoning of so serious a scholar as Max Weber, in part, follows the same course in *Wirtschaft und Gesellschaft*).

F. A. Hayek took Mises's solution as the starting point of his own critique of socialism to reach a less drastic interpretation. He showed that Mises's reasoning demonstrates not the theoretical, but the practical inability of socialism to develop a rational economy. Hayek, like Robbins and others, considers that Pareto's argument as expanded by Barone is theoretically correct. Accordingly, the central planning body can obtain the optimum use of means on the condition that it

[1] L. von Mises, 'Die Wirtschaftsrechnung', quoted from *Collectivist Economic Planning*, ed. F. A. von Hayek, 1935, p. 92.
[2] *Ibid.*, p. 104.

behaves consciously, *ex ante*, and analogously to a perfect market mechanism. However, this planning body would have to take account of all the mutual interrelationships in an economy and would, simultaneously, be obliged to solve a system composed of hundreds of thousands of equations with hundreds of thousands of unknowns. As such it assumes perfect accuracy of data on the number of goods produced, prices, production coefficient, and needs of services. Because, at best, it would seem difficult to fulfil this kind of condition, a rational socialist economy, although theoretically conceivable, cannot exist in practice.

Therefore, the advocates of socialism must try not so much to prove the theoretical possibility of a rational socialist economy, but rather they must try to show that it is possible to construct a mechanism which guarantees optimum decisions when the means of production are socialized and planning is centralized. Fred Taylor, in 'The Guidance of Production in a Socialist State'[1] made the first attempt to produce a solution along these lines. (It is noteworthy that the article had to await publication of Lange's book to make an impact.) A further important contribution is the article 'Price Formation in a Socialist Economy'[2] by the English economist, H. D. Dickinson. Yet it was Abba Lerner and Oskar Lange who made the most important contribution to the inter-war discussion through a series of articles (in part a mutual polemic) in the *Review of Economic Studies*.[3] Lastly our summary must note a certain similarity to the Lange–Lerner solutions in earlier but less precise German works.[4]

For the purposes of the ensuing review of the period it will be sufficient to extract the most representative of these studies and to use it as an example in considering the proposed mechanism of the functioning of a socialist economy. As that representative the best choice is Lange's work in its final version and as subject to modification by the comments of Lerner (hence the frequent allusions to the 'Lerner–Lange solution').

Briefly the argument runs as follows: in order to solve the problem of managing the factors of production, what is required is not prices in the narrowest sense (the actual exchange relationship between two commodities on the market) but in the most general sense (an index of choice alternatives). Hence the prices to be used for allocating

---

[1] *The American Economic Review*, 1929.

[2] *Economic Journal*, 6/1933. Dickinson's book, *Economics of Socialism* (1939), seems to be less clear than his article.

[3] Lerner in years 1934–7, Lange in years 1936–7.

[4] E.g. C. Landauer, *Planwirtschaft und Verkehrswirtschaft*, 1927, E. Heinemann, *Sozialistische Wirtschafts- und Arbeitsordnung*, 1932; H. Zassenhaus, 'Ueber die Oekonomische Theorie der Planwirtschaft', *Zeitschrift fuer Nationaloekonomie*, 5/1934.

factors must not be established by actual exchange among various owners but must be ones calculated by the central planning office. (The former alternative based on the private exchange of producer goods is excluded by the nature of socialism and social ownership of capital.) The centrally calculated prices are parametric in so far as managers of socialized enterprises cannot influence price determination, but, on the contrary, are given prices by the central planning office as a basis for their own decision-making. If it is the case that such prices are not arbitrarily established then the problem is at an end. Given the following assumptions which are not at variance with the principles of a socialist system, objective price structure can be constructed:

1. There is freedom of choice in the consumer goods market; with given incomes, the prices of these goods will establish themselves as equilibrium prices similar to those of a competitive market.

2. There is freedom of choice of occupation and place of work which in the same way tends to establish an equilibrium in the labour market.

3. There are established principles for the distribution of income among members of society; here arbitrariness is limited by the assumption of a labour market.

4. Managers act according to definite principles: a. the minimization of the average cost per unit of output; b. regulation of production of output to the point where marginal cost is equal to price. Consequently marginal rates of substitution will be equalized.

5. The rate of accumulation is directly established by references to the central planning office; while the allocation of capital to branches of production and to enterprises is achieved by using a rate of interest which equalizes the demand for and supply of capital.

On these assumptions, price is the single determinant of the supply and demand of not only consumer goods but also of producer goods. 'The conditions of equality between supply and demand determine a set of equilibrium prices—the only one guaranteeing the consistency of all decisions.' Equilibrium prices—and hence, not arbitrary ones but such as are objectively determined by the whole set of complex interconnections—are achieved by trial and error (successive approximations). Far from requiring the simultaneous solution of hundreds of thousands or millions of equations, what is needed is the observation of the movement of supply and demand. This movement, of course, is the independent result of the decisions of consumers and managers constrained by the general conditions listed above. Successive approximations, raising the price of goods or services in short supply and lowering those of goods in the opposite situation, allow the central planning office to obtain an equilibrium price structure.

In this summary of Lange's views I have omitted the problem of the criteria for establishing objectives of the central planning organ and the definition of the optimum allocation of available factors (for the latter we must have a standard of evaluation). These interconnected difficulties, long the intensive subject of welfare economics, are related to the principle of consumer's sovereignty—which amounts to the adaptation of the composition of production to consumer preferences expressed as effective demand. Lange, at first, included this principle in the foundations of his socialist system. Later, expanding his theory, he showed that the procedure for achieving price equilibrium by the use of successive approximations can also be applied when production is adjusted not to consumer preference scales but to a specific scale of preferences set by central planners.[1]

Theoretically this thesis arouses few outcries, for when given preference scales are assumed, it is possible to say that by trial and error optimum allocation can be achieved in line with those preferences. In the abstract it is possible to agree that the economy in the assumed conditions will tend towards the situation which Lerner describes thus: 'If we so order the economic activity of the society that no commodity is produced unless its importance is greater than that of the alternative that is sacrificed, we shall have completely achieved the ideal that the economic calculation of a socialist state sets before itself.'[2] Obviously this idealized picture of the equalization of marginal rates of substitution does not correspond to any economic reality. It is, however, further removed from reality (even as a tendency) when the specific preferences of the central planning body are decisive than when the consumer is 'sovereign'. Such an abandonment of reality, it seems to me, is related to the extreme decentralization of Lange's model. He tries to show that the socialist system is able, at least as well as capitalism, to achieve what is described as the

---

[1] Lange correctly distinguishes between consumer's sovereignty and freedom of choice in the market for consumer goods. 'But freedom of choice in the market for consumer goods does not imply that production is actually guided by the choices of the consumers. One may well imagine a system in which production and allocation of resources are guided by a preference scale fixed by the Central Planning Board while the market prices are used to distribute the consumer goods produced. In such a system there is freedom of choice in consumption, but the consumers have no influence whatsoever on the decisions of the managers of production and productive resources' (O. Lange and F. Taylor, *On the Economic Theory of Socialism*, pp. 95–6). It is quite clear, in this case, that the price structures of marketed consumer goods and the prices paid to the producers (and hence the price structure of producer goods) must be separated from one another, e.g. by a system of taxes and subsidies.

[2] A. P. Lerner, 'Statics and Dynamics in Socialist Economies', *Economic Journal*, 1957, 47, p. 253.

optimum in the conceptual apparatus of 'welfare economics'. He points out that it can, perhaps, do it even better, thanks to the accurate information in planners' hands concerning the situation in the entire economy. In Lange's model the central planning board differs from the market only in that it prescribes the rate of accumulation and puts into practice the principles of income distribution. In all its other functions in accordance with the rules established for managers it merely replaces the market. The suitability of this model is more for controlling output under pressure from direct reactions of the 'sovereign consumer' than for controlling output under the influence of separate overall social preferences. Hence doubts arise as to the universal applicability of the theory.[1]

The most noteworthy achievement of Lange and the other participants in the discussions which led to the competitive solution was to show the baselessness of the assertions of Mises, Hayet, Robbins, etc., that rational economic calculation under socialism was impossible. This does not mean that Lange's and Lerner's articles of that period went unchallenged. However, their opponents refrained from repeating old arguments, attempting instead to put forth new ones often on a completely different basis. Hayek, for example, attacks Oskar Lange and Dickinson,[2] not by opposing their general line of argument but by concentrating on questioning the possibility of organizing quasi-competitive conditions without private ownership. The weakest points he uncovers are the difficulty of separating independent productive units where there are strong central preferences; the question of incentives for lowering costs of production; the state of official entrepreneur dilemma with regard to the position of the director of production who is obviously not in a position to bear actual material responsibility for the consequences of his decisions. Another general set of criticisms hinges on the question of how far practically it is possible for the central planning authority to fulfil the role of the market (this is a question of the speed of reaction to changed conditions).

It is not my intention to minimize the importance of such criticisms. Practice has shown no simple solutions to the marginal autonomy of the enterprise from the centre, no greater results have been obtained for the problems of criteria, incentives, and managerial responsibility. By the light of experience we would certainly be more cautious in judging Hayek's arguments than, for example, Schumpeter. The

[1] Some of the ideas in this section have been developed in chapter 4, especially in the discussion of the criteria to be employed in the choice of investments and their relation to the law of value.

[2] F. A. Hayek, 'Sozialistische Wirtschaftsrechnung', 3—'Wiedereinfuehrung des Wettbewerbs' in *Individualismus und Wirtschaftliche Ordnung* (Erlenbach–Zürich, 1952).

latter replies affirmatively to the question 'can socialism function?' on the basis of arguments put by the advocate of the 'competitive' solution. As evidence of the possibility he points to the behaviour of corporate managers.[1] On the other hand the difficulty in developing satisfactory managers—a group mandated by society to manage production—is among the negative results of the underdevelopment of capitalism in Poland. (In this, Poland is not unlike the majority of other contemporary socialist countries which have had insufficient (or poor) experience in operating state-owned or corporate enterprises). It is unquestionable that the high degree of separation of the function of management from ownership visible in contemporary capitalism constitutes a basic material precondition for socialism; the more so in the setting of the development of various forms of state capitalism.

Independently of actual present situations where the obstacles foreseen by Hayek may cause some difficulties, they form no insuperable barriers to ensuring economic effectiveness. (It is also assumed that the conditions necessary for this end are fulfilled.) That Hayek and Mises were aware of the insignificance of these arguments is witnessed by their later shift from proofs of the economic inefficiency of socialism to purely political criticism concerning the relationship between planning and individual freedom. Bergson, generally very careful in his formulations, writes that 'it must be conceded, too, that the emphasis that the critics of socialism have lately placed on this issue [planning and freedom] sometimes has the appearance of a tactical manoeuvre, to bolster a cause which Mises's theories have been found inadequate to sustain.[2] No more need be added to this.

Leaving aside many other notes and comments of varying importance we shall pass now from consideration of the 'competitive solution' to consideration of criticisms of our theme from those whose positions we could constitute as the 'left'. These are the Western Marxist economists who base their positions on the planned socialist economy as it emerged during the inter-war years in the Soviet Union. Included in this group are Maurice Dobb,[3] Paul Baran,[4] Paul Sweezy,[5] and Charles Bettelheim.[6] Although they were

[1] J. Schumpeter, *Capitalism, Socialism and Democracy* (London, 1957), chapter entitled 'The Human Element'.

[2] A. Bergson, *Socialist Economics*, pp. 412–3.

[3] A number of his articles were published in *On Economic Theory and Socialism* (London, 1955); see also *Soviet Economic Development since 1917* (London, 1948).

[4] P. Baran, 'National Economic Planning', Part 3, 'Planning under Socialism' in vol. 2 of *A Survey of Contemporary Economics*, edited by Bernard Haley, 1952.

[5] Paul Sweezy, 'Socialism', *Economic Handbook Series* (New York, 1949).

[6] Ch. Bettelheim, *Les problèmes théoriques et pratiques de la planification* (Paris, 1946).

not entirely in agreement with each other, I will concentrate on one, Dobb, who immediately and vigorously took up the cudgels against Lange. In part I also want to take up an article by Baran and to return later to some problems raised by the other two of the quartet.

At the time of NEP when he wrote his first book devoted to the development of the Soviet economy, Maurice Dobb[6] was very close to the views of Dickinson and Lange. However, evidently under the influence of the changes which had taken place in planning and organization of the Soviet economy, he later declared his previous views mistaken. This point is emphasized in one of the footnotes in *On Economic Theory and Socialism*. His doubts about the 'competitive solution' derive from a fear that such a model does not make it possible to show the superiority of the planned socialist economy. More than that, regarding the mechanism, it is at best an imitation of capitalism on the basis of the social ownership of the means of production.

In reply advocates of the 'competitive solution' might state that their model contains two assumptions of cardinal importance which distinguish it from the model of a capitalist economy.

1. the assumption that the rate of accumulation is determined by the central planning authority on the basis of general social preferences, and hence that it guarantees the optimum growth rate. At the same time, this means the elimination of one of the chief causes of cyclical movements in the process of reproduction;

2. the assumption that the central planning authority determines the principles of income distribution—principles based on justice and economic stimulation. This is a basic condition for the socially rational allocation of factors by the market mechanism (a proper structure of consumer demand). As with the above this is also impossible to achieve in capitalism.

However, the advocates of the 'competitive solution' did not reply to criticisms that their proposed model contained internal inconsistencies. Of these the most noticeable is the extent to which it was possible to achieve general social preferences while simultaneously observing the other principles which had been adopted for the functioning of the economy. For example, the model can be questioned on the grounds that an ideal allocation of factors conflicts with efforts to transform the socio-economic foundations of output and distribution of national income. (This is a very basic problem especially in the transition period when certain sacrifices in production may be required of society in order to transform the socio-economic structure and to achieve a more rapid long-term growth

[1] M. Dobb, *Russian Economic Development* (London, 1928).

rate.) Even apart from this special situation it is doubtful whether that mechanism which guarantees the 'ideal' allocation of means in any given period is also capable of guaranteeing the postulated growth rate.

It is on this plane, that of general economic equilibrium, that Dobb offers many of the criticisms of Lange's model. Put forward as a series of articles on economic calculation in socialism[1] they were subsequently made more concrete by examples.[2]

Here, rather then repeat Dobb's argument, I would merely like to emphasize his main idea. He feels that it may prove impossible to establish simultaneously the investment rate and use any 'equilibrium interest rate' to reduce the demand for investment funds to desired levels and to allocate funds among users. Simplifying somewhat, we may assume that the magnitude of funds available for investment is equal to the difference between the price of consumer goods and their cost of production. The greater the rate of investment I/Y (where I is investment and Y is national income), the greater is the profitability of the production of consumer goods and hence the greater the propensity to invest. Built into the system there is a cumulative process which makes it impossible to achieve equilibrium at the rate of interest previously assumed.

This difficulty can be overcome by the introduction of a tax (on turnover) which will limit excessive profits resulting from an increase in the investment rate or by the introduction of subsidies when there are deficits. However, to Dobb, this procedure is very complicated especially since it may be necessary to differentiate the approach for different branches. Thus, if the demand and supply of investment funds is not automatically equalized, and if special methods of balancing are complicated and fraught with the probability of error, would it not be better to abandon attempts at influencing management indirectly and to allocate the funds directly through the central authority and thereby to ensure realization of social preferences? Dobb argues further against decentralizing investment decisions by holding that individual enterprises are too limited in their scope; they are unable to appreciate society's point of view in assessing the merits of a decision and they are incapable of making the proper allowances for the time factor. (The types of decisions which come up for special mention are those dealing with the division of investments between departments 1 and 2—investments in capital which produces investment goods (1) and in capital which produces consumer goods (2). Within each of them he alludes to decisions about scale of enterprises, the number of units in each branch, and their location.) He

---

[1] M. Dobb, *On Economic Theory and Socialism* (London, 1955), pp. 34–41.
[2] *Ibid.*, 'A Note on Saving and Investment in a Socialist Economy', pp. 41–55.

favours centralizing decision-making because of the need to make
co-ordinated calculations for the whole complex of investments, and
in this shows a special lack of faith that the trial and error procedure
can be applied to a long-term rate of interest given a considerable
time-lag between the decision and its effect.

In the article of 1939 Dobb points out that unlike investment
decisions, decisions concerning current problems of production can
under certain circumstances be decentralized.[1]

Even if all questions of investment were decided (or had to be
finally sanctioned) centrally, questions of class 1 above (the volume
of output from a *given* plant) might still be settled according to Dr.
Lange's and Mr. Lerner's rule; i.e., of equating *M.O.C.* (marginal
operating cost) with price. This would mean that 'short period'
questions could be decentralized; i.e., day-to-day decisions about
the intensity of utilization of plant, and as much adaptation to unforeseen circumstances as would be possible . . .

Admittedly Dobb indicates a number of difficulties in decentralizing day-to-day decisions but ultimately, he feels, they can be overcome. It is apparent how his view corresponds to the trends of
development in the Soviet system of planning at that time.[2] Moreover
in an article published in 1953 entitled 'Review of the Discussion
Concerning Economic Calculation in a Socialist Economy'[3] he goes
even further in the direction of centralization. Briefly his arguments
are as follows:

1. A decentralized model involves recognizing the principle of consumer's sovereignty. However, the unconditional adoption of this
assumption is incorrect (though important, the consumers' desires
are neither the only nor the most important factors) because of a. the
frequently irrational behaviour of consumers on the market, b. the
necessity of earmarking a certain amount of income for communal
consumption, and c. a factor recently of increasing importance, the
simple conventional origin of some needs ('keeping up with the
Joneses').

2. The justification for using a decentralized decision-making
mechanism is largely based on the premise that only in this way can
the number of possible alternatives involved be lessened. Concentrating all decisions in the hands of the central authority confronts it
with the problem of choosing among an enormous number of complicated alternatives which in practice makes rational procedure
impossible. On the other hand, such an argument depends on the

[1] M. Dobb, *On Economic Theory and Socialism*, pp. 102–3.
[2] M. Dobb, *Soviet Economic Development*, p. 378.
[3] M. Dobb, *On Economic Theory and Socialism*, pp. 104–70.

assumption of the classical theory of equilibrium in which the number of possible choices is infinite, while the ability of resources is absolute, i.e. the function is continuous. In reality, however, discontinuities can frequently reduce the number 'of alternative positions or allocation patterns from which the planner can choose', and he lists some causes of 'discontinuity'. a. the appearance of bottle-necks; b. the relative stability of technical coefficients of production, due, among other things, to the increased specialization of the factors of production; c. complementarity in the supplies and demands of both capital and consumer goods; d. sudden spurts in the demand for durable consumer goods as a result of equalizing incomes under socialism. ('Where there are no large inequalities of income, the market demand for a thing is likely to be negligible above a certain price level and then highly elastic within the neighbourhood of that price ... The practical consequence will be that no intermediate position may be practicable for planning between not putting the commodity into mass production at all and producing it on a very large scale indeed'.)[1]

The significance of this is that the central planning body does not confront a plethora of relatively minor problems which it is incapable of rationally resolving. Rather it faces a comparatively small number of major problems, and these few can be most rationally dealt with centrally, because the interests of the entire economy can be considered. This facet of the problem is sharply stressed by Paul Baran, who denies that the discussion of the optimum allocation in socialism has any theoretical value at all. 'In the advanced and backward countries alike, the problem facing the Board would be not slow adjustments to small changes—the main pre-requisite analysis—but choice among few technological alternatives involving large indivisibilities and fixed coefficients. Attempting to cope with such perplexities, the Board would look in vain for guidance to the literature on socialist economics.'[2]

[1] *Ibid.*, p. 85.
[2] P. Baran, *National Economic Planning*, p. 385. On the other hand, Baran adds: 'At the peril of some oversimplification it may be said that the Board would permit consumer's preference to determine the composition of output *within* the Board's relevant "priority classes" ... It goes without saying that most of these problems [the limitation of the effect of consumer preference on production] disappear or lose much of their urgency as soon as the Board's autonomous programme has accomplished its purpose ... Loosening the Board's priorities schedules, this development would, at the same time, widen its "priority classes"—in other words—increase the area of the Board's indifference with respect to the allocation of resources. Where the Board's "autonomous programme" was small from the very beginning, where—in other words—developmental requirements loomed less large in the early stages of economic planning, the transitional period would be accordingly shorter and

The tremendous import of these condensed arguments is to put in relief the weaknesses of a model which assumes that it is possible to attain automatically optimality in the refined, if somewhat unreal sense, intended in 'welfare economics'. In fact, literally interpreted, Lange's model does not provide the most favourable conditions for utilizing the potential elements in socialism which make it superior to capitalism. The adoption of the frame of reference dictated by Mises and Hayek had the virtue of making it possible to oppose basic theoretical criticisms but was less favourable to the development of practical solutions. Especially for investment, the market or quasi-market process of achieving equilibrium by trial and error has an extremely limited application. In that area it threatens to eliminate such valuable elements of a planned socialist economy as the possibility of determining the effectiveness of investment from a general social point of view, of a high concentration of investment outlays, and of direct co-ordination of decisions.

The argument between the critics and advocates of the 'competitive solution' prompts the philosophical reflection that no discussion should resemble a duel in which the only aim is the defeat of one's opponent. If we accept most of Dobb's argument, it is impossible not to notice some basic weaknesses which can only be eliminated by adopting some of the elements of the decentralized model. At this point I would like to give some important examples.

1. We confront difficulties in ensuring a uniformity of reproduction processes and this is related in turn to the proper organization of restitution investments and in smaller, secondary investments. Here it is difficult to expect an appropriate solution with strict centralization of decision-making, especially when the economy has achieved those overriding priorities to which all else was subordinated. And if, even to a limited extent, some decentralization even of investment decisions is necessary, a price structure becomes an indispensable instrument of proper allocation.

2. Although it is difficult to assume an infinite number of alternatives (especially for key problems) one cannot agree that the actual number is so limited that no difficulties are created for the central planner.

---

simpler' (*ibid.*, pp. 386–7). These assertions, although there is a great deal of truth in them, cannot be entirely reconciled with the description (cited above) of the problem with which the Board is faced 'in advanced and backward countries alike'. The sequential division would seem to be somewhat mechanical: in fact both types of problem are always interconnected, although not always to the same degree. Finally, Baran seems to connect the possibility of decentralization exclusively with 'the area of the Board's indifference' without perceiving the possibility of realizing general social preferences from a given system of decentralized decisions.

Practice indicates an enormous number of daily problems which cannot be solved effectively at the centre. This holds not only for problems of adopting the supply structure to the structure of consumer needs but also of the choice of productive techniques used to satisfy the desired supply structure at the lowest cost.[1]

3. Although Dobb rightly stresses the advantages of *ex ante* adjustments as opposed to those made *ex post*, he overlooks two considerations. First, *ex ante* decisions are not necessarily synonymous with direct decisions (obligatory planned targets). Such a non-direct change is one in which changes in the price structure improve profitability and thereby leads to an increased supply. Second, *ex ante* decisions are neither always possible nor always correct. If either of these is the case a decentralized mechanism of adjustment yields more advantages than a system in which the necessary corrections must be made by the central planning board.

4. In all Dobb's arguments there seems to be the tacit assumption that the whole problem of management in socialism is reduced to making the optimum decision. Problems of decision-making, the efficiency of enterprises from society's point of view, and of incentives, are neglected. This is so, even though for management purposes an examination of the part played by prices and other economic instruments and a study of the respective spheres of decentralized versus centralized decision-making is absolutely indispensable.

In these few remarks I do not claim to have the answer for those problems to which the entire book is devoted. My concern is merely to indicate that the problem is far more complicated than either of the alternative presentations examined hitherto. Moreover, today both representatives of Marxist thought whose views have been outlined here recognize these complexities. As much of his present work manifests, Oskar Lange is far from overrating the possibility that a

---

[1] It should be noted that both Dobb and Baran seem to understand substitution in its limited sense as the technical substitutability of factors. It can also be understood in a broader *economic* sense, e.g. as the choice between alternative possibilities of reducing outlays. Even when there is no choice between the use of steel and the use of aluminium (i.e. when it is technologically necessary to use steel for the production of good *A* and aluminium for the production of good *B*) there always exists a practical problem of the choice between steel and aluminium in the sense of establishing the relative efficiency of economizing in the use of one or the other of these materials. In this sense substitution is practically unlimited, and the problem of equalizing marginal rates of substitution (not, obviously, in textbook form) appears in a new light. From this point of view the importance of the price structure is undoubted. On the other hand, the technical coefficients of production can be altered, among other things, by changes in relative prices. In this case to assume that the coefficients are stable is less than agreed upon. (Edward Taylor has drawn attention to this, though in a different context. *Teoria Produkcji (Theory of Production)*, Warsaw-Lódz, 1947, p. 354.)

socialist economy could function automatically, especially with regard to investment. Maurice Dobb has also adjusted his stand in view of the experiences of a planned economy and of recent theoretical discussions. He has recognized that he was, perhaps, too severe in his criticism of decentralized projects[1] and is more concerned than ever with the problems of the law of value and prices in a socialist economy. That is not to imply that all differences of opinions have disappeared. However, the signs of a growing agreement are there and it is with considerable satisfaction that we note them.

Jumping forward in time from the inter-war period to the present we must, at least, allude to the fact that post-war non-Marxist literature is very little concerned with the question of economic calculation in a socialist economy. At most, it is interested in the usefulness of applying one form or another of this calculation and with the assumptions on which it ought to be based. An illustration is the international symposium on the subject of 'Economic Calculation and Organization in Eastern Europe' organized by the University of California at Berkeley in June, 1958.[2] Not one of the papers presented there dealt with the Mises-Hayek problems, although, from different positions, they are all interested in the examination of the methods of calculation applied and the lines of discussion followed in socialist countries.

The reasons for this shift of emphasis are not difficult to find. They issue from the eloquence of the economic experience of the socialist countries and from the changes which have led to an increase in the economic role of the state in some capitalist countries. It is not my whole intent, in noting this, to rouse a sense of satisfaction among us, socialism's supporters, I would like also to indicate that we are faced with a new situation. More now than ever, it is necessary for us to study Western writings on economic planning, especially since we have become concerned with many problems of the functioning of a socialist economy which we did not deal with hitherto.

Soviet economic discussions in the 1920s and the functioning of a socialist economy

For obvious reasons one would expect to find the most important contribution to the solution of the problems of the functioning of a

[1] See his article 'Uwagi o roli prawa wartości w gospodarce socjalistycznej i systemie cen' ('Remarks on the role of the law of value in a socialist economy and on a price system'), specially written for the Polish edition of M. Dobb's book *On Economic Theory and Socialism*, pp. 452–68. See also 'A comment on the discussion about price policy', *Soviet Studies*, vol. no. 2.

[2] The papers were published in *Value and Plan*, edited by Gregory Grossman, University of California Press (Berkeley and Los Angeles, 1960).

D

socialist economy being made by Soviet economists. As a result of the
October Revolution, they were able to work in a marvellous 'labora-
tory' and obtain first-hand experience in the working of a planned
economy. Yet much remains to be accomplished before it will be
possible to appraise fully the economic discussions which took place
in the 1920s and early 1930s. It has been difficult (at least, until
recently) to gain access to works published in the period, and little
reference was ever made to them in current publications. True, signs
seem to indicate that the situation will improve gradually,[1] but for the
moment we are still in the early stages of reconstructing this important and unusually interesting period in the history of the Marxist
economic theory of socialism. From these circumstances arise the
reservations we must make, initially, regarding the fairness of the
analysis concerning the past. Shortly we would expect a fuller
appraisal of the literature as a closer study of archives progresses.

The studies and results of discussions during this period are to be
found not only in academic but also frequently in political practice
and official economic actions. Party and state documents frequently
contain materials of prime importance. Apart from that, even in the
best theoretical writings, we sense a close connection with the
pressing problems of actually building socialism. (Among the few
exceptions are the scholastic discussions on the works of Rubin.)
Deep involvement is witnessed both by the choice of questions discussed and the acerbity of subsequent exchanges. The latter not only
did not try to avoid the political consequences of a theoretical position but were aimed at laying them bare. (It is obvious that I am
thinking of the work of Marxist economists at the time universally
termed Communist to distinguish them from bourgeois economists in
the university faculties and economic institutions.) Politically sharp
as they were, the discussions were characterized by a great freedom
of opinion, originality, and factual argument. This is in contrast to
the later period when a political argument was used as a proof of
condemnation and was final in any controversy.

In the foregoing it is not meant to imply that disputants' positions
were reached without certain *a priori* assertions which were rather
difficult to oppose. Among these untested assumptions was the one
which held that there was a contradiction between socialism and a
commodity economy and between every form of plan and market.
Communist economic thinking, especially just following the Revolution, was dominated by the conviction that the progress of building
socialism was inseparably linked with the unfolding of a system of

---

[1] Another sign is to be found in the republication of several works from this
period, e.g. *Na planovom frontie* (Moscow, 1958), a collection of Strumilin's
articles.

physical allocation. Thus, under 'war communism' (and even later), practical attempts were made to solve the problem of direct calculation in labour units by the so-called reduction method (the reduction of complex labour to simple labour).[1] Here, too, can be found the roots of the early attempts to treat hyper-inflation, during and shortly after the Civil War, as a process of eliminating money. As such, it is a concept which seemed to agree with the corresponding point in the programme of the Russian Communist Party.[2]

With the transition to the New Economic Policy the circumstances in which the theoreticians worked were slightly altered. The need arose for a theoretical study of the role of market links between town and countryside and of the effects induced by the revival of a money–commodity economy *(khozraschot)*, in the socialist sector itself. Analyses of market processes and the resultant conclusions for planning were important both in economic policy and in theoretical work.

The first signs of change in Marxist views toward market-plan relationships came when the idea of their mutual negation transformed itself among some circles into the conception of the market as a special kind of planning mechanism. The system of physical allocation 'war communism' was no longer generally treated as an economic synonym for paradise, lost.

In the discussion aroused by Preobrazhenski's book (cf. *infra*) Pashukanis, a prominent lawyer and economist, emphasized the importance of using value forms. Failure to employ them would lead to a reversal to such unpopular and ineffective economic methods as compulsory mobilization of labour, allowing no freedom of movement for workers in their jobs, rationing, etc.[3]

G. Sokolnikov makes some interesting comments on the part to be played by money. As a specialist in monetary policy and long-time Commissar for Finance he wrote:[4]

> By itself money bears a certain right to choose goods on the market for everyone who possesses it . . . This freedom of choice on the market is absolutely necessary for the small (commodity) producer. To what degree is it indispensable for the worker, and were we correct in going over to this form of freedom from coercion which existed during the Civil War? I think so. Trying to

[1] See, for example, E. Varga, 'Reckoning of the Value of Production in a Moneyless Economy', *Ekonomicheskaya Zhizn*, no. 259, 1920, which provoked much discussion.

[2] See above, pp. 15–16. Some typical statements on this subject are quoted by Dobb in *Soviet Economic Development since 1917*, pp. 121–2.

[3] *Vestnik Kommunisitcheskoi Akademii*, no. 14, 1926.

[4] G. Sokolnikov, 'O korennykh voprosakh denezhnovo obrashchenya v perekhodnuyu epokhu', *Sotsialisticheskoye Khozyaistvo*, no. 5, 1925.

organize the economy so much that the consumption of each human unit is regulated compulsorily is to set oneself an essentially incorrect task and, for the present, one which is quite unfeasible. The regulation of consumption must be carried out in a different manner—a much more complicated manner—through wages and price policies, etc.

I. Smilga puts the problem even more generally:[1]

What does the principle of *khozraschot* mean? It means economic management in order to obtain the maximum effect for the minimum of outlay. In theoretical terms it means the restoration of the operation of the law of value, constrained by a series of specific orders issued by the state . . . The law of value can be compared to a machine gun which serves the man who fires it. To attempt to treat the law of value and planning as mutually exclusive factors is no less than an attempt to reopen the problem of plan and market, which has already been settled in practice in the conditions of the New Economic Policy.

Not only can there be found opposition to using administrative measures[2] in Soviet literature of this time, but there are even attempts to give a general description of socialist economy based on economic motives[3] and stressing the need to preserve marked equilibrium in planning.[4]

On the basis of the fragmentary materials available it is hard to say whether, and to what degree even these writers extended their outlook to the socialist economy in general. Did those who were emphasizing the market as an instrument of a planned economy limit themselves only to the multi sectoral (public and private) transitional economy? Perhaps, the last alternative is best supported by the documentation cited above. At any rate some of the chief representatives of the old guard Marxist economists stubbornly clung to this view supporting the physical allocation used under war communism, Lev Kritzman, the author of a comprehensive monograph on war communism, wrote:[5]

[1] Smilga, 'Piat let NEPa', *Planovoye Khozyaistvo*, no. 2, 1926.

[2] 'Where *khozraschot* is employed, administrative means of influence are by no means the best', A. Mendelson, 'Planirovaniye promyshlennosti', *Planovoye Khozyaistvo* no. 3, 1926.

[3] Every economic organization ought to find itself in an economic environment such that by the exclusive pursuit of its own advantage it will fulfil the will of the economy as a whole. Y. Repshe, 'Nashi ekonomicheskiye problemy', *Planovove Khozyaistvo*, no. 2, 1926.

[4] V. Novozhilov, 'Niedostatek towarov', *Vestnik Finansov*, no. 2, 1926.

[5] L. Kritzman, *Geroicheskiy period Velikoy Russkoy Rewolustii. Opyt analiza tak nazyvayemogo voennogo kommunizma*, 2nd ed., 1926, p. 177.

War communism was the first large-scale experience of a proletarian economy run in physical terms, the experience of the first
steps in the transition to socialism. In essence it was not a mistake
made by some people or a class. Rather despite certain distortions
and its lack of purity, it was an anticipation of the future, a transformation of the future into the past (a present which already
belongs to the past).

The situation was also clearly expressed by Kzhyshanovski, the
first president of the Gosplan:[1]

Was it intended under war communism to create the outline of a
moneyless economy? It is easy to show that there was a clear
intention to create such an outline ... the transition to free turnover of commodities and to a more or less explicit money economy
... constitutes a tactical retreat.

Thus, one can say that even in the middle of the 1920s when the
area covered by money–commodity relations and the degree to which
they were used were at their apex, it was still strongly held that the
reasons for the appearance of the money–commodity relation were to
be found outside that socialist economy itself and that the 'market'
was a synonym for 'spontaneity'. And, although the development of
a new socialist-type market as an important element in the operation
of the economy did make some headway, it did so only with very
great difficulty.

Towards the end of the 1920s, as the first five-year plan went into
operation, anti-market views decisively won the upper hand. In
practice, all theoretical 'concessions' in this sphere were sharply condemned as everywhere 'planned economy' because equal to direct
administrative methods of operation, and the market was just as
clearly identified with spontaneity. A 1930 article by Strumilin dealt
with this relation between plan and market in the NEP.[2]

By opening up a certain area for the operation of spontaneous
market relations in the name of peace with the countryside, the
New Economic Policy *had serious and long-term, but no permanent
intentions*. It was intended, as it became possible to plan the
economy more and more fully, gradually but quite consistently to
limit the spontaneity of the market until this element had been
entirely replaced by planning.

[1] G. Kzhyshanovski, 'K voprosu ob ideologii sotzialisticheskogo stroitelst-
va', *Planovoye Khozyaistvo*, no. 1, 1926.
[2] S. Strumilin, 'Pervye opyty perspektivnovo plainrovanya' in his book *Na
planovom fronte*, p. 247, (italics are in the original).

In dissecting the theoretical views of these Soviet economists, it must be remembered that their negative attitude towards markets derived from practical conditions of that period as well as a particular line of thinking which appeared on the theoretical front. Generally, the practical causes of this attitude towards the market are to be found in the fact that the private sector (including capitalists) contrived to adapt itself to the market better than the socialized enterprises did. To this extent it is fair to say that the market was a spontaneous element hindering the planning activity of the state and the development of socialism.

At the same time, in the theoretical realm, representatives of bourgeois economics came out in defence of the market; views in no way different from those of Mises were expressed by Boris Brutzkus, later an emigrant, who tried to prove the impossibility of having a national economy without a market in his lectures at the University of Petrograd during 1920.[1]

Another group of economists, while accepting the Soviet system and a planned economy, advocated an NEP-form of market as an indispensable component of any planning system. Further, they held that market phenomena must be treated as the starting point for determining the aims of the plan, and they held that changes in market conditions must be the most essential element for assessing the fulfilment of those tasks. The stand of this group of economists received a good deal of attention from Strumilin in an article referred to above. Thus, he quotes the following statements of Bazarov from archival material (protocols of the meetings of the presidium and committees of the Gosplan):

> Basic assumptions of NEP, i.e. *the existence of a market and khozraschot* constitutes the basis of *all possible planning*, independently of whether a world revolution takes place or not. Historical experience shows a *healthy interest* in the result of his work. But that is not enough: only the market in the present conditions allows the creation of *an automatic control* of all operations, an automatic meter, showing the results of the operation of each branch of the economy and of each enterprise individually.

---

[1] These lectures were later included as part 2 of a book by Brutzkus, *Economic Planning in Soviet Russia*. (London, 1935). In 1937, in the Warsaw *Economist*, he published an article entitled 'Plan i rynek w Rosji Sowieckiej' (Plan and market in Soviet Russia) where he describes these lectures as follows: 'The basic ideas of my lectures are the same as those to be found in the critique of natural-economy socialism in the well-known book by the Viennese professor, Ludwig von Mises, *Die Gemeinwirtschaft*, although the author of this article had no access to Western literature as he was living in Russia' (*Ekonomista*, 4, 1937, p. 51).

Groman and Kondratiev, as Strumilin writes, subscribed un-reservedly to Bazarov's views.[1]

I agree with Bazarov's thesis (says Kondratiev in the same pro-tocol) that the existence of the NEP is not only not contradictory to the plan, but constitutes one of its foundations. The market and prices, undoubtedly, constitute a basis for formulating the plan, even if only because, otherwise, we lose all possibility of a commensurate view of economic phenomena.

Obviously it is difficult to judge these views without being able to undertake a more extensive study of the content and context of each of their statements. This may be especially needed as Strumilin's article was written in 1930, hence in the period when there had just been a transition to centralist forms of planning and marked intensi-fication of ideological campaigns in economics. It appears from his article that they made a fetish of the market, proposing the adapta-tion of the tasks of the plan and the forms of its fulfilment to the current and predicted market situation. Hence they seemed to advocate a *sui generis* supremacy of the market over the plan.

The statements of Kalinnikov, the then director of the industrial section of the Gosplan, also manifest this clearly. 'The production plan should correspond not to the theoretical needs of the state and the population for products, but to their ability to pay ... This assertion should be recognized as basic, since all departures from it will cause over-production and market crises, with all its conse-quences in the form of unused enterprises, unemployment, etc.'[2] The real interrelations appearing in a socialist economy are inverted, but disagreement with this approach to the plan–market problem does not necessitate adopting the conclusion drawn by Strumilin when he denied that it was possible to reconcile socialism with the market:[3]

In accepting the market as an indispensable basis for all possible planning, we would have to pay too high a price—it would mean relinquishing socialism as a system, since it is incompatible with this basis.

Our subject demands consideration of yet another aspect of the theoretical discussions of this period. This was the long, passionate dispute about the main regulator of economic processes in the Soviet economy of that time. True, it was not mainly concerned with the problems of the mechanism of the functioning of the economy (and hence the forms of its operation); it dealt chiefly with the content of

[1] S. Strumilin, *Na planovom fronte*, pp. 253–4 (his italics).
[2] *Ibid.*, p. 257.
[3] *Ibid.*, p. 254.

planning and with the character of its proportion between various macro-economic magnitudes such as major sectoral growth rate and type of output and between savings and investment. However, indirectly this particular dispute is very important to our undertaking, since it so closely relates to the theory of socialism.

The core of the debate was a book by Preobrazhenski *Novaya ekonomika*[1] containing a number of theses which were attacked by Bukharin.[2] The dispute culminated in the several-day debate in the Communist Academy over that chapter dealing with the law of value in a socialist economy. Although, Bukharin did not actually take part in the verbal struggle, an article of his was read as a co-report and during the discussion views very similar to his were expressed by many of the participants.[3] Thus Preobrazhenski and Bukharin may be considered the main protagonists in the great debate, and this feeling is reinforced by their respective positions as the most important Marxist economic theorists for the contending wings of the opposition within the communist party; Preobrazhenski was one of Trotski's chief representatives, while Bukharin was the leader of the right-wing opposition.

In relating our discussion to the problem of a socialist model the analyses of commodity trade and the experiences of the contemporary Soviet economy are particularly important. Here our chief source is Preobrazhenski's book and the summary of the discussion in the Communist Academy. Leaving aside problems particular to the USSR of that time (the relative magnitude of private trade, the nature and structure of foreign trade etc.), we note the attempt to differentiate markets on the basis of the types of parties dealing on them and the influence of the state on the exchange processes. Among others Preobrazhenski differentiates:

1. Turnover between state enterprises, where, he feels, only the *forms* of commodity exchange make their appearance and the law of value operates exclusively through the labour force and then to an extent which varies directly with the number of wage-goods purchased from private producers and retailers.

2. Turnover in which the state appears as a monopoly producer, but not as a monopoly seller (mainly where manufactured goods are

[1] Preobrazhenski, *Novaya ekonomika Opyt teoreticheskovo analiza sovietskovo khozyaistva.* Kommunistitsheskaja Akademia, Moscow, 1926, vol. 1, part 1.

[2] N. Bukharin, 'K Voprosu o zakonomernostyakh perekhodnogo perioda. Kriticheskiye zamechanie na knigu tov. Preobrazhenskogo 'Novaya ekonomika',' *Pravda*, 9. nos. 148, 150, 153, 1926.

[3] The discussion, together with Preobrazhenski's summing up, was published verbatim in *Vestnik Kommunisticheskoi Akademii*, nos. 14 and 15, 1926. Among those taking part were Stetski, Mendelson, Pashukanis, Motilev, Chernomordik, Rosenberg, Bogdanov and Kritzman.

sold in the countryside). This sphere is controlled by the state, which determines prices, but which must reckon with a structure of demand, considerably influenced by incomes from private holdings. Thus, it forms a 'field of battle' between the new laws regulating economic processes and the law of value, which retains a certain influence.

3. Turnover in which the state appears as a purchaser (most frequently along with other purchasers and hence not as monopolist). This case applies mainly to the purchase of agricultural raw materials. Here the direction of influence is contrary to previous cases since the basic price ratios are established by the law of value, and state price founded on new economic laws policy can only operate within this framework. (The maximum price—the world market price, the minimum—dictated by profitability.)

4. Retail turnover in consumer goods (mainly sales to the urban population). Preobrazhenski feels that the operation of the law of value is manifested through the necessity of maintaining equilibrium between demand and supply by price policies. However, price should not necessarily affect the distribution of labour (and hence the pattern of output) in production (e.g. the automatic rise in output where price exceeds value.)

Preobrazhenski's market morphology is striking because he attempts to avoid a schematic reply to whether exchange in the Soviet economy of that time is commodity exchange in its economic content. There is an attempt here to interpret Lenin's thesis that the product of a socialist factory is ceasing to be a commodity (*possessed of an absolute monetary value by virtue of the direct and indirect labour input*); hence products are part of a process which proceeds in different ways depending on the sphere of turnover. Preobrazhenski's division of markets into different spheres according to the strength of the operation of the law of value, in itself, indicates his standpoint with regard to the question of commodity turnover in the condition of socialist production relations. Directly put:[1]

Market relations within the area of state property are by no means the result of immanent laws of development and the structure of the state's economy itself. Market relations are here formal and imposed on the state economy from without, by the form of its mutual relations with the private sector.

It is characteristic that Preobrazhenski differentiates between the operation of the law of value in the sphere of state ownership and in the sphere of co-operative ownership. 'The co-operative sector is considerably weaker than state organs in resisting the law of value.'[2]

[1] E. Preobrazhenski, Clarendon Press Ed., *Novaya ekonomika*, p. 160.
[2] *Vestnik Kommunisticheskoi Akademii*, no. 16, 1926, p. 62.

His view that commodity relations within the state-dominated sphere are formal and that this character results from external factors, is interesting since he stated it a quarter of a century before Stalin's similar conception in *Economic Problems of Socialism in the USSR.* It is not at all impossible that we have here the roots of Stalin's theoretical inspiration.

However, Preobrazhenski was more precise than Stalin, chiefly because he attempted to distinguish clearly between the use of money–commodity forms and the operation of the law of value in the strict sense. 'The sphere in which money exchange appears is not identical with the sphere in which the law of value operates.'[1] The book's text and related discussion, show Preobrazhenski and his supporters (Solntsev, Kogan etc.) as concerned with at least two problems:

1. The essential feature of the operation of the law of value is spontaneity, while a socialist economy demands a planned determination of proportions (between the different branches and economic categories of the economy) to the end that even if we use market forms to establish these proportions, the law of value no longer operates.

2. The operation of the law of value is connected not only with the specific *method* of achieving the proportions within the economy, but above all with a definite content of the proportions. In other words, the operation of the law of value leads (or at least, tends to lead) to equivalence of exchange where price conforms to cost and therefore no surplus for investment is generated. And it is just this which Preobrazhenski feels cannot be tolerated in the Soviet economy, especially at this period. The problem is to obtain exchange relations other than those which would develop as a result of the operation of the law of value. Clearly other types of exchange relations would also involve other proportions in the distribution of social labour and other proportions in the growth of individual branches of production.

Obviously, the second problem is the most important. It is associated with Preobrazhenski's thesis on the law of primitive socialist accumulation, which is in conflict with the law of value in the role of economic regulator in the transition period. The law of primitive socialist accumulation is well known from later references in Soviet literature, in handbooks of the history of the Communist Party of the Soviet Union, and in handbooks of political economy. It became a kind of theoretical symbol of the anti-peasant tendencies of the Trotskyites. Undoubtedly, such an assessment of the political content of the law of primitive socialist accumulation is not ground-

[1] E. Preobrazhenski, *op. cit.,* p. 158.

less, especially given the actual conditions of the period. Nevertheless, I feel that the way in which Preobrazhenski's theory was elaborated at the time was decidedly over-simplified, especially if the actual course of later events is taken into account (the extent and way to which the countryside participates in ensuring the needs of accumulation in the USSR). *In toto* his argument goes as follows:

The basic problem of the socialist revolution, especially in backward countries, is the creation of the conditions for economic development on the basis of new productive relations. This means that radical change is necessary in the prevailing relative importance of different branches. To accomplish this task with relative rapidity requires the accumulation of a large supply of means, because the normal process of accumulation, corresponding to market proportions, would be too slow. It is doubtful whether the latter would have been feasible bearing in mind external conditions and the requirements of the socialist rebuilding of the countryside. Hence there is a need to accelerate the process and to enable a 'supernormal' accumulation concentrated in strictly delineated sectors. This process Preobrazhenski describes as the law of primitive socialist accumulation, by analogy to its capitalist counterpart. Obviously, no analogy is to be found in the methods, but in the fact that in both cases normal market processes are not sufficient (too slow) for the triumph of the new relations of production and thus demand special intervention. Conclusion: the law of primitive socialist accumulation requires that exchange be non-equivalent (or not in conformity) and hence contradicts the law of market exchange and *sensu stricto* the law of value.

As we can see, Preobrazhenski is not proposing to discard money–commodity *forms*. The main issue for him is not *forms*, but the economic content of exchange relations. The content constitutes a conscious non-equivalence (of value and price), redistributing means in favour of socialist industrialization. It is meant not as a concession but as a norm, a part of the pattern of the period. He openly cites the behaviour of monopolies, and emphasizes the importance of accumulation of the monopoly of foreign trade. In Soviet conditions exporting grain and selling manufactured goods to peasants at a higher price than in the open market provides another instrument for redistributing income.

It would be incorrect to think that this redistribution of income from the countryside to industry is the sole source of accumulation. He credited the importance of accumulation in socialist industry, and with a frankness to be respected, he noted that 'the terrible poverty of the period of war and revolution . . . became and remained one of the elements of socialist accumulation, in the sense that in the light

of this recent expression, it is easier for working class itself to limit its needs in the years when the task of socialist accumulation is the main one'.[1] Furthermore, Preobrazhenski held one source of accumulation insufficient, since, among other things, the low level of the maturation of productive forces (technological attainments) hinders the growth of labour productivity and the reduction of cost. An additional point of interest here is the remark that some features of the socialist organization of production, which are in themselves advantageous, have a negative effect on the accumulative ability of socialist enterprises. This is a reference to the development of labour protection, social services, the shortening of the working day, the abolition of intensive labour, etc.

From the preceding is derived the necessity of finding considerable means outside the socialist sector, mainly in the countryside. Thus Preobrazhenski feels the chief purpose of primitive socialist accumulation, for planning in the transition period, is to create changed proportions and structure of division of labour different from those that derive from the unimpeded operation of market forces. In this sense the law of primitive socialist accumulation is an economic regulator, but it is not the only one since the basis for commodity production and the operation of the law of value as a regulator in certain areas have not vanished. From this arises the thesis of two regulators and of the conflict between them; the law of primitive socialist accumulation versus the law of value, non-equivalence versus equivalence. These are the basic indications of the main contradiction in this transition period, the contradiction between socialism and capitalism.

Bukharin strongly attacked this theory of two regulators together with Bogdanov, Eichenwald, Pashukanis and to some extent Motilev, though there was never complete agreement among them. In the article mentioned above, 'A contribution to the problems of the patterns of development in the transition period' (later in brochure form) Bukharin advanced his own concept of the regulator. As in the preceding discussion, although Bukharin's theses refer mainly to the transition period, they do contain a number of elements of general significance for the functioning of a socialist economy.

Briefly stated his position goes as follows:

The socialization of the means of production makes it possible to replace the *spontaneous* regulating mechanism of the economy by a planned mechanism. In the sense of a spontaneous regulator the law of value disappears from the scene as the socialist economic base develops. But the law of value in its material content is something more than a mere spontaneous regulator of private commodity

[1] *Ibid.*, p. 137.

production. It is the particular historical form taken by the general law of the proportional division of labour in society (or, as it was then often expressed—the law of the proportionality of social labour outlays). Two passages from Marx are cited in this connection, which later in the course of the discussion are interpreted in every conceivable way.[1]

> No form of society can avoid regulation of production in one way or another, by means of the labour time which is at the disposal of society. However, so long as this regulation is performed not by direct conscious control of society over its labour time (only possible when property is socialized) but by the movement of prices of goods, then everything which you have already stated correctly in the *Deutsch–Franzoesische Jahrbuecher* remains in force.

The second passage is from the letter of 11th July 1868 from Marx to Kugelmann:[2]

> Every child knows that any nation which ceased to work for two weeks, let alone a year, would perish. Every child also knows that in order to produce a mass of products satisfying a variety of needs, various and quantitatively determined amounts of joint social labour are indispensable. Hence it is *self-evident* that a *given form* of social production can in no way dispense with the *necessity of distributing* social labour in definite proportions; it can only alter the manner in which it makes *its appearance*. The laws of nature cannot be done away with. In different historical conditions, only the form in which these laws appear can be changed. Hence in a social system where the interdependence of social labour exists in the shape of private exchange of individual products, the form in which proportional distribution of labour manifests itself is the exchange value of these products.

Bukharin develops his argument in the same spirit: in socialism the law of value is transformed into a law of the proportionality of society's labour inputs, a universal law of economic equilibrium. The spontaneous division of labour is replaced by a planned division without the capitalist tendency to achieve equilibrium by continually disturbing it. But the material content which was always concealed

---

[1] Letter to Engels, 8.1.1868, (from Marx and Engels, *Listy o 'Kapitale'* (*Letters on 'Capital'*) Warsaw, 1957, p. 148). In referring to the *Deutsch-Franzoesische Jahrbuecher* Marx had in mind Engels' *Outline of Critique of Political Economy* printed in his periodical in 1844, (See Marx and Engels, *Selected Works*, vol. 1). In this essay Engels gives a critical account of capitalist competition.

[2] *Letters on 'Capital'*, p. 188.

behind the form of the law of value remains; the share of a given branch of enterprise in society's income is proportional to the amount of indispensable labour contained in the products of this branch or enterprise. The plan anticipates these proportions, which in perfect circumstances (one might say in conditions of perfect competition) would be developed as the result of the operation of market forces. As Bukharin states the plan is 'an anticipation of what would establish itself (*post factum*) if regulation was spontaneous.'[1]

In asserting that the plan may not disturb the proportionality of the division of society's labour (i.e. that society ought to observe the principle of recompensating labour outlays) Bukharin has a theoretical basis for rejecting the principle of the non-equivalence of urban–rural exchange. It will be recalled that the latter was elevated by Preobrazhenski to the rank of the law of primitive socialist accumulation. Non-equivalence endangers the normal conditions for reproduction in individual branches and enterprises, and particularly farms. For this reason Bukharin finds in Preobrazhenski a symptom of 'economic futurism' which threatens to sever vital links between various spheres of the economy, (chiefly between industry and agriculture).[2]

> According to Preobrazhenski the proletarian plan consists in systematically jolting society out of balance by systematically disturbing the socially necessary proportions between different branches, i.e. a systematic conflict with the most elementary conditions for the existence of a society.

This is a concept of extreme importance in understanding Bukharin and other economists of his period, proponents of the laws of the proportionality of social outlays and hence the equivalence of exchange. One of the basic tasks of a planned economy is to guarantee equilibrium or correct proportions between branches of production and, in addition, between all the spheres of economic life (industry, agriculture, production—consumption, demand and supply structures etc.). To ignore these broadly conceived proportions spells instability. In a later article just prior to the attack on him as the leader of the right-wing deviation, Bukharin wrote: 'Elements of crisis which jar the course of reproduction can be found only in the disturbance of the foundations of economic equilibrium, i.e. they result from an improper juxtaposition of the elements of reproduction (including consumption)'. He continues with the following significant remark: 'the disturbance of the necessary

[1] *Pravda*, no. 150, 1926.
[2] *Ibid.*

economic interdependances has its obverse in the disturbance of political equilibrium of the country.'[1]

Again we have here a clearly formulated 'theory of equilibrium' we know from numerous later presentations sometimes of a rather simplified nature. One of the main oversimplifications was the identification of the concept of equilibrium and the law of proportionality of society's labour outlays with the thesis that the Soviet economy ought to preserve the pre-war proportion between industry and agriculture. This proportion (1:2) was said to correspond to 'the optimum economic conditions of Russia.'[2] However, this accusation hardly seems justified by an analysis of Bukharin's statements. In an article directed against Preobrazhenski, Bukharin clearly emphasizes that the proportions established under the influence of the law of the proportionality of labour outlays will differ basically from the old capitalistic proportions. This is primarily because of radical changes in the distribution of the national income, in the demand structure and in the whole complex of conditions which determine the proportions of an economy. He does not hold that the law of the proportionality of labour outlays fixes immutably some rate of growth which does not allow, say, acceleration. Rather he was chiefly concerned to maintain an *equilibrium* in the growth process, to ensure what we now call *balanced growth*, Bazarov also focused attention on the question of balanced growth[3]

> The economic plan ought to solve two cardinal problems which constitute the goal of the plan; determination of the condition of the line of transition from the present system of equilibrium to the future one.

Bukharin yields a similar formulation:[4] 'The task is to determine the foundations for a proper connection between different spheres of production and consumption, or in other words—the foundations of a moving economic equilibrium.'

Obviously he realized that in the mixed Soviet economy of his time, the process of transforming the law of value into the law of the proportionality of social labour outlays, was only in its initial stage. In many sectors the law of value still operated in its old form favouring the rebirth of capitalism and elements of the plan and elements of

---

[1] N. Bukharin, 'Zametki ekonomista', *Pravda*, no. 228, (4080) 30.9.1928.

[2] Among those who interpreted Buhkarin's conception in this way was A. Leontiev in his article, 'Zakon trudovych zatrat, yevo metodologicheskye korni i prakticheskie sledstviya', *Sotsialisticheskoye Khozaistvo*, no. 5, 1929.

[3] V. Bazarov, *Kapitalisticheskye tsykly i vostanovitelnyi khozyaistva USRR*, Moscow-Leningrad, 1927.

[4] N. Bukharin, *op. cit.* See also the criticism of this conception in G. Glezerman, *Teoriya rivnovahy i Marksizm* (in Ukrainian), Kharkov, 1930.

spontaneity were continually at war with each other. Nevertheless he, unlike his principal antagonist, considered that only the form of the operation of the law of value, and not the material content concealed within it (equivalence), hindered the development of socialism. He thought that it was possible and necessary for the socialist state, founded on socialist economic sectors, to utilize the market and the law of value.

Preobrazhenski replied to Bukharin's criticisms at length in the second edition of this book and in the discussion in the Communist Academy.

He doubted whether there was any validity in the statement that the law of value is supplanted as a regulator by the planning element merely because of social ownership. This statement is meaningless if it is not known what is meant by the plan and hence how economic proportions are to be shaped. Bukharin's reasoning on the latter subject, the proportionality of labour inputs, can be considered correct only when the socialist mode of production is completely developed. This eventuality exists not only when new productive relations hold absolute way, but also when the same is true of the new productive forces corresponding to socialism.

According to Preobrazhenski every regulator of the economic system has two functions: 1. the satisfaction of the needs of society in a way appropriate to the given conditions; 2. the self-preservation and development of the system (expanded reproduction of the means of production). If it were merely a question of the former function, the whole problem of planning would boil down to allocating society's labour so that the demands of the law of the proportionality of outlays would be fulfilled (where the most intensive need of the final consumer appeared, there, the relative amount of social labour would be the greatest and *vice versa*). It is the necessity to reckon with the second function which means that frequently specific proportions are required 'which can be formed neither under the influence of the pure form of law of proportionality of social labour outlays i.e. in conditions where production is designed only to satisfy needs.'[1] Again and again this same *leit-motiv* reappears. The chief difference of opinion lies in the proportions which are to be achieved; the question of the mechanism is secondary. Markets and their prices cannot provide indicators sufficient for determining the proportions which are to change the economic structure radically. Today's structure of investment (and hence also the structure of the production of investment goods) must, to a certain degree, correspond to the structure of needs which have not thus far manifested themselves in

[1] E. Preobrazhenski, *op. cit.* Introduction to the second edition. (Moscow, 1926).

effective demand but which are, in part, created by today's investments. For this reason it is not possible to limit planning to the anticipation of the operation of the market; this would be to transform the
plan into a *sui generis* instrument of the law of value.

I have attempted to render as true an account of the argument as
possible, leaving out all the secondary elements. Although not everything in this discussion is, perhaps, clear to us today, one thing is
certain: we have here a consideration of the same problem from two
sides. Preobrazhenski devotes his main attention to the acute
development problems of Baran's 'steep approach' in which a
sudden change of proportions becomes of particular importance.
Bukharin, on the other hand, attaches much greater importance to
allocation, the correct distribution of social labour, the preservation
of equilibrium and the balanced development of every branch of
production and consumption. The former concentrates mainly on
large-scale investment and primarily on investment in the production
of the means of production. The latter is the sphere not directly connected with the current structure of consumer demand and with the
market. Bukharin's reasoning clearly emphasizes the fullest possible
use of the existing productive apparatus with a more gradual growth
of investment and allowing for needs indicated by the market situation. The distance between their ideas has to do with their different
approaches to the make-up of class forces (especially the peasantry)
and to the speed of reconstruction of socio-economic relations.

The importance of the Preobrazhenski–Bukharin controversy for
the theory of the functioning of a socialist economy is found
primarily in general methodological conclusions. Although these conclusions are not always explicit in their statements they are implicit
in the method which they both employ to deal with the problem—in
spite of the profound differences in opinion, they have a largely
similar method. Both Preobrazhenski and Bukharin differentiate
between the operation of the law of value and the existence of money–
commodity forms. Bukharin, for example, in defending the need to
preserve equivalence (in accordance with the law of the proportionality of social labour outlays and, hence, with the material content of
the law value) did not identify this with the application of market
forms. On the contrary, in the long run he foresaw an appropriate
solution in directly determined proportions by planning bodies, but
so as to guarantee equilibrium on the basis of equivalence. For
Preobrazhenski the essence of the problem could be found in non-
equivalence as the source of primitive socialist accumulation. Again,
however, this was not identical to abandoning money–commodity
forms or commodity exchange as an instrument of redistribution;
furthermore, as we have seen from extracts, Preobrazhenski clearly

E

emphasized the differences between the law of value and money–commodity forms.

This is not the right place to analyse distinctions between the law of value and commodity forms. We only note it in order to deal with it later as one of the essential elements in the theory of the functioning of a socialist economy.[1]

We would be underestimating the importance of the Preobraz-henski–Bukharin discussion if we limited its significance for defining a model to this methodological conclusion. Although the chief point of contention was that of the areas of expansion and the proportions of them in the process of reproduction—bearing in mind existing conditions—each of these two concepts ultimately brings us to the question of the mechanism of the operation of the economy. Without a doubt the policy contained in Preobrazhenski, a more violent change of structure and a greater straining of industrial effort, is nearer to the practice of large-scale applications of direct administrative methods of management than the economic policy implicit in Bukharin. I do not intend to judge which concept was correct (such a judgment would be problematical since both contain correct and incorrect elements). I am concerned only to emphasize that there is a certain—though by no means automatic—connection between the content of the tasks of economic planning and the forms by which they are achieved. The latter point is quite clear from statements by each of the authors. In Bukharin's case, while discussing the Five-Year Plan in 'An Economist's Notes', he emphasizes the need for realistic investment targets (especially in relation to available supplies of material and labour) and warns against the consequence of allowing disproportions between the development of industry and agriculture to evolve. ('From the long-term point of view the greatest rate of development is obtained when a rapidly developing agriculture accompanies the development of industry.') At the same time he formulates a series of what we would call today postulates of the model.[2]

> We ought to set in motion the maximum number of economic elements working for socialism. This requires an extremely complicated combination of different forms of initiative—personal, group, mass, social, and state. We have overcentralized everything. We should ask ourselves whether we would not be better to take a few steps in the direction of a commune-state. This does not mean letting go of the reins, since basic decisions and the most important problems ought to be more strongly and much more categorically

---

[1] See in particular chapter 5.
[2] N. Bukharin, *op. cit.*

(and thereby more carefully) handled by decisions made at the top. Bodies at lower levels already operate within the strict terms of such decisions, responsible for their own domain. Over centralization in many areas means that we deprive ourselves of additional forces, means, resources, and possibilities. We are unable to employ many of these possibilities because of a multitude of bureaucratic hindrances. We could operate more elastically, with more of the necessary manoeuvrability and with much better results, if, beginning with the individual state enterprise, we were better able to adjust to real conditions. In this way we could avoid making thousands of more or less stupid mistakes which in the end constitute a large total.

The debate broadly outlined here obviously does not exhaust the history of discussions of a model in USSR. However their character was changed in the following period which also marked a turning point in the history of Soviet economic science. The total condemnation of both the achievements and the whole trend of development of Soviet economics up to that time ended many creative and extremely promising theoretical discussions and studies. Traces of controversies on various subjects including the problems of a model should be sought from them not so much in public statements of economists, as in the authoritative pronouncements of political leaders (above all Stalin) who laid down the obligatory interpretation of practical economic measures.

The economic literature of the 1930s and the 1940s was devoted either to particular elements of the existing highly centralized economic mechanism or to general theoretical considerations and interpretations of the system which was taken as given. This derived from the general atmosphere of those times and also no doubt from a broad and deeply-rooted conviction that a planned economy was to be identified with the maximum centralization of all economic decisions. Changes occurred only in the 1950s and then especially after the 20th party congress of the Communist Party of the Soviet Union.

Because of the circumstances of economic theory, the centre of concern about the functioning of a socialist economy shifted to the practical process of the formation and development of a system of management. At the end of the 1920s the practical manner of achieving the general Party line in the struggle for the building of socialism was defined. Above all the rate and methods of industrialization and the collectivization of agriculture were fixed. In the period which followed a system of economic management crystallized,

which basically was to last almost a quarter of a century forming the only known pattern of a socialist economic model.[1]

Before recapitulating, one point needs to be made. Irrespective of how this system is regarded today,[2] beyond a doubt the shaping of the first socialist economy was a contribution of historical importance for the development both of socialist economic practice and of theory, which cannot progress without a reality from which to generalize.

Our brief survey of the theoretical heritage of the principles of the functioning of a socialist economy may be summarized as follows:

The works of Marx and Engels and other Marxist writers prior to the October Revolution provide a number of valuable general premises for a planned economy. However especially because these general conceptions were rather hastily applied to more detailed elements of the functioning of the economy, some of their suggestions have been interpreted as arguments favouring the elimination of all forms of market relations and founding the socialist economy on the principles of in-kind distribution.

Western discussions during the inter-war years not only discredited

---

[1] The principles of the Soviet system of management were laid down at that time in a resolution of the Central Committee of the All-Union Communist Party (b) 5th December 1929 on the reorganization of industry. This resolution is one normally cited as strongly emphasizing the role of the enterprises ('the enterprise is the main link in economic control'). However, for the enterprise this was a promotion due to the liquidation or severe restriction of the trusts which, hitherto, had been the basic institution in the industrial organization, and had operated on the principle of profitability within the general limits of the plan. The new reform gave enterprises juridical independence but not by any means the breadth of decision-making which the trusts had possessed. The unit immediately superior to the enterprises was then the 'obyedinenye' (Association), which rapidly developed into an administrative organ as it took over the main functions of the old syndicates along with certain elements of economic autonomy. The elimination of 'Associations' in 1934 and the transfer of their functions to the central branch director's offices which served as organs of the Ministries gave formal recognition to this evolution.

The subordination of all aspects of an enterprise's activities to a system of planning directives proceeded concomitantly with the expansion of the directing managerial organs. They rapidly changed from centres of economic policy to centres of operative control. In 1932 the Supreme Council of the National Economy was broken into four industrial commissariats (ministries) which increased to 21 by war's outbreak.

Corresponding to the changes in the organization of industry, the organization of planning and the financial system (unification of the tax system, credit reform 1930-1) were also altered.

[2] Attempts are made to make an analysis of this kind in chapter 3, and to some extent in chapter 4.

the view that socialist economic calculation is impossible, but in a polemic among socialism's adherents, produced a series of interesting interpretations of the problem of the plan and market and of centralism and decentralism in a socialist economy.

The importance of the Soviet debate of the 1920s lies in the attempts to formulate the economic theory of socialism on Marxist methodological assumptions and in the connection between the problems of building models and economic socio-political practice. It is especially important that the Soviet debate faced the problems of the relationship of the law of value to money–commodity forms, of the plan and the market, of centralization and decentralization etc. Moreover, the way in which these problems were handled demonstrates that they arise directly from practice and are not merely invented by theoreticians.

In general, then, it is fair to say that the history of the functioning of a socialist economy has a great deal to say about the problem. It is worth examining and as far as possible filling the lacunae especially in the Soviet debate. On the other hand, it is difficult to expect these sources to give direct answers to the problems now facing us, since in the past the problems were raised rather than solved.

The point of asserting this truism is to indicate the complete lack of foundation of the accusation that the quest for new solutions in this field is an attempt to overthrow long established maxims of Marxist science.

3   The centralized model

The discussion of the model of the functioning of a socialist economy revolves about two problems: plan and market—centralization and decentralization of economic decision-making. Basically these are not even two separate problems but two aspects of the same problem; for it is impossible to extend the areas of an enterprise's decision-making without simultaneously increasing the role of the market from which the criteria for such decisions are largely taken. It is not intended that the market and plan or centralization and decentralization should be read as alternatives. True there are some economists (their number is shrinking) who regard the problems as one of choosing one of two mutually exclusive possibilities. But, from earlier discussion (certain aspects of which are in chapter 2) and from current debates it is apparent that the solution of the problem must be sought on a different plane; it is a question of the way in which the plan and the market are connected and of the optimum areas for centralized and decentralized decisions. On reflection it becomes increasingly obvious that the contradiction between the two points of view, which have always appeared and still do on occasion, in discussing the model—economic growth on the one hand and the optimum allocation of resources on the other—is only an apparent one. A contradiction, let us say, between economic growth and optimum resource allocation would only be real if the purely static criteria for the rational allocation of resources supplied by traditional bourgeois economics were in fact correct. However, to admit this would be difficult since the criterion for the optimum resource allocation must itself incorporate the need for growth. This need and optimum resource allocation do not stand opposed to one another; an allocation which does not guarantee the full use of the dynamic potential of the economy is not the optimum one. Likewise it is difficult to expect optimum growth in the long term without rational administration of existing resources. Hence the title of Peter Wiles's article 'Growth versus Choice', may be useful as a catch phrase but it is doubtful whether it will help us to make any progress in the proper understanding of this crucial problem in economics.[1]

[1] Peter Wiles, 'Growth versus Choice', *Economic Journal*, vol. 66, June 1956. In a recent article based on a paper read at the Berkeley Symposium referred to

The general limits of centralization and decentralization in socialism

The co-existence of the plan and the market, of centralized and decentralized decisions, is the cardinal feature of a socialist economy; it cannot endure if it is unable to make direct, centrally-planned decisions on basic macro-economic problems—for instance the rate and main areas of expansion, the basic principles of the structure of income distribution etc. Similarly, in the foreseeable future, it is hard to imagine a socialist economy lacking some form of market relations independent of the level of development of the productive forces (at the minimum this holds for consumer good and labour markets).

Schematically, economic decisions in a socialist system can be divided into three groups: first, basic macro-economic decisions as a rule taken directly by the central authorities; second, decisions on personal consumption given consumer incomes and the free choice of profession and place of work (these are taken in a decentralized manner by means of the market except for exceptional periods); third, residual decisions which are the most difficult to categorize although they are often called 'current economic decisions'. (These are decisions concerning the size and structure of output in individual enterprises and branches, the size and structure of inputs, the areas of marketing and of supply procurements, smaller investments, detailed forms of rewarding workers, etc.). *The real area for studying the model is basically limited to this last group: models of the functioning of a socialist economy, if they are truly to correspond to the foundations of the system, can only differ from each other by the centralization or decentralization of the decisions in this third group.* Obviously these are significant differences, leading to a whole number of important consequences. But it is very important to remember that the differences among socialist models are not unlimited.

It is for this reason that, even at a purely theoretical level, it is difficult to agree with the method some economists employ of constructing 'varying' models of a socialist economy without considering limits to the validity of their approach. The failure to see a necessary delineation of spheres for the market on one hand and for planning on the other is manifested variously. Some writers allow different

above. Wiles develops his striking paradoxes further. 'An attempt', he writes, 'may be irrational on account of factors on the part of the consumers or on the part of the planners and in spite of that form very quickly and achieve startling successes. Irrationality is a serious fault but not a fatal one' ('Rationality and the Market Principle, Planners and Models', *Soviet Survey*, London 4, 1958). Naturally everything depends on one criterion of rationality which in this case seems to be rather peculiar . . .

variations of model solutions from the completely centralized to pure market solution.[1] Some take as their answer an extreme variation as for instance Stefan Kurowski, the Polish economist. He holds that the market mechanism is of superior importance to the central plan, which is reduced merely to the function of co-ordinator; '. . . the plan ought to guarantee that the process of adaptation in an economy governed by the law of value, will progress evenly and smoothly.'[2] In a sense, Wakar[3] also fails to account for limitations on the different types of variation when he allows as one variation (groundlessly attributing it to the Yugoslavian practice) a market economy, unlimited by a central plan.[4] A book by the German, K. Paul Hensel,[5] on the theory of a centrally managed economy serves to illustrate the other extreme. He analyses a model of a completely centralized economy, lacking free choice in consumption, in employment, and place of work—an economy in which planning is conducted almost exclusively in physical units. However, it must be said that Hensel does not describe this model explicitly as a socialist model and that he deals with the problems in a purely formal manner.

The proper point of departure for any analysis of the problem 'plan—market, centralization—decentralization' is a tentative generalization of the experience of the system which was the sole form of a socialist economy from the end of the 1920s to the beginning of the 1950s (Yugoslavia excepted). Obviously, I do not intend to present a detailed description of a concrete system, but merely an abstract

[1] See, for example, Wiles, *op.cit.*, in which he gives six variants and then with the reservation that he is limiting himself to only one aspect of the problem. Similar, though he employs different criteria for differentiation, is the approach of the Hamburg economist, Karl Schiller, in *Sozialismus und Wettbewerb*, Hamburg, 1955. Arbitrary model and socio-economic elements are, I feel, also adopted by Edward Taylor who in his *Teoria produkcii* (*The Theory of Production*), differentiates individualistic-competitive; individualistic-planned; collectivist-competitive; and collectivist-planned.

[2] S. Kurowski 'Demokracja a prawo wartości' ('Democracy and the Law of Value') in *Ekonomiśći dyskutuja o prawie wartości* (*Economists Discuss the Law of Value*) Warsaw, 1956. See also by the same author *Szkice optymistyczne* (*Optimistic essays*), Warsaw, 1957.

[3] A. Wakar, *Wybrane zgadnienia z ekonomii politycznei socjalizmu* (*Selected Problems in the Political Economy of Socialism*), Oddział Wydawniczy Studiów Zaocznych SGPiS, Warsaw, 1957, In the second edition *Ekonomia socjalizmu. Wybrane zagadnienia* (*The Economy of Socialism, Selected Problems*), Warsaw, 1958, there are some changes.

[4] Gabriel Temkin gives an interesting critique of the views of these Polish writers from a similar standpoint in his, unfortunately unpublished, work, 'Planowanie centralne a modele gospodarki socjalistycznej' ('Central Planning and Models of the Socialist Economy').

[5] K. P. Hensel, *Einfuehrung in die Iheorie der Zentralverwaltungswirtschaft* (*An introduction to the Theory of a Centrally Managed Economy*), Stuttgart, 1954, 2nd ed., 1958.

picture of its principles and hence a centralized model of the functioning of a socialist economy.

A centralized model

The basic feature of a centralized model is:

1. *The concentration of practically all economic decisions on the central level* (*except for individual choice in the fields of consumption and employment*). It is secondary, though not without significance, whether the central planning organ (the planning office) has the right to make decisions and deliver executive orders or whether it is concerned exclusively with planning in the strict sense. The chief factor is that the final decisions, along with the organization and control of the execution of the plan, are left to the central administrative organs of the state, perhaps subject to sanctioning by the representative body. The basic feature is thus the concentration of decisions at one level.

Most important among the decisions made centrally are the groups which fix the basic economic proportions. Among these should be included: a. Determination of the rate of accumulation and the rate of investment, which in turn determine the growth rate. b. Determination of the portions of investment funds allotted to particular sectors, which not only shapes the economic structure in the current planning period, but also the future growth rate. The current investment structure largely determines the future structure of production and hence the real base of the future rate of accumulation. (The adjustment of the real structure to the proposed distribution of national income takes place partially through foreign trade.) c. Division of the consumption fund into collective and individual consumption. d. Determination of the main proportions of current output in accordance with the adopted structure of income distribution.[1]

For the present I will ignore the criteria for making these decisions. It is sufficient to state that they are *autonomous* and hence are not meant to anticipate the directions of micro-economic repercussions. They reflect the specific preference scale adopted by the central authority and thus are the reflection of a national and long-term point of view. The basic assumption often explicitly formulated by political leaders and theorists, is that the greatest possible growth rate is the most important means for best satisfying economic and

---

[1] Where different forms of ownership exist, in particular where the means of production in agriculture are privately owned, some elements in these decisions are based on estimates (this especially concerns the extent of private accumulation). As noted in the introduction these problems are not dealt with in this book.

political needs. This assumption when juxtaposed to economic possibilities and socio-political circumstances underlies the determination of the so-called *leading links* (aims recognized as of first priority and to which all other aims are subordinated). The principle of employing leading links plays an important role since they provide criteria for economic choice in all, or nearly all, areas. Once a set of leading links is established as optimum, the decisive criterion for optimum solution and all later stages becomes the greatest possible satisfaction of the 'needs' of those leading links. It is here that the *method of balances* plays its special role.

This method is usually defined as a method of producing co-ordination in the plan, internal coherence, as opposed to calculations of optimization which aim to establish the most effective programme. Lange distinguishes the difference in this way.[1]

> The theory of programming divides itself into two parts. The first of these deals with the internal coherence of programmes, i.e. the co-ordination of individual, mutually inter-dependent decisions, which must be co-ordinated in order that the programmes may be realized. The second part of the theory of programming deals with the problem of optimum programmes. As a rule, there can be a large number of internally consistent programmes (theoretically an infinite number) thus the problem is to choose the best programme from all possible programmes (the optimum).

Then, the balance method, both in its simple form and in the form of input-output analysis, allows one only to state what *can* be produced but not what *should* be produced. In general, this restriction is undoubtedly correct. On the other hand, once the leading links are chosen, the method of balances becomes a *sui generis* method for the calculation of the optimum, in that it is possible to select from the various alternatives those which best assist achievement of primary aims. Less effective alternatives from the point of view of the initial assumptions are eliminated. The balance method can also be applied as an instrument of *choice* if there is full or a very high degree of utilization of capacity. Our present survey does not mean that through the use of quantitative balance, choice problems can always be exhausted, especially if the complex possibilities of substitution and change of technical coefficients is allowed for. Nevertheless for understanding some aspects of the centralized model this point seems to be vital.

It is the basic instrument of central planning in this model where planning is understood not only as the determination of the lines of

[1] O. Lange, *Introduction to Econometrics*, PWN—Pergamon Press, London, 1962, p. 222.

expansion, and general acquisition of the means of achieving those lines (more detailed decisions are left to the lower levels) but as the direct assignment of tasks to all economic units (at least in the state sector). Assuming the basic proportions and the leading links and given the expected technical coefficients, specific production tasks are calculated directly or indirectly by the method of balances and the technique of successive approximations. They are meant to be broken down to the enterprise level. Thereby central decisions embrace the size and structure of labour and material inputs, marketing and sources of supply. (Labour is controlled through detailed regulation of employment by category, and the distribution of tools and materials through established use norms.) As it is concerned with the internal consistency of the plan, the central authority makes itself responsible for plan-synchronization during the period of its effect. Thus preferences expressed in key decisions of the long-term plans are split up into smaller sections—yearly, quarterly, and monthly; in special circumstances even shorter periods. The allocation of means, since it is closely connected with predetermined aims (i.e. output-size, output-mix, its time sequence etc.), cannot be accomplished independently; this applies especially to changes in their designation at a lower level, although in practice, planning discipline is not always observed.

We see then, that all the most essential economic choices including both aims and methods are made centrally. Lower levels are assigned executive functions; their freedom of choice limited by the narrow boundaries prescribed by central decisions or decisions derived from those central decisions. The lower the level the more restricted becomes the already narrow scope in which decisions can be freely made. The longer such a system as this endures the more detailed becomes the decisions, and the greater the number and variety of choices made by the central authority. I believe that this tendency, noted by many students of planning, must be considered as inherent in the model. This is a model in which it is less convenient to operate with aggregates as they may imply the possibility of some uncontrolled structural changes. By the terms of this model there is a preference to handle quantities as concretely as possible or, as one might say, as individually as possible. Hence there is the tendency to universalization and secondly towards increasingly detailed central decisions (all-embracing plan).

A number of other features of the centralized model stem from the concentration of economic decisions at the centre.

2. *The hierarchical nature of plans and the vertical links between different parts of the economic apparatus.* A plan based on central decisions is directed to a particular unit at a lower level. The function

of each successive level in the hierarchy (e.g. of a ministry) is analogous in relation to the next lower level (e.g. a central board of a ministry) down to the individual enterprise; but at the same time the ministries and central boards frequently have very limited rights even to allot and specify centrally determined global tasks, since central decisions refer directly to enterprises.[1]

Since the plans of every unit form a part of the plan at the higher level, the structure of the plan must be adapted to the organizational structure of the economy (planning by ministries). This causes vertical connections (between levels in the hierarchy) to be dominant, while horizontal connections (between deliverer and consignee) play no independent active role. Instead they are established by the vertical relations and form a supplementary, almost technical element. In any case, no basic change in horizontally made arrangements can be instituted before the appropriate decision has passed through the hierarchy and before it has been incorporated into the system of vertical relations by altering output goals, the allocation of means etc. In these circumstances the chief form of economic initiative open to enterprises or to lower units in the economic administration lies in presenting their proposals for the plan, and even these are usually within limits of targets set at a higher level.

3. *The imperative form of transmitting decisions is downwards.* The plan tasks are sent down to the successively lower levels in an administrative way, as so called imperative plan orders.[2] This means

---

[1] However, the enterprise as a part of the hierarchical economic system, has a different place in a centralized model than that accorded to ministries or central bodies which are simply administrative extensions of the central organs. This special position is due to a certain economic separation related to the so-called *khozraschot* (cf. *infra*.)

[2] The expression 'imperative' was adopted in Poland not long ago as being less ambiguous than 'directive'. Plans are said to be directive when they establish real lines of action and are equipped with effective means for implementation. Conversely, plans of a forecasting nature do not give any such lines and are not equipped with means guaranteeing the achievement of targets. Plans based on social ownership and able to effectively implement by centrally controlled incentives rather than direct orders do not readily fit into the latter category. Thus, to avoid misunderstandings, the term 'directive planning' was applied to all types of socialist planning equipped with effective means for executing the plan, while the expression 'imperative planning' means a form in which the plan was executed by means of orders. Thus we read in 'Tezy Rady Ekonomicznej w sprawie niektórych kierunków zmian modelu gospodarczego' ('Views of the economic council on some trends in economic model changes'): 'National long-term and annual economic plans are directive acts and are obligatory to all controlling organs of the economy at all levels. The directive nature of economic plans as a rule does not demand the passing of tasks to enterprises in the form of plan orders' *Dyskusja o polskim modelu gospodarczym* (*The Discussion of the Polish Economic Model*). Warsaw, 1957, p. 263.

that the tasks embodied in the plan must be treated by lower levels as imperative regardless of their own preferences resulting from the current economic situation. Apart from plan orders superior organs also utilize administrative measure in the course of the plan period. They are closely associated with the centralization of decisions and the hierarchic structure of plans. They are basic to the workability of the centralized model, in which a symbiosis occurs between strictly planning activities and the direct administration of the economy.

The imperative form of plan targets (usually treated as minimums) become the fundamental, if not the only, indicator of the efficiency of both enterprises and the superior units, and even of the overall economic and political leadership. Such an indicator is, at least tacitly, founded on the assumption that the plan correctly reflects real needs and economic possibilities and that it gives a correct scale of valuations. (Perhaps, here are the roots of the theory that the plan is an economic law, one which was formerly widely broadcast and suddenly condemned by Stalin in *Economic Problems of Socialism in the USSR*.)

When the execution of the plan is based on administrative measures, the application of economic incentives is not excluded, especially when there is a freedom of choice of profession and place of work, a freedom involving the differentiation of remuneration (we shall deal with this later). Thus an order may be supported by a material incentive to execute it. However the appearance of economic incentive does not change the character of the model, since the incentives do not stimulate the making of independent choice, but serve (or should serve), merely to guarantee or to foster the achievement of decisions taken at a higher level. Here they become an auxiliary instrument of

---

The second terminological problem is to be found in the expression 'administrative measure'. The adjective 'administrative' is not popular in the context of economic problems and its use is often opposed. Attempts have been made to show its inappropriateness by arguing that the achievement of any decision of a state institution is an administrative act. Why then should an alteration in the price structure or taxation be called an economic measure and a production target of a million light bulbs in the fourth quarter of a year be described as an administrative order? Obviously all terminology is open to discussion and cannot, in every case, be used without precise definition. It may be that, from a certain point of view, there is no difference between a decision to alter prices and a decision dealing with the production of light bulbs. But from the point of view of our subject the difference is basic. In one case we have a direct order to produce a given quantity of goods within a definite time period, regardless of whether economic conditions are favourable to accomplishing the task. In the second case we are faced with an act of shaping economic conditions in order to induce certain decision-makers to behave in accordance with the desired aims. The difference is clear, and the expressions 'administrative measures' and 'economic measures' will be used henceforth in this sense. These need not, of course, be always mutually exclusive.

execution. On the other hand, it should be noted that even in this form, the incorporation of incentives in the system is not easy and that they can turn out to be something of a Trojan horse. Linking incentives with plan orders produces a number of unintended results. At the executive level it creates a special preference scale which transforms the intent of decisions established for the executives into a subtle network of alternatives which are often at odds with the social interest.[1] Multiple choices not only threaten the general level of indices (by virtue of inducing tendencies to lower planned targets) but also the internal consistency of the plan. Especially if instead of monetary indices an elaborate system of physical indices is used, some of them prove easier to obtain than others. Often the quantitative index of output takes preference to the detriment of all others.

4. *The predominance of economic calculation and planning in terms of physical units.* In a centralized model there is a need in macroeconomic decisions to consider not only proportions in terms of value, but also in terms of use-value. This consideration is the root of the whole system of orders dealing with the detailed structure of production and outlays in physical units.

The complicated network of material balances for the plethora of outputs which serves as the basis for centralized distribution, is in itself the cause of planning tasks becoming more and more detailed. It is in the very adaptation of the physical structure of supply to the structure of demand that aggregates are useless (even within commodity groups) and therefore they must be broken down to homogeneous groups. Also in their advanced form economic calculation and planning *in natura* give each item in the plan an individual mark and thus limit economic substitution.

Hagemejer puts it well:[2]

It is assumed in a centralized system that the central planning authority can be supplied with complete information about the productive capacities of all plants. This leads to the postulate that the centralized plan be formulated in such detail that it would conform to the information given. There was a tendency to build up a

---

[1] The Hungarian economist, Janos Kornai, in his critical study of light industry, *The Hyper-centralization of Economic Management*, The Economic Institute of the Hungarian Academy of Sciences (Budapest, 1957—in Hungarian), calls this 'planned-economic speculation'. 'It is possible everywhere to find managers', writes Kornai, 'who are real artists in this kind of speculation. They are not guilty of any formal abuses but they skilfully exploit the economic contradictions and ambiguities in planning indices which affect their bonuses.' It is perhaps unnecessary to cite Polish examples . . .

[2] W. Hagemejer, 'Agregacja a planowanie', ('Aggregation and Planning') *Ekonomista*, no. 6, 1958, p. 1443.

plan based on individual norms of labour productivity and of utilization of different types of productive equipment. Among the obligations of enterprise managements, the result of this way of constructing the plan is to stress good administration and careful supervision of the fulfilment of those productivity norms and of the techno-economic indices. The part of this group in creating and continually improving the plan itself becomes continually smaller, and the more and more difficult tasks of calculating individual technical norms in a detailed plan are concentrated in one planning body.

We might add, ourselves, that such detailed specification in a centralized model often includes not only the overall capacity of each plant but also the particulars of assortments while the techno-economic norm must account for the actual material's availability as well as the composition of the labour input by groups and categories.

5. *The passive role of money within the state sector* (i.e. in relations between the economic administrative organs and enterprises and between enterprises themselves). To understand the assertion that planning and economic calculation in physical terms is dominant demands a more detailed examination of the following aspects of the model: planning in money units, embracing both the size of output and a comparison of inputs with their results (plans of costs and profitability, etc.), allocation of means in money terms to individual parts and units of the economy, the price system, expansion of a network of financial and credit institutions, the whole complex of elements involved in *khozraschot* in enterprises.

The passive and active role of money

To understand clearly the passive role of money in the state sector it is, perhaps, easiest to take as a point of reference an analysis of two areas of economic activity in which money is not prevented from playing an active role in the centralized model. They are the labour market and the consumer goods market.[1]

Above all what the *labour market* needs is *de jure* recognition in the political economy of socialism. Specialists and publicists in the subject use this term in practice, but it is hardly used at all by Marxists dealing with general theoretical problems of the socialist economy. Reticence in employing the term derives from a conviction that it implies recognition of the commodity nature of labour power. This

[1] Again I would remind the reader that I abstract from the possible existence of sectors other than that of the state.

is not the place to examine such a complicated problem.[1] but I do think that there is no unqualified link between the two categories. In socialism the socio-economic position of the working class undergoes fundamental change. The size of the consumption fund, including the wage fund and the level of minimum wages, is set not by the antagonistic conflict of owners of capital and sellers of labour, but by planned decisions. And the latter determine income distribution in light of the social needs and potentials even though this does not obviate the possibilities of a certain type of contradiction arising or remove the need for properly representing workers' interests.

There remains the question of the distribution of the wage fund among branches, professions, labour categories etc. We say that this is accomplished in conformity with the law of distribution according to input of labour. However, the direct form of distribution according to labour input—i.e. comparing labour contribution in standard physical units—can only be effected in special cases; mainly within the enterprise and then only where the differences can be technically measured. In all other cases, especially work in different branches, different professions and at different levels of responsibility, direct comparison is impossible. The law of distribution according to labour input operates by trial and error, by means of a special market mechanism, in which the wage level (earnings) becomes 'the price of labour'—an index of the alternatives of choice made freely by employees.

A socialist labour market has many specific features: the main one of which is that it is contained in a plan which not only co-ordinates the supply and demand for labour but also determines a whole series of other elements which need not be enumerated. Having a plan does not alter the fact that, when there is a free choice of employment, the distribution of labour according to the planned current needs cannot be instituted without employing a 'price of labour', and hence without using money as an active factor affecting demand. To prevent being misunderstood I should say that I do not mean that *only* wages can be instrumental in correctly distributing the labour force and in creating an equilibrium between the supply and demand for labour. Many factors are at work here: the state has available a number of expedients for coping with a deficit on labour supply (e.g. mechanization) as well as a number of other non-wage instruments to ensure fulfilling a given size and structure of the demand for

[1] Zofia Morecka attempted this in 'Placa w gospodarce socjalistycznej' ('Wages in a Socialist Economy') in *Zagadnienia ekonomii politycznej socjalizmu (Problems of the Political Economy of Socialism)*, ed. O. Lange (Warsaw, 1960), pp. 457–513. Also 'Płaca ekonomiczna czy socjoekonomiczna' ('Wages—Economic or Socio-economic?'), *Zycie Gospodarcze*, nos. 8 and 9, 1959.

labour. As numerous are the criteria on which the individual's choice of jobs is based: wages are only one of them, like price in a commodity market. But price is a factor, in the first place indispensable and in the second place the most elastic. When other elements are relatively stable, it plays a special role in creating equilibrium between the advantages and disadvantages connected with any particular type of employment. To surmount the impediments to a sufficient supply of labour for underground work in coal mines, the heaviest labour is mechanized, working conditions are improved so far as safety and hygiene are concerned for a given wage level. But if all these elements are given or if they are only slightly subject to change (especially in the short term) an increase in the 'labour price' is needed either directly or indirectly. It must be borne in mind that the adjustment of labour supply to its demand is never a problem of distributing the whole of the labour force, only (as usual in factor allocation) a marginal problem of *changes* in the existing ratios. These changes come about by transferring (a few of) those already employed (to a limited degree only because of rigidities in the reservoirs of skills) and chiefly by an appropriate distribution of fresh labour supplies.

The function of the relative levels of remuneration (wage differentials for different branches, professions etc.) is therefore greater than it appears at first. It is worth emphasizing that the socialist labour market, while retaining many features of the imperfections found in capitalist markets, exhibits wage flexibility in labour since full employment removes one of the most significant brakes on labour mobility.

Therefore using the term 'labour market' is fully justified in a socialist economy, and we might note that this fact greatly influences what are called prime costs in socialism. All current costs, in principle, can be ultimately reduced to wages: if, then, at least, the relative wages are determined on the market as described, the connection of costs with market processes is obvious.[1]

---

[1] In practice the problem is more complicated. Primarily because of the large number of non-wage material advantages received by workers (communal or social consumption). The principles of distribution of the 'social dividend' and the manner in which it enters into cost calculations must be resolved (Lerner and Lange discussed this point in the 1930s). Recently the problem has aroused more interest than ever before in socialist countries. Strumilin considers it at length in *Drogi rozwoju społeczeństwa komunistycznego* (*Paths of Development for a Communist Society*), Warsaw, 1959. The connection between social consumption and cost–price determination is handled by the Hungarian economist, Csikos-Nagy Bela in 'Preisbildung fuer Industrielle Erzeugnisse in Ungarn', *Wirtschaftswissenschaft*, no. 7, 1959 and by the Yugoslavian, Bogdan Pilič, in 'Ekonomiski razvoj i politika cena', *Ekonomist*, nos. 1 and 2, 1958. The importance of the social dividend in the transition to communist principles of distribution has been emphasized by Nikita Khrushchev at the 21st Congress of the Communist Party of the Soviet Union.

F

What is the effect of the existence of a labour market on a centralized model? Here the magnitude and detailed structure of the demand for labour is fixed in close connection with investment and current production decisions, after which they are transmitted to lower echelons as obligatory indices. Such a centralization of the labour plan means concentrated control of the measures for its implementation. In the past practice of the Soviet and People's Republics non-economic measures for labour distribution of free changing of employment, and the penitentiary system have been seen. However they cannot be regarded as an indispensable feature of a centralized model. Fundamentally, the centralization of economic decision-making can be reconciled with freedom of choice of employment and place of work but only if the economic instruments, like the wage policy, which are used to influence it, are also centralized. Hence in the centralized model, the lower echelons are stripped of initiative in wage policy, wage funds, and the average wage level of each category. In such a centrally-determined wage system there is a clear preference for piece-rates which are best suited for attaining the plan's quantitative indices. However, unlike many other centralized decisions, centralization of wage policy must reckon with the situation in a market, in this case for labour; many other types of decision are not directly subject to market influences (take for example the so-called supply prices). Centralized labour policy decisions must be even more flexible than the ones utilizing market prices since disturbing the equilibrium especially in key sectors (e.g. building and heavy industry) leads to detrimental consequences throughout the entire economy. Thus a contradiction arises between the need for flexibility in the conditions of choice offered in employment and the limited ability for rapid and co-ordinated manoeuvres of a short-term type (i.e. changes which do not amount to basic alterations in proportions). The contradiction derives not so much, or not only, from the limited flexibility of the administrative apparatus but from the model's characteristic rigidity in all its more important economic links. Nevertheless some minimum requirement of flexibility must be achieved since in this sphere the central planning authority is faced with real market phenomena. Resort is usually made to *ad hoc* measures which change relative wages without affecting the rest of the elements dependent on wage differentials. The most obvious example is the continual relative disparity between actual levels of earnings and the fixed scale of wages.

We have dwelt at length on the active role of money in the labour market because of the somewhat scant attention paid to its theoretical aspects. A similar problem faced in connection with the *consumer market* requires rather less attention. The principle of free choice of

consumer goods[1] necessitates using a market mechanism to balance supply and demand. In the principles of the centralized model the size and structure of the supply of consumer goods is determined in detail by the plan. Consumer income size and structure is also set except to the extent necessary to bring equilibrium in the labour market (and this in turn cannot but affect the planned structure of the supply of consumer goods). This creates the need for a price policy to adapt the structure of demand to the structure of supply. Practice has always differed from theory to some degree and this field is no exception. Two forms of the difference are: 1. rationing, either total or involving only selected articles; 2. setting non-equilibrium prices without rationing but also without having goods in the shops while guaranteeing the purchase of the commodity at the established price to privileged categories of consumers, or in privileged spheres of supply. The causes of these exceptions were various and not always purely economic, and as in the previous case need not be regarded as inherent in the model. In practice the unfavourable effects of these features are noticed and produce a continual tendency to reconcile supply, demand, and the prices of consumer goods. Here, too, should be noted the difficulty arising from insufficient flexibility of the whole economic structure.

Summarizing, we can say that *money in a centralized model plays an active role in the labour and consumer goods markets, in the same sense that the economic magnitudes expressed in them (wages and prices) affect the choice made by individuals (workers and consumers), so that the central authority achieves its own preferences for the structure of employment and consumption by means of these magnitudes. Therefore, they cannot be regarded as conventional accounting magnitudes.* Hence we have phenomena which are similar to a degree with those portions of Lange's model which deal with the formation of equilibrium of prices in the labour and consumer goods markets (see pp. 30 ff.).

The part played by money *in the relations between the central authority and enterprises and between enterprises themselves* is quite different.

---

[1] Again I draw the reader's attention to the comment on p. 32 n. that this is not identical with the principle of consumer's sovereignty but is only a particular procedure for distributing consumer goods, independently of the degree to which the structure of supply of consumer goods is determined either by the preferences of the central authority or by consumer preferences (see also A. Bergson, *Socialist Economics*, C. Bettelheim, *Problemes théoriques et pratiques de planification*, R. Mosse, *L'economie collectiviste*, Paris 1939). We shall return to the problem of the relation between freedom of choice and the consumer's sovereignty in the following chapter.

Nationalization does not eradicate the necessity for separate production units in the form of enterprises. All social production cannot be contained within one enterprise where the division of labour would take place in a form similar to that of a factory.[1] That is because of the efficiency of information media (in the wide sense). The separation of the technical organizational unit known as the socialist enterprise must be accompanied by some degree of economic autonomy; otherwise it would be practically impossible to make any calculation of inputs and outputs, or to analyse resource use and the movement of resources through successive stages of the social division of labour. However, the actual degree of autonomy and its economic significance can differ very greatly; and it is these variations which are the major features distinguishing different socialist economic models.[2]

The economic separation of enterprises in a centralized model amounts to assigning them a certain amount of means, establishing their external relations in money and commodity forms, and adopting the principle of compensating outlays by revenues possibly with some excess profits. This means that the enterprise must reckon its own outlays and results in money, while the central authority must

[1] Cf. Z. Fedorowicz, *O prawie wartości i rozrachunku gospodarczym* (*The Law of Value and Khozraschot*), Warsaw, 1957, p. 149 ff. I would like to note that while I generally agree that it is necessary to separate enterprises within the sphere of state ownership, I do not share all the views expressed in this book as will be clear from my further argument.

The Czech economist Jaroslav Vojvoda demonstrates the need to separate state enterprises in a way similar to that of Fedorowicz: 'For a given level of the development of production forces . . . the whole society organized in a socialist state cannot directly centrally manage the operation of state enterprises but, nevertheless, the operation of these enterprises must be controlled. Consequently, *operational control of production must be left to autonomous state socialist enterprises* . . . The state socialist enterprise, although it is the property of the entire nation, receives an entirely *objective economic autonomy* which becomes the basis for realizing the operational aspect of the centrally planned process of production'. 'Produkcja towarowa w ramach sektora państwowego' ('Commodity Production in the State Sector'), *Materialy Ekonomickeho Ustavu Československe Akademie Ved.*, no. 1, 1959 (mimeographed in Russian, p. 18). Vojvoda uses the concept of an enterprise as user of the national means of production (user in the sense of an economic category which acquires an appropriate legal form) on the basis of *property separation*.

[2] For the same reason to include basically differing types of 'relations of separation' (Fedorowicz's term) under one heading 'economic accounting' (*khozraschot*) and to seek its general 'essence' seems to me an unpromising approach. I would prefer to use the term 'economic accounting' for that form of the 'relations of separation' which is to be found in the centralized model. This is consistent with the way in which the expression has evolved and enables a real analysis of its 'essence' which cannot be separated from model solutions as a whole.

use both physical and money terms for distributing resources within the state sector.

It does not mean, however, that magnitudes, expressed in money, form indices of alternate choices open to an enterprise—as a purchaser of means of production and employer of labour, or as a seller of goods. They are not this kind of index because a separate enterprise is in principle deprived of the right of choice. Economic decisions of the central authority fix in detail (as orders) all the more important elements of the economic operation of an enterprise and, above all, the size and structure of output, methods of production, sources of supply, and to whom output is sold.[1] Money is not an active instrument affecting the movement of factors in the reproductive process, but on the contrary, is its passive reflection. An enterprise does its reckoning before not after taking (i.e. receiving) a decision. In this way it limits itself to recording the outlays considered necessary for the tasks and methods of production dictated from above. The planned financial result (profit or loss) is a passive reflection of the prevailing set of indices and prices. In principle, substitution of material inputs or changes in technical coefficients in response to prices are impossible, since the use of particular machinery or raw materials is decided by allotment. Hence, favourable financial results are not the deciding factor in expanding an enterprise and unfavourable results do not necessarily lead to curtailing economic activity. This holds not only when profits or deficits are planned but also when the outcome differs from the target. A financial gain due to good management in itself does not confer the privilege of purchasing additional means of production or of employing more than the planned number of workers. So, too, a deficit in finances does not in itself limit the additional influx of factors as laid in the plan. At the most they involve additional administrative arrangements or even merely financial bottle-necks. The passive role of money is evident in the use of fixed capital not only in expanded reproduction (central decisions dealing with particular investment items, subsidies, etc.) but also in simple reproduction (the centralization of the amortization fund).[1] *Khozraschot* as a

---

[1] Cf. J. Kronrod, *Osnowy khozaystvennogo rashchota*, (Moscow, 1952), p. 31 ff. In one chapter he gives a long (although incomplete) list of the obligatory indices used as the basis for elaborating the enterprises so-called technical industrial financial plan. Typically it is entitled 'The most important element in the organization of the process of reproduction according to the principles of economic accounting in the state sector of a socialist economy'.

[2] In view of this it seems fallacious to attempt to justify a low price on machines and equipment (often lower than cost) on the grounds that in this way technical progress is stimulated. This transfers an argument correct when it refers to a unit making a free choice between the cost of a machine and the economies it

crude attempt to derive a profit or loss account (but, as has been shown, not the development of an investment criterion), is not, therefore, without significance in a centralized model. Quite the contrary, I think that it is of great importance but mainly as an instrument for recording and verifying the execution of the decisions of the central authority. These are the main functions of the selling-and-buying (market) relations between enterprises in the financial and credit system and of the incentive system for management personnel; in this sense the incentive system is connected with *khozraschot*. However, these functions of *khozraschot* do not contravene the supremacy of planning and *in natura* economic balance in a centralized model. There movements of money generally follow movements of the material elements in the reproduction process which are carefully regulated from the centre.

One feature of the centralized model is a deep mistrust of money calculation because it is held too general, anonymous, and lacking in individuality. Therefore it is not conducive to evaluating adequately an enterprise's situation from the centre. Profitability as the basic category of money calculation, affected by complex factors and sensitive to elements beyond an enterprise's control, plays a secondary role. An increase in profit due to lower costs unaccompanied by output increases, may be judged quite differently from the same result achieved by increasing production without raising costs. An economy of material by itself does not compensate for a rise in labour outlays, although the amounts may be identical. Each element forms a part of a separate central balance and cannot, in spite of equivalence in money terms, be substituted without a decision from above. It would even appear that in this same case it is the cause of the apparently incomprehensible use of gross instead of net output indices. The former's superiority as an indicator for evaluating actual productive effort is obvious, since the size of net output (value added) is hardly unambiguous from the point of view of balancing. Net output is the residual of two factors: the size of gross output and the extent of material outlay; in an extreme case an increase in net output can be achieved without any increase in gross output by reducing materials outlay.

But, is it necessary to hold all this as a feature of the centralized model as such? Are we not in fact faced with a practical consequence

---

engenders, into the situation in which enterprises cannot make such a choice and are indifferent to the cost of equipment. If the central authority assigns a machine to an enterprise at a lowered price, it assigns a smaller investment fund and, hence, a lower amortization quota for cost calculations which in turn leads to a correspondingly lower price of the finished product (or to a smaller share in the surplus received by the enterprise.)

of widely known deficiencies in the price system which ceases to be capable of reflecting actual effects and outlays? Undoubtedly these deficiencies form an important aspect of the problem, but they are largely the product of certain foundations of the model, and not an independent cause of practical deviations. Otherwise, why does an economy acquiesce in a defective price system not just as a casual occurrence but as a rule holding for a number of years?[1] Typically, in the history of the centrally controlled economy rather major deviations were frequently permitted from the theoretically accepted principle of basing prices on branch average costs. Broad prices of key significance to the economy operated for long periods at a loss. A trend toward eliminating deficits arose because of their negative influence on the growth of output,[2] but usually only after considerable delay. In spite of great changes in cost structure supply prices would remain unchanged for many years.[3] Moreover, as a rule they were completely at odds with other economic conditions besides cost-price ratios in the world market, relations of technological substitutability among various products designed for the same purpose, or the degree of scarcity in the economy.[4] I am ignoring the question of 'constant' prices for calculating the rate of growth of output.

In the model it is difficult to say that centrally established prices must always be dissociated from the economic conditions moulded by central decisions. The fact that a disruption can occur, and that it

[1] We refer here to prices in the turnover between state enterprises—supply as opposed to market prices.

[2] Deficit production greater than planned leads to losses unforeseen in the plan which may mean that if plan 'balance' additions are made and the financial results are included in a bonus system, this deficit production will hamper attempts to maximize quantitative indices.

[3] See a description of supply pricing in Soviet heavy industry prior to World War II in D. Kondrashev, *Tsenoobrazovanye v promyshlennosti SSSR* (Moscow, 1956), pp. 116–19. As early as the First Five-Year Plan, price level diverged from cost (in spite of the fact that the growth of nominal wages was curbed by a system of rationing); the divergence became even more pronounced in the Second Five-Year Plan. The reform of 1936 was ineffective and again within a year or two, heavy industry showed a deficit as a result of further rise in costs. 'In the next period', writes Kondrashev, 'the deficit grew larger by the year, since wholesale prices were not changed until 1949, although costs of production (apart from military production) rose.' He comments further that 'the planning authorities made the same mistake in several revisions of wholesale prices; they failed to see the problem in its proper perspective and set the original level of costs together with the planned price too low' (p. 118).

In Poland the divergence between cost and price structures increased throughout the whole period of the Six-Year Plan without producing any change in prices.

[4] Cf. H. Fiszel, *Prawo wartości a problematyka cen w przemyśle socjalistycznym* (*The Law of Value and the Problem of Price in Socialist Industry*), Warsaw, 1956 (especially chapter 4).

appears and endures for entire long-term planning periods confirms the thesis that the role of money in a centralized model is chiefly one of recording and verifying. In such a model, equilibrium within the state sector is achieved not by means of economic magnitudes in money terms but mainly by means of direct physical resource allocation. Here again the difference between a system of market wages and prices continually needing adaptation to changed conditions, and a system of supply prices deserves stress.[1]

As usual in such circumstances a cumulative process takes place in practice: the supremacy of planning and balance in physical units leads to a lessening of the importance of prices; since they no longer need reflect adequately actual conditions, this in turn increases their uselessness and raises the importance played by physical quantities. Limits obviously exist to the 'passive feedback', since, as we know, the market mechanism in a centralized model is not and cannot be completely eliminated.

Deviations from the model's assumptions and their significance

Clearly (it follows from the concept of a 'model' itself) the centralized model described here does not correspond in detail to the actual practice of centrally managed economies like that of the Soviet Union and other countries. Moreover, variations over time increase the lack of correspondence. Even eliminating concrete differences in time and space, it is quite certain that not all the features of the centralized model described above will be found in each case. The cardinal questions of centralized economic decision-making (the obverse of which is the right of choice on the part of enterprises) and the connected problem of the role played by money are not exceptions.

Many examples exist of economic choice on the part of enterprises in a centrally managed economy. They can be divided into several groups:

1. Some problems of detail can be solved neither centrally nor at the dependent echelons. This is because of technical reasons (the impossibility of decision-making at the centre) and the existence of a certain number of alternatives which are indisputable even for the most enthusiastic advocates of centralism. For this reason, the obligatory indices of assortment need not always cover 100 per cent of an enterprise's capacity (especially for small ones); the specification of the

---

[1] At the very inception of absolute centralist methods of management, attempts were made to justify this model theoretically. S. Turetski, for example, a specialist in price policy, wrote in 1929, 'Socialist industry as a whole may be considered as a gigantic combine of successive stages of production. The price of means of production in these circumstances retains only a quite formal meaning important only in accounting (*schotnoye*)', 'Tsenobrazovanye v sistemye narodnogo khozyaystva', *Planovoe Khozyaystvo*, no. 10, 1929.

assortment plan is not and cannot be equally detailed in all branches and in all enterprises; there is an area within which it is possible to organize independent supplies of non-basic materials (especially local sources); etc. In all such examples an enterprise makes economic decisions by reference to results and outlays in money terms. However most often the chief role in an enterprise is not played by cost–revenue comparison in specific money units used only for calculating purposes. Such prices are used for computing the aggregate size of output, for the basic index for plan fulfilment, and consequently for bonuses awarded to managerial personnel. Depending on the principle of computation adopted it would be the constant price, the comparable price or the actual market price. It is apparent that the profit calculation is not completely meaningless since among the plan indices there are also those of cost and financial results. But it is secondary in nature, making its appearance only when a decision based on profit does not conflict with the achievement of the main quantitative targets.

2. In practice an enterprise has some influence on choice within the terms of the plan and is not limited merely to the range beyond imperative orders. Of the indices which reach the enterprise as orders not all can be wilfully laid down by the superior planning authority. The number of indices is simply too great; just as the number of producers subject to planning is also too great to coincide with Kautsky's hope for a high degree of concentration of production to obviate this kind of difficulty. Effective control and independent assessment of information as the basis for planning the indices cannot cope with everything. (There is some truth in W. A. Lewis's remark that 'If the government takes upon itself a few tasks, we are all in a position to check it, but if it undertakes to be responsible for everything, it cannot even itself provide a check on its own activities.')[1] Some indices issued as orders are thus based on suggestions offered by enterprises, with their own scale of preferences in mind, and using criteria which were previously discussed. This is an indirect form of economic choice.

3. If an enterprise (especially in a key industry) is encompassed in a system of direct allocation it has little opportunity for substitution in the usual sense of replacing a reduced amount of one production factor by an increased amount of another with factor prices in mind. (Even if it should succeed in effecting a substitution, the improved financial result will have to be justified as due to factors unrelated to the efficiency of the enterprise itself, for efficiency is indicated only by a reduction in physical outlays.) There are, however, some instances

---

[1] W. A. Lewis, *The Principles of Economic Planning* (London, 1949).

of what might be called substitution in a wider sense.[1] Within the limits of its total aptitude for reducing outlays over those planned, an enterprise may concentrate on economizing on those factors which most strongly affect costs and the overall financial result. Here the price structure of means of production (especially materials) plays relatively the most active role as witnessed by the effects of erroneous price ratios. But this is only possible when economies can be obtained without additional outlays, especially in investment, since no enterprise can make them independently. The hierarchical ordering of indices is another obstacle; when the economies threaten the quantitative results, they must be foregone.

4. Finally, there is a hard-to-delimit sphere in which a 'freedom of decision' also costs; it acts by infringing the tenets of the plan. This is the 'speculation in a planned economy', mentioned above by the Hungarian Kornai, and which he has called the phenomenon of utilizing inconsistencies within the plan's indices against the social interest.

Other examples could be added to these four and in particular some instances of the active role of money in *khozraschot*. However, these are phenomena which, although exaggerated in some descriptions,[2] are actually of rather marginal importance; and if they sometimes play a larger role, this is not because of the system, but in spite of it.

In conclusion, we can say that although in special cases the decisions of the central authority are not as far reaching as would seem from our outline, nevertheless, in its broad outlines the picture is accurate. Returning to the controversial three groups of economic decisions, a centralized socialist model attaches the third group to the realm of central decision-making. Therefore money–commodity forms of exchange in the state sector are assigned a passive role.[3] As a rule in the centralized model only an indispensable minimum is beyond the reach of direct decisions of the central authority—choice

[1] See the footnote on p. 40.

[2] E.g. in the first and second parts of my book *Prawo wartości a problematyka bodźców ekonomicznych* (*Law of Value and Problems of Economic Incentives*), Warsaw, 1956.

[3] This view is not universal. Recently I discovered a contrary position which is interesting in so far as it uses the same criteria for distinguishing between the active and passive roles of money. The Hungarian economist, Peter Erdöss, (in *Voprosy Ekonomiki*, no. 5, 1955, 'Tovarnoe proizvodstvo i stoimostuye kategorii v sotsialisticheskom khozyaistvye') goes so far as to say that 'If material supplies were entirely centralized and central direction so strict that enterprises had no influence on the allocation of resources and could not affect them by financial methods, the system of material and technical supply would no longer be one which could be held to have something in common with a commodity system.' However, he thinks that 'the socialist system of economic accounting, affords

in individual consumption, employment, and place of work; and even here the central authority influences these decisions through market mechanism. Thus in these areas money maintains an active role.

Various criticisms of the centralized model

A system of management which corresponded essentially to the centralized model was established in the USSR in a period when conditions provided several objective pre-conditions for centralistic tendencies. The initial stage of industrialism was marked by a sudden acceleration of the growth rate with major and rapid structural transformation in an enormous country possessing vast unused reserves. Thus certain features of the centralized model were of special value. It was essential to ensure an extraordinarily high degree of concentration of means, especially investment, on a small number of key goals regardless of the consequences in other sectors. The problem was not so much of equilibrium as of disturbing equilibrium in a special sense; to give the economy the type of impetus which would avoid— at least, initially—imbalance (disproportions) and bottle-necks. In a situation of this kind the advantages of far-reaching centralization of decision-making and allocation in kind is to be clearly seen. It lies not only in the celerity of operation but also (perhaps even chiefly) in what I would call a high selectivity—the ability to operate intensively in strictly defined and sometimes very narrow sectors, while simultaneously excluding others even in the immediate vicinity. Such selectivity, which enables short-term uneven development by successive leaps forward, cannot always be guaranteed by the market mechanism even assuming sophisticated instruments and very subtle planning methods. Nor can the market provide a quantitative increase in output with such a ruthless disregard for other indices.

The connection between centralization and the specific problems of an abrupt and violent acceleration of economic growth was recognized at the inception of the centralized system of management. Prevailing opinion then expressed in the programme document of the Communist Party of the Soviet Union and the Communist International (cf. chapter 2) was in accordance with the process of ever greater concentration of economic decision-making at the centre, and with the transformation from market forms to resource allocation *in natura*. This was treated as a sign of the maturity of strictly

---

sufficient room for the operation of enterprises as sellers and purchasers' to ascribe to money an active role in it. It is not clear whether the author is referring to the situation as it existed some years ago or to the situation today when the degree of centralization has been considerably diminished everywhere.

socialist planning and as the correct pattern of development. Consequently, the political economy and planning theory of the time failed to deal with the limitations of centralization, its disadvantages, the interdependence between growth and equilibrium etc. As Czesław Bobrowski wrote:[1]

> The problems of the limits to useful planning is considered non-existent. On the contrary, an abundance of detail is regarded as the basic feature of a good plan and hence the tendency to break up (indices) into as short time periods as possible and intervene at the lowest level (where possible right down to the level of the individual worker) leaving no room for improvisation and individual initiative... Only categorical directives supported by checks and sanctions are considered effective instruments ... The concept of effective planning is thus identified with the principle of order and imperativeness.

In the following years no basic alterations were effected, though some excesses had to be corrected (the attempt to base criteria for credit on plan indices and not on the actual course of its fulfilment; the tendency to preserve indefinitely the system of direct distribution of consumer goods, and thus to enter an 'era without trade and without money' etc.). Shortcomings and difficulties in the functioning of the economy were interpreted as the result of too little rather than too much centralization. This meant ever more detail in planning, extension of direct allocation of the means of production, and development of a system of bonuses (and sanctions) connected with each separate individual indicator.

Politics, just as did the petrification of doctrine, exerted a very important influence on the system's development. The centralized, hierarchical organization of the economy, was a perfect counterpart to the political system called the 'cult of the individual'.

History repeated itself in the European People's Democracies. Again the economic conditions to some extent justified centralistic tendencies. Again in Communist circles, no one paused to consider the optimum degree and the duration of centralization; and again the centralized model was identified with socialist planning. Moreover, the authority of nearly twenty years of Soviet experience supported centralization and meant that Soviet principles were adopted as the main guide for managing the economy.[2]

[1] C. Bobrowski, *Formation du Système Soviétique de Planification* (Paris, 1956), p. 83.

[2] In Poland's case some aspects of the discussion of late 1947 and early 1948 are significant from this point of view. The only published work dealing with this discussion is found in Hilary Minc's, 'O właściwe metody planowania w Polsce', ('The proper methods of planning in Poland'), *Nowe Drogi*, no. 8, 1948.

Moreover at that moment a comparison of model solutions with the conditions and needs of economic growth was needed even more than in the Soviet Union in the 1930s. The question was not only of change in the general disposition of forces in the international arena, but also of economic conditions which were not identical. Economically the European People's Democracies differed in their degree of development, structure, and potentialities both from the USSR and from each other. These factors should have been of great importance for assessing the optimum degree of centralization even in those countries undergoing the tense initial stage of industrialization, not to mention those which already had this stage behind them. The advantages of a highly centralized system of resource allocation are greater in a country which has vast natural resources and a high percentage of unemployment (open or disguised). In a country which would have to wait a long time for balanced development to work, the possibility of rapid geographical or sectoral concentration of investment may prove so effective that it justifies, to some degree, a disregard for the other aspects of the problem. On the other hand, the same problem assumes a rather different form in a country where there are no reserves of this type and hence where development depends much more on the need for intensification.[1]

The depth of the conviction that the centralized model was the only legitimate form of socialist planning, particularly in the state sector, is demonstrated by the processes initiated in 1953—the moment when the most immediate cause of the petrification of Marxist economic thought ceased to be valid. Major agricultural reforms were introduced almost immediately (in a resolution of the Supreme Soviet of August 1953 approved by the Central Committee of the CPSU in September of 1953) which put an end to excessive centralization and expanded the realm of money–commodity relations. It is highly probable that this indicates an already long-standing conviction that radical changes were needed in co-operative agricultural ownership. Often the very principle of this ownership had been interfered with in relations among central planning organs, local organs and the *Kolhozi*. They felt that what was required were favourable circumstances to make a break with the system which was fatal in its very operation. The changes were slower in industry and came only later. Initially action continued to be confined to treating symptoms, leaving an attack on the causes of the disease to be begun later. Perhaps their very inception was due to agricultural reforms which, more than anything else, destroyed the myth of the identity of

[1] Some interesting Czech material on this subject is to be found in the papers published in *Problemy nove soustavy planovani a financovani československoho prumyslu* (Prague, 1957), p. 5.

Socialist planning with central planning and demonstrated the far greater effectiveness of the new methods. In 1955 the outcome of the Industrial Conference in May and the Plenary Meeting of the Central Committee of the CPSU in July produced the first signs of the transition to a new stage. The Council of Ministers produced the outcome—decisions to increase the powers of enterprise directors, new principles for establishing and distributing the enterprise fund from profits, and decentralization of bank lending decisions for smaller, quickly-maturing enterprise investments. Today these may hardly look revolutionary but they were then of immense significance. However, it was eighteen months after the 20th Party Congress before the Rubicon was crossed. Then it was decided to conduct a thorough decentralization of the whole economy which meant the liquidation of industrial ministries, and establishment of territorial councils of the national economy—*Sovnarkhozy*. This was the time when theoretical writings began to break with the absolutism of the previous system by making new and bolder proposals.[1]

At first this process was imitated closely in other socialist countries but later they developed features of their own. In Poland one of the main features of this process was a far-reaching criticism of the principles of the functioning of the economy which had applied up to that time. The product of this analysis found expression in resolutions passed at high party levels.[2]

[1] Liberman's article published at this time made a particularly strong impression ('Khozyaistvennyi raschot i materyalnaya zainteresovannost' rabotnikov promyshlennosti', *Voprosy Ekonomiki*, no. 6, 1955).

[2] Part of a resolution of the 7th Plenary Meeting of the Central Committee of the Polish United Workers' Party runs as follows: 'The shortcomings in executing the Six-Year Plan have their roots chiefly in the violation of the Leninist norms of party life and the principles of socialist democracy in the effects of the cult of the individual and the lack of collective leadership in economic policy. These found expression in excessive centralization and bureaucratization in economic planning and management methods, in the lack of candour in economic life, in the stultification of initiative, and an inadequate development of material incentives combined with a lack of democratic control by the working masses over the activity of state and economic administration. As a result of errors in planning, disproportions caused by objective factors were not always corrected quickly enough, where it was possible to do so. In the Six-Year Plan we did not fully utilize rational economies which our socio-economic system makes possible'. Further, it was said that 'an indispensable condition for mobilizing the internal reserves (hidden productive potential) in our economy is the introduction of major changes into the existing management system. The general trend of these changes must be towards the deepening and expansion of the democratic feature of our system, *the liquidation of excessive centralization in planning and management together with further increases in the rights granted to socialist enterprises*, the creation of a ground work for broad social initiative and the control of the economy by the working masses . . . The necessary condition for the exploitation of the reserves of socialist enterprises is an increase in the direct material interest

A large number of quite basic criticisms were directed at the centralized model in the course of the Polish economic debate. Gleaning the views of Baran (and also of Dobb) in chapter 2, parts of the discussion seem to demonstrate that economic reality does not by itself confront planners with the choice between 'a small number of alternatives'. Rather they are only capable of direct rational choice between a small number of basic alternatives and that if they take responsibility for practically all acts of choice, the effects can only be detrimental. Polish experience indicated the following main fields visibly subject to the harmful effects of the centralized model.

1. Inelasticity of production not justified by objective conditions, mainly in the adaptation of the assortment output to needs in the sphere of production (co-operation) and in the sphere of consumption. This is associated with an unsatisfactory level of quality in manufactured goods.

2. Excessive costs involved in achieving plan targets deriving from excessive inputs per unit output (especially material) within an enterprise and from a faulty division of the production programme among enterprises on the basis of cost considerations.

3. Exclusion, or at any rate powerful repression of all forms of 'self-development' in enterprises and branches. There is inadequate concern for technical progress both in methods of production and in product refinement which could have been obtained with the aid of continuously applying comparatively minor modifications. Thus the centralized model puts a large share of new investment in the expansion of production while passing by opportunities afforded by the existing structure (especially those of reconstruction). It also leads to excessive disproportionality of development among branches and individual enterprises unjustified by objective conditions.

4. Weaknesses and internal contradictions of the system of economic

---

of employees in their plants economic results'. *7th Plenum Komitetu Centralnego PZPR, 18–20 lipca, 1956 (The 7th Plenum of the Central Committee of the Polish United Workers' Party)*, Warsaw, 1956, pp. 162, 115–16, 117, (italics in the original).

Three solutions of the 7th Plenum were approved and expanded at the 8th Plenum of the CC in October 1956 in a resolution and in a speech by Władysław Gomułka when he said: 'The problem of change in the management of industry is a profoundly structural one. Our socialist model must be improved . . . in our socialist economic system every factory ought to be based on real, and not—as with frequently previous practice—on fictitious *khozraschot*. While preserving the needs of central planning, our socialist economy ought to heed the necessity for independence on the part of enterprises. We cannot have the situation in which all the factories form one enterprise, headed arbitrarily by the state.' *Nowe Drogi*, no. 10, 1956, pp. 30 and 33. The 2nd Congress of the Polish United Workers' Party (March 1959) accepted this appraisal and the changes in the economic system introduced after the 8th Plenum.

incentives which undermine instead of strengthening the connection between the interests of the state and those of the individual.

5. Bureaucratization of the state and economic apparatus, which led to all kinds of extremely unfortunate economic and socio-political results.

Finally and most controversially, there were criticisms of the central planning authority for some of its crucial investments, which were felt to be irrational. This could occur because there was no proper system of prices, which made the accuracy of economic calculation inadequate and overburdened central authority with current problems of economic administration.

The views of a significant number of economists (and in my opinion the theoretical criticism of the centralized model and its proposed changes) were founded in the belief that too little account was paid to the role of the law of value in a socialist economy.[1] Such a position (as can be clearly seen from some of the pronouncements in the publications I have just named) did not gain universal support and furthermore, was not even uniformly interpreted by its adherents. Undoubtedly the entire discussion was hampered by too little clarification of even some of the most fundamental elements of the Marxist theory of value in a socialist economy. And this says nothing of the chronic lack of verbal precision.

Therefore a vital condition of progress in discussions of the model is an analysis of the operation of the law of value in a socialist economy and careful definition of several concepts employed in such discussions. This will be mainly theoretical though not lacking in important consequences for practical facets of the problem. Otherwise there is a danger that we shall find ourselves imprisoned in a circle of paralysing misunderstandings which will not only prevent practical, rational solutions but will even make impossible unequivocal definitions of disputed points. Even though this is a subject for which Gladstone's remark quoted by Marx has significance: 'Not even love has made a greater number of men into idiots than brooding on the subject of the essence of money', consideration of this problem is necessary to verify the above inferences about the centralized model which we shall discuss later.

[1] Examples: *Ekonomiści dyskutuja o prawie wartości* (*Economists Discuss the Law of Value*), Warsaw, 1956; *Dyskusji o prawie wartości ciag dalszy* (*Discussion of the Law of Value Continued*), Warsaw, 1957; *Dyskusja o polskim modelu gospodarczym* (*Discussion of the Polish Economic Model*), Warsaw, 1957; W. Brus, *Prawo wartości a problematyka bodźców ekonomicznych* (*The Law of Value and Economic Incentives*), Warsaw, 1956; the book by H. Fiszel referred to above, *Prawo wartości o polityka cen w przemyśle socjalistycznym* (*The Law of Value and Price-Policy in Socialist Industry*); and Z. Fedorowicz, *O prawie wartocśi i rozrachunku gospodarczym* (*The Law of Value and Khozraschot*).

4   The law of value in a socialist economy

This chapter will be chiefly concerned with clarifying the following questions: What ought we to understand by 'the operation of the law of value' in its strict sense and to what extent does this law really operate in a socialist economy? Among other things considering these problems ought to make it possible to clarify whether in socialism the existence of money–commodity relations necessarily means the operation of the law of value.

The analysis will not, however, touch on the causes of the existence of commodity production in socialism. Here I will merely draw attention to a point which follows from discussions in the Soviet Union.[1]

The vast majority of economists have now discarded the formulation, (one found in my book *The Law of Value and the Problem of Economic Incentives*) adopted after the appearance of Stalin's last work, which held that money–commodity relations within the state sector are the result of the law influencing the socialist production from without. Quite apart from fairly basic differences of opinion on the origins of commodity production and the law of value in socialism, the prevalent view is now, that money–commodity relations are not just some kind of moon-like reflection of external light but are derived from the inherent features of the state form of socialist ownership as well.[2]

[1] Cf. reports of special sessions on the problem of commodity production and the law of value in socialism: 1 *Zakon stoimosti i yego ispolzovanitye v narodnom khozyaistve SSSR*, report of a discussion organized by the Economic Institute of the Academy of Sciences of the USSR, ed. J. Kronrod, Moscow, 1959. The views of 50 economists including all the best-known specialists in the field are contained in 514 pages. The only fragments of the discussion omitted were those dealing with the relations between the MTS and the *kolkhozi* which *ceased* to be of interest when the MTS were dissolved in accordance with decisions of the central Committee of the CPSU. 2 *Zakon stoimosti i yevo rol pri sotsjalizme*— a similar report of a discussion organized in January 1958 by the Faculty of Political Economy in the Economic Department of Moscow University, ed. N. Tsagolov, Moscow, 1959. I shall refer to these publications as the *Soviet Papers on the Law of Value*, nos. 1 and 2 respectively.

[2] To avoid misunderstandings, I must clarify my opinion that money–commodity relations may exist in the state sector. This is not the same as asserting the identity of their economic content with money–commodity relations between

G

General definitions

In approaching the problems considered here I would like to concentrate on the connection between the operation of the law of value and the proportions of the division of society's labour in a socialist system. The problem is very closely related to our understanding of the law of value in socialism and has a basic significance for the model of the functioning of the economy.

In Marxist literature the general concept of the law of value and

---

different owners (including of course, the co-operative market but also the market for consumer goods and the labour market). Thus I maintain the point I made at the second conference of Polish economists, that it is necessary to distinguish between the transfer of a product from one owner to another and the exchange without change of owner. See my paper 'O roli prawa wartości w gospodarce socjalistycznej' ('*The role of the law of value in the socialist economy*'), *Ekonomista*, no. 5, 1956, pp. 91–2. The peculiarities of money–commodity relations among state enterprises or between enterprises and state organs are seen in at least two interconnected points: (1) In the process of exchange there is no real redistribution of income. (2) Money–commodity relations are not the only means by which the social division of labour (adjustment of the structure of production to the structure of needs) is achieved; there are even cases when they do not fulfil this role at all. K. Ostrovitianov upholds a similar opinion in *Soviet Papers on the Law of Value*, no. 1, p. 2.

Stalin's view, it will be recalled, was that the law of value 'influences production' since 'consumer goods, which are needed to compensate labour input into production, are produced and sold in our country as commodities coming under the operation of the law of value'. (*Economic Problems of Socialism in the USSR*, p. 23).

Literally taken, this theory is obviously inadequate especially as an explanation of the appearance of money–commodity relations within the state sector. However, if it is not treated literally and if it is remembered that Stalin identified a planned economy with the centralized model, then does it contain an interesting and valuable concept of the labour power as a factor linking the peculiar market in the state sector with the markets for consumer goods and labour. As I have tried to show, in the latter money always plays an active part, as far as it is indispensable for adjusting demand for consumer goods or the supply of labour respectively to the structures of consumer goods output and of employment which are fixed in the plan. This link is apparent not only in Stalin's point that consumer goods enter the market which ultimately determines their price and thereby affects the restoration (*restytucji*) of labour power; but it is also apparent since relative costs of production are determined by the amount of labour and relative 'prices' which are also ultimately specified by market means (the labour market). Therefore, there can be no talk of separating the money-commodity relations within the state sector from the market where prices must reflect also conditions of demand and supply. Even when the prices of the means of production within the state sector are reduced to the role of units of account market processes still penetrate 'to within' through costs (assuming given freedom of profession and place of employment). This is even more easily seen when allowance is made for the market in agricultural products and foreign exchange which is not handled here.

its functioning in competitive capitalism are usually interpreted in an unambiguous way. This concept corresponds more or less to that expressed in a Soviet textbook on political economy in the following way: 'The law of value is a law of commodity production; its essential meaning is that commodities are exchanged according to the amount of socially necessary labour used up for their production.'[1]

Ignoring the question of what constitutes labour outlay and under what circumstances it becomes a socially necessary one (the problem will not be discussed in this work) one can say that where the law of value operates, the exchange *ratios* of goods are established by the ratios of their values, i.e. the socially necessary amount of time used up for their production.[2]

Approaching the problem less generally, viz. for the commodity money economy, the operation of the law of value means that *price* ratios are determined by the ratios of value. Of course, this is not tantamount to asserting that in every case price ratios are identical with the ratios of value. However, *the tendency* is in this direction. Bearing in mind these few comments we would define *the operation of the law as a continuous tendency towards the adaptation of price ratios to those of value.*

Sometimes the general fear is voiced that the definition of the law of value as the law of prices may restrict its meaning to an excessive degree. Paul Sweezy, for example, writes that 'what Marx called the law of value summarizes those forces at work in a commodity producing society which regulate a. 'the exchange ratios among commodities', b. 'the quantity of each commodity produced', and c. 'the allocation of the labour force to the various branches of production . . . the law of value is essentially a theory of general equilibrium developed in the first instance with reference to simple commodity production and later on adapted to capitalism.'[3]

Other writers emphasize the tendency of the law of value to reduce individual labour outlays to the socially necessary proportions, to reduce socially indispensable outlays by technical progress and so on.

Of course, an analysis of the law of value in a commodity economy cannot be limited to the problem of fixing price ratios. It must comprise not only the elements included in the definition of the law itself, but also a description of its role and its effects in a commodity-type economy. What is important, however, is that the law of value

[1] *Ekonomia polityczna. Podręcznik* (*Political Economy. A Handbook*), Warsaw, 1955, p. 104. (The Polish translation is based on the first edition, Moscow, 1954).
[2] Obviously, here it is possible to talk only of the comparative ratios and not of absolute quantities which cannot be directly measured.
[3] P. Sweezy, *The Theory of Capitalist Development*, (New York, 1942), p. 53.

touches different aspects of social reproduction not in spite of, or parallel to price regulation, but through it.[1]

For example, take the question of reducing individual labour outlays to those which are socially indispensable. A uniform price for a given commodity (and such a price is created on the market by competition) always means greater gains for those who make smaller outlays. By reducing the uniform price to the level of the socially indispensable outlay (more strictly, by reducing the ratio of price to the ratio of inputs) the law of value allows producers with lower than the socially indispensable level to obtain greater gain while those who have higher outlays have smaller gains. Thus, the law of value 'persuades' producers (I assume we are dealing with producers guided by the motive of money income) to keep within the limits of socially indispensable outlays; drives the incompetent producers from the market; and spurs technical and economic progress.

The law of value appears even more clearly in regulating the output of goods and the allotment of labour power to particular areas of production with which Sweezy deals. The classical mechanism for regulating the social division of labour by tending to eliminate the continual deviations of price ratios from value ratios operates here. I would like to emphasize the word 'eliminate' since what is important for the operation of the law of value is not so much the appearance of deviations but the release of economic springs which reduce price ratios to value ratios. A downward deviation caused by a relative excess of supply over demand at a price corresponding to value *ceteris paribus* causes the movement of a certain amount of social labour away from the production of a given good; an upward deviation leads to the flow of labour towards it because of high profitability. The convergence of price ratios with value ratios is thus inseparable from the regulation of the social division of labour in such a way as to bring about a state of equilibrium (e.g. the balancing of supply and demand at price ratios which reconcile with value ratios). Thus the mutual relationship between conditions of production and conditions of exchange find their reflection in the operation of the law of value, though in the final analysis the conditions of production retain superiority. I feel no proof is needed for the generally accepted fact that in private commodity production (conditions of competition between individual producers) the whole process occurs spontaneously, without possibility of attaining a

---

[1] 'Price is a manifestation of the law of value. Value is the law of prices, i.e. a generalized expression of the phenomenon of price.' V. I. Lenin. One more Defeat of Socialism—marginal notes on Struve's book 'Economy and Price', *Works*, vol. 20, p. 205 (Polish Edition).

The law of value in a socialist economy 93

state of relatively stable equilibrium. This results in economic losses and leads to definite social effects.

The functioning of the law of value in a developed competitive capitalism is modified by the motive of maximizing the return to capital as the direct aim of production. It is manifested, primarily, in the appearance of the category called production price (Marx's *Produktionspreis*) which replaces value in the strict sense as the median of price oscillations. Disregarding the famous 'problems of transformation' (of value into production price) and assuming that the production price really is a modified form of value, the above definition of the law of value may also apply to a situation peculiar to competitive capitalism (a tendency in the direction of the convergence of price ratios and the ratios of production prices). It should be noted that the relative proportions of the division of social labour between branches, which are established in an equilibrium based on production prices, differ from those which would prevail if value were the norm of the median of price oscillation.[1] However, we are not interested in this aspect of the problem; we are exclusively concerned to learn whether the operational mechanism of the law of value (in its modified form) works in a similar, though more complex, way to the one described. The gravitation of prices towards the 'norm' (the level determined by the conditions of production) will occur only along with the regulation of the sectoral allocation of labour by means of a continual interaction of production and exchange conditions. Henceforth the notion of 'the law of value' will be used whether the median of price oscillations is value in the strict sense or the production price as a modified form of value.

Monopoly capitalism changes the situation greatly. Monopolies employ their power to hinder the process of adaptation based on the interaction of production and exchange conditions. Hence in mono-

---

[1] Strumilin rightly stressed this fact in 'Zakon stoimosti i planirovaniye', *Voprosy Ekonomiki*, no. 7, 1959, although he draws a number of important and highly controversial conclusions from it. He feels that the appearance of the production price and the law of the average rate of profit is not identical to the operation of the law of value which he interprets strictly as the law of the equivalence of goods exchanged or what amounts to the same thing—'prices proportional to values.' Strumilin adopts the view that 'the points at which the law of value has fully realized its demands, with respect to the proportions of production and exchange, are optimum from the viewpoint of economizing society's time and labour outlays.' In so doing he treats equilibrium based on production prices as a continual deviation from the optimum allocation of social labour (another argument against capitalism); and he feels that 'increasing divergencies in the organic composition of capital lead unavoidably to increasing divergencies of prices from value and in growing disproportions of exchange' (and in production, as follows from his reasoning), pp. 124–5.

poly capitalism, due to the activities of monopolies and the development of state intervention, the deviations of price from production
price become significant and more importantly are of longer duration
(monopoly prices). Obviously the tendency to reduce price ratios to
'normal' production price ratios is not and cannot be completely
eliminated since monopoly is never complete and the mechanism of
competition, though very distorted, does not cease to function.
Thus to the extent that competition succeeds in destroying monopolistic barriers and enables 'normal' changes in the structure of
labour allocation, the law of value operates in agreement with its
unequivocally defined content.

On the other hand, the non-equivalence of exchange becomes
more and more a rule. It results from the strength of monopolies
and makes the tendency towards equilibrium lead to patterns of
supply and demand different from those of free competition.

The above definition gives rise to the question, whether we can
speak about the operation of the law of value at all in monopoly
capitalism without serious reservations.[1] Generally Marxist literature
does not touch this problem and is instead inclined to speak about
modifications of the law of value in capitalism. However, this is not
the same thing. Modification implies that the law of value in monopoly capitalism is fully operative and that its form is changed. How
can this assertion be justified in view of the obvious non-equivalence
of monopoly prices? Here the meaning of the law of value undergoes
a metamorphosis. In many works, in which authors begin with the
above definition and apply it to competitive capitalism, there is an
unexpected transition to a completely different position in analysing
monopoly capitalism. The problem of equivalence in the operation
of the law of value is ignored and attention is focused on problems
like the equivalence of the sums of values and the fall of prices
when there is a long-term rise in labour productivity.[2]

The first of these latter arguments is tautological. In reality the
sum of prices can never differ from the sum of the values of all
commodities. Changes in the general level of prices are—in given
productive conditions—merely the expression of a change in the
purchasing power of money, while changes in price ratios lead to a
different distribution of value created. The second argument makes
a real connection between price movements and increases in labour

[1] Strumilin's formulation is in the above cited article. Similar though less
clearly Paul Sweezy, *The Theory of Capitalist Development*, and as well R. L.
Meek, *Studies in the Labour Theory of Value*, Chapter 7.

[2] Cf. eg. *Ekonomia Polityczna, Podrecznik*, p. 314; K. Ostrovitianov, 'Stoimost',
The Great Soviet Encyclopaedia, 2nd ed., vol. 41, and the article 'Zakon Stoimosti
pri kapitalizmie and monopolnaya tsena' in *Krakti ekonomi-cheski stovar*,
Moscow, 1958.

productivity (nominally visible only if the value of the monetary unit is assumed constant) but it is a connection of a different type from that enunciated in the prior definition of the law of value. If the connection between labour productivity and the price level in the long run were to constitute the content of the law of value, it would not concern the regulating of the division of social labour; the attainment of equilibrium, etc. Therefore to make this factor of prime importance is little more than a way of admitting that the principle of equivalence of exchange is not (or tends not to be) found in its full form in monopoly capitalism.

Typically, analyses of the law of value in competitive capitalism or as a simple money commodity do not treat as a separate element interrelations between prices and labour productivity. This may happen even though this interrelation appears more clearly than in the monopolistic stage.

There are no reasons for abandoning the idea of applying the general definition of the law of value to monopoly capitalism. On the other hand, as a rule, the equivalence of exchange is distorted here. Then does this fact justify the conclusion that there are, at least, far-reaching limitations on the law of value? Not quite, since a distortion of equivalence may be symptomatic to the violation of an objective economic law, and the economic results may be harmful in themselves. Therefore, we must first clarify whether we are dealing with a violation of this law or with the results of major transformations in the economic base which are limiting the operation of the law of value in an objective sense. It is beyond the scope of this book to examine such a problem. However, it seems that the frequently expressed view which holds that many negative aspects of monopoly capitalism derive from disturbances in equivalence, is based on a number of oversimplifications.

A thorough study and clarification of the problem of the operation of the law of value in monopoly capitalism would be of great significance for the theory of value in socialism. Though this view is not a new one, it can be found in Preobrazhenski's book and in Blumin's *Subjektivnaya shkola politicheskoy ekonomii* (*The Subjective School of Political Economy*)—unfortunately, even today Marxist literature has made no real progress in its study of the problem.

The formulation of the problem for a socialist economy

In hardly any other theoretical problem has confusion reached dimensions similar to those reached in examining the law of value in a socialist economy. Primarily this was due to a lack of precision in defining the concepts used; in turn the result was an illusory

accord, or difference in point of view. This is true also of my own articles and even of my paper before The Second Congress of Polish Economists[1] which displays vestiges of a bad habit particularly common in this field—the habit of engaging in complex theoretical discussions without previously lending due precision to the terms and concepts used. To some extent I shall try to remedy this now.

To begin with, I think we should finally reject the idea that the mere existence of money–commodity categories is evidence in itself, of the operation of the law of value. This view was first expounded in the article 'Niekotoriye voprosy priepodavaniya politicheskoy ekonomii'—the first, semi-official interpretation of the famous conversation of some economists with Stalin in 1941. It was in the course of this conversation that Stalin, like a bolt from the blue, recognized the operation of the law of value in socialism.[2] We read that 'the errors of earlier teaching which denied that the law of value continues to operate in a socialist society created insuperable difficulties in clarifying categories like money, banks, credit, and so on in socialism.' Since then many different versions of this view of the operation of the law of value have been expressed. J. A. Kronrod wrote: 'The money form of value is the economic form that is used by a socialist state and which thereby employs the law of value in managing the economy.'[3] This quite obviously confused position probably stems from an unwarranted parallel to the classical competitive situation. There, indeed, the mere fact of the existence of money–commodity categories presumes the operation of the law of value, since the mechanism of equalizing the ratios of prices with those of values (or prices of production) functions freely. However, when control over economic resources reaches a degree of concentration such that those who exercise it can effectively influence the whole system of economic quantities, the existence of money—commodity categories can no longer presume the law of value. (Contrast this with conditions approaching the so-called perfect competition when those who control the factors of production must accept the system as given and adjust themselves to it.) This is true of monopolistic capitalism; it is also true (indeed, to such a degree that it amounts to a qualitative difference) of a socialist economy in which control over the bulk of economic resources is in

[1] W. Brus, 'O roli prawa wartości w gospodarce socjalistycznej', *Ekonomista*, no. 5, 1956.

[2] No proper account of Stalin's conversations with the economists (in connection with the proposed alterations in the *Handbook of Political Economy*) was ever published. The article cited here, unsigned and later distributed as an offprint to universities as a programme document, appeared in the journal *Under the banner of Marxism*, no. 7–8, 1943.

[3] J. Kronrod, *Diengi v sotsialisticheskom obshchevstvye* (Moscow, 1954), p. 147.

the hands of the State as founded in social ownership. When the state controls proportions and social production by means of a plan, the appearance of money–commodity categories cannot be defined as the 'utilization of the law of value' if price ratios differ from those of values not accidentally and temporarily, but because of a conscious policy. At any rate, to view any system of prices as proof of the operation of the law of value is to deprive the law of any objectivity; it would not provide any basis, or framework for a national price policy.[1]

More concrete is the conclusion, adhered to since the publication of Stalin's *Economic Problems of Socialism in the USSR*, that 'the law of value retains, of course with certain limitations, the role of a regulating factor' in the sphere of the exchange of commodities. Generally this statement is interpreted to require that prices of consumer goods be set at a level which equalizes demand and supply.[2] Today almost all Marxist economists consider that under socialism, too, the price which does not equalize demand with supply is economically unjustified (at least, for goods sold in a market, i.e. without physical rationing).[3] The question arises then: Why is it justified to say that the need to fix *equilibrium* prices must be a

---

[1] 'They sometimes call price policy the conscious exploitation of the law of value.' In my opinion this is inaccurate; it is perhaps better to talk about the conscious exploitation of value categories. P. Erdoss, *Tovarnoe proivzodstvo i stoimostnye kategorii v sotsialisticheskom khozyaistve*, p. 100.

[2] It was this interpretation that I adopted in my paper at the Congress of Economists: 'The role of the law of value as a regulator in commodity turnover is to be found chiefly in adjusting market prices to that level at which demand and supply are in equilibrium.' A similar interpretationi s offered by K. Ostrovitianov writing roughly about the same time: 'The operation of the law of value in commodity turnover is revealed in the movement of supply and demand . . . when the prices of foodstuffs and consumer goods are too high, a commodity surplus (*zatovariwanye*) arises, when prices are too low—a shortage, etc.' 'Stoimost', *The Great Soviet Encyclopaedia*, 2nd. ed., vol. 41, p. 21.

[3] This was shown by the Ukrainian Economist A. Kasevina, in her contribution to *Soviet Papers on the Law of Value*, no. 1, pp. 384–7. On the other hand, it is difficult to understand the reservations made by one of the participants in the discussion. A. Kulikov, who begins rightly by stating that price policy must heed the relation of supply and demand. Then he speaks of the need of a non-mechanical flexible application of this principle, taking as examples the establishment of low prices for goods of primary need (especially children's goods, medical supplies, etc.), *ibid.*, p. 99. It is obvious that the state, guided by social considerations, can and ought to set low prices for those goods whose consumption it feels warranted increasing. But this should not violate the principle of a price which equalizes demand and supply since at a low price there ought to be a corresponding increase in supply. In these circumstances it is a question not of lowering a price when it is impossible to buy a commodity but of actually increasing consumption and hence mutually adjusting supply and demand at a lower price.

manifestation of the regulating role of the *law of value* in the sphere
of commodity exchange? It is obvious that market equilibrium can
be attained also at a price considerably different from the value.
Price ratios which equate supply and demand are treated as identical
with those of values only by the crudest schools of economic theory.
These are the schools which deny any 'internal value' of the commodity and confine themselves only to superficial observation of
market phenomena. Equilibrium prices which are set to deviate
from values can be regarded as an element in the operation of the
law of value only when such deviations induce the convergence of
equilibrium price ratios and value ratios by means of changes in the
pattern of production.

As Stefan Kurowski writes.[1]

> This mechanism [the alignment of prices with value] operates as it
> were in two stages. In the first stage the price of the commodity
> strives to establish itself at a level for which the demand for a
> given good is equal to the existing supply. If after the first stage
> nothing happens . . . there would be no movement of prices towards
> value. Hence, after this first stage there must be a second stage in
> the aligning process . . . the producer either increases or decreases
> the total outlay of labour per unit of production or he *shifts* the
> existing resources of labour from the production of one set of
> commodities to the production of another.

Herein lies the crux of the matter. Inquiries into the working of the
law of value in a socialist economy usually refer to the relationship
between price and value.[2] However, this connection is described in
a very enigmatic fashion as there is commonly a reluctance to define
terms and a usage of the least precise definitions in this context.
'Prices are based on value'; 'value forms—price, cost, etc.—should
reflect socially necessary outlays, to a greater extent'; 'value constitutes the economic essence of price'; 'a socialist state takes as a
point of departure the value of goods produced'— these are typical
expressions of the relations between price and value. Moreover,
frequently even such a flexible definition is circumscribed by a
provision that it does not mean that prices must correspond to

[1] S. Kurowski, 'Demokracja a prawo wartości' ('Democracy and the Law of
Value'), *Kierunki*, no. 14, 1956.
[2] L. Gatovski summarizing a discussion in the Economic Institute of the
Academy of Sciences of the USSR said: 'At the base of prices lies value. Very
many people now agree to this. It was pleasant to hear many comrades who once
rejected the idea acknowledge it now' (*Soviet Papers on the Law of Value*, no. 1,
p. 504). I know of no post-war work in which the connection between price and
value is directly denied—perhaps Gatovski was thinking of some unpublished
statements.

values. In a socialist state it cannot mean this, since there the opportunity provided by the law of value is seized and prices are set to deviate from values in a planned way.[1] Some of Marx's pronouncements are frequently quoted to justify this paradox. He has made statements to the effect that the law of value operates through a continual divergence of prices from values and in particular that 'the possibility of non-equivalence between price and value, i.e. a deviation, is to be sought in the *form of the prices as such*.' At the same time it is forgotten that these are circumstances in which a deviation of price from value is the medium through which disproportions in the division of labour is spontaneously manifested. The deviation is an indispensable feature which sets in motion the mechanism for realigning of price with value.

In a reference to the possibility of quantitative non-equivalence between price and value Marx emphasized that: 'It is not a defect of this form, on the contrary, it admirably adapts the price form to such a method of production whose inherent laws can only secure expression as the average result of apparently blindly operating irregularities that compensate one another.'[2]

In this sense the law of value operates essentially through the deviation of prices from values; the inherent law (for this is the ultimate idea) works its way through disorder. But why describe as a use of the law of value the *planned* deviation of prices from values? This is a process which not only fails to set in operation the mechanism aligning price and value but, on the contrary, consciously excludes it. Without the use of sophistry (which is sometimes offered as dialectical argument) it is not possible to answer the preceding question. And it is of no use to observe that deviations do not affect the law of value since the sum of prices remains equal to the sum of values.

In my opinion the reason for the vagueness of the definitions of the law of value can be found in the genuine difficulties of reconciling the law with the tenet that proportions of production in socialism are not based on it but on other economic laws. (At this point it is customary to quote the basic economic law of Socialism and the law of planned balanced growth.) 'The law of value operates, but it is not a regulating factor of production.' This premise is explicit or

---

[1] One of the participants in the discussion at Moscow University, G Khudokormov, said quite simply: 'Correct, economically justified deviation of the prices of particular goods is in agreement with the mechanism of the operation of the law of value . . . the limitation of the regulating role of the law of value [in planning price] not only does not conflict with the conception of the use of the law of value in socialism, but directly constitutes its content.' *Soviet Papers on the Law of Value*, no. 2, pp. 193 and 195.

[2] K. Marx, *Capital*, Everyman, London, 1940, vol. 1, p. 79.

implicit in the enormous volume of printed pages devoted to the problems of that law in socialism.[1] And yet the law as it regulates production requires that all social labour be apportioned among the production of different goods; and it must be done so that the quantities of various outputs produced enable (a tendency towards) the balancing of demand with supply and the convergence of price ratios with the ratios of values. Therefore to deny the regulating role of the law of value and to maintain simultaneously that it operates under socialism is a contradiction in logic. Rejecting or timidly omitting the sole definition which expresses the sense of the Marxist law of value (that price ratios tend to correspond to value ratios) is, of course, not a way of escaping the contradiction. A true escape may take the form of one of three possibilities:

Either socialist production is totally regulated by the law of value, then we can speak of its validity without qualification.

Or socialist production is regulated to some extent by the law of value—under certain conditions, in certain branches, etc. Here the thesis which holds that the law operates within certain bounds is maintained. If objective economic conditions do not warrant directing the pattern of production towards a convergence of price and value ratios it cannot be validly argued that 'the law of values is made use of' and 'it operates although it does not regulate'. It is better to say that the operation of the law under given conditions and in a given field, etc. is limited (or non-existent).

Or, finally, socialist production is not regulated by the law of value. In other words, there is no need to develop patterns of production in such a way that price ratios correspond to values and a price policy should be based on entirely different premises. In order to be consistent this statement should be accompanied by another assertion that the law does not operate in socialism; this is not to exclude the possibility even the necessity of employing money–commodity forms (some authors use the term 'value forms or value categories').[2]

---

[1] In my paper at the Second Congress of Economists I identified the operation of the law of value as the regulator of production with *spontaneous* regulation and on these grounds denied the regulating function of the law of value in socialism: 'We are faced here with a function of the law of value which is qualitatively different from its function in capitalism.' I think it was right to draw attention to the difference in forms of operation, but this does not solve the basic problem.

[2] Peter Erdöss supports a similar view with admirable consistency not only in title (*Commodity Production and Value Categories in a Socialist Economy and not the Law of Value*) but also throughout the paper in which he speaks always of the employment of value categories and not of the law of value. I made no differentiation of this kind in my paper to the Second Congress of Economists. This was undoubtedly one of the reasons why some critics found nothing more in it than a statement of managing the economy by means of money–commodity

To generalize we could say this: to the extent that the law of value operates, it is the regulating factor of production also under socialism. I have already suggested (in dealing with monopoly capitalism) that the question of whether the law of value operates cannot be answered by mere empirical observation of the actual ratio of price to value.

This is particularly true of a socialist economy where the concentration of economic power is on a scale hitherto unknown.

Social laws differ from natural laws in being mutable. The most brilliant acrobat and the best cosmic rocket cannot defy the law of gravity for a moment. Man, on the other hand, with a certain use of force can behave, at least temporarily, in defiance of social laws. Prices can be maintained which are at variance with the law of value and, given appropriate adjustments in proportions of production or appropriate administrative measures, not even the least symptoms of infringing the normal course of the economy's functioning will appear. If in a given situation it is actually functioning, the objectivity of the law of value ought to reveal itself in harmful economic results; underemployment of the available resources of social labour, both live and 'embodied'; insufficient satisfaction of needs; or succinctly— the impossibility of attaining the situation described in economics as the optimum. Unfortunately, the operation of the law of value and the area covered by it cannot be demonstrated experimentally. That task requires theoretical proof made even more complicated because it must be conducted with the aid of imperfect instruments. Particularly complex is the concept of the optimum resources allocation. It can be theoretically defined only in terms of an arrangement of assumptions specific to this question. Attempts to supplement them with other, vital elements are extremely complex and science has yet to solve the issues involved.

Thus we are faced with the question: *If the pattern of production and exchange do not match patterns that the law of value would form, does it impair the objective economic law and result in economic waste? Or is it justified by new regularities formed by new economic conditions?* In socialism this question assumes greater importance than in monopoly capitalism. A socialist planned economy enables conscious control of the distribution of economic resources in the public interest on a hitherto unknown scale. Such a great opportunity involves an equally high degree of responsibility for the negative effects of an incorrect allocation of means of production.

---

categories (proportions unconnected with the law of value) while others found in it a complete and unqualified subordination of the economy (including investments) to the law of value. In fact, as I am still trying to show, my views were not and are not so one-sided.

One form of an attempt to answer the requirements may be sought in a paper read by Edward Lipiński at the Second Economists' Congress.[1] There he opposed separating the law of value from the regulation of the structure of production. The law of value operates as a regulator and is the law of economic equilibrium; that is to say the law of proportional distribution of available labour resources. The difference in the operation of the law in capitalism and socialism does not touch the heart of the matter but merely the form in which it appears (especially the degree of planning). In a planned socialist economy it is much easier to adjust prices to values and to guarantee the proper distribution of available labour and the pattern of output. Lipiński identifies the operation of the law of value with what is called the law of proportionate development. He goes on to emphasize that in a centrally *planned* socialist economy the potential for planned development as a growth policy can reduce dislocation, waste and bottle-necks to a minimum and thereby can allow growth without crisis.

It follows from Lipiński that—abstracting from the particular social or political aims of economic policy—activity which contravenes the law of value makes an optimum distribution of labour impossible and hence is responsible for economic losses. However, it should be stressed that this view often lacks reasoning which is satisfactorily precise and properly developed. Moreover multiple interpretations are possible due to the fact that his paper is no more than an outline of the problem.

Strumilin's approach

Stanislav Strumilin constructs a similar argument in an article published early in 1957.[2] Although his main subject was the method of calculation of approximate values in socialism, he reflects his position on and the great importance of the law of value. A fuller development of those ideas appeared in his *Zakon stoimosti i planirovaniye* referred to above.[3]

For him the law of value has a broad meaning since it is the form assumed in a commodity economy by the general law of 'time

[1] E. Lipiński, 'O przedmiocie ekonomii i prawach ekonomicznych' ('On the subject matter of economics and economic laws'), *Ekonomista*, no. 5, 1956. See especially pp. 24–32.

[2] S. Strumilin, 'Zakon stoimosti i izmereniye obshchestvennykh izderzhek proizvodstva v sotsialisticheskom khozyaistve,' *Planovoye Khozyaistvo*, no. 2, 1957.

[3] He also published a pamphlet with the same title which is an expanded version of the article. In 1961 it appeared in a book, *Problemy sotsializma i kommunizma v SSSR (Moscow)*.

saving' which regulates the division of labour. As already indicated, Strumilin considers the equivalence of commodity exchange (proportionality of price to values) a direct requirement of the law of value. Equivalence can be attained only when the structure of production—hence the distribution of available labour resources—corresponds to the structure of needs as expressed in effective demand given the income distribution. 'Only when all disproportions in production are eliminated will the proportionality of prices to values be reached with an absolute equilibrium of supply and demand.'[1] Elsewhere he writes: 'The requirements of the law of value can be expressed in a condensed form by the words: away with disproportions in production. Long live equivalence in exchange.'[2]

Although Strumilin never used the expression 'the law of the proportionality of outlays of social labour', which was used in Soviet discussions of the 1920s, there is no doubt that he is close to some of the important economists of the period. For him the law of planned balanced growth is the socialist 'embodiment' of the law of value. The essentials of any qualification of the law are that in the new conditions society is conscious of its requirements and they are fulfilled not through compulsion but in a planned fashion of goodwill and therefore with better effects.[3] Socialism's advantages over capitalism in operating with the law of value (for Strumilin these are among the most important elements in socialism's superiority) are outlined in seven carefully chosen points. He vigorously stresses the possibility of a degree of *ex ante* satisfaction of the law in socialism by taking account of foreseeable changes on the side of both output and consumption. Also basic to his analysis is the possibility (engendered by freely redistributable resources in conditions of social ownership) of shaping the structure of production in a planned way according to the law of value. Private capitalistic ownership may be a hindrance to the redistribution of means and especially in material form.

The following forms the grounds for Strumilin's forceful opposition to violations of equivalence.[4]

Strict observance of the law of value as well as the complete elimination of disproportions in output and exchange in a commodity guarantee the maximum exploitation of the existing productive forces while simultaneously maintaining a balanced satisfaction of all society's needs.

[1] S. Strumilin, 'Zakon stoimosti i planirovaniye', *Voprosy Ekonomiki*, no. 7, 1959, pp. 1–25.
[2] S. Strumilin, *Problems of Socialism and Communism*, p. 139.
[3] *Ibid.*, pp. 135–9.
[4] S. Strumilin, *The Law of Value and Planning*, p. 130.

Individual cases of deviations from the law can only take place when particular social preferences regarding the structure of consumption arise and especially when political considerations play a part.[1] These, however, are only exceptions to a rule which ought to be as closely adhered to as possible to avoid the risk of not attaining the economic optimum. He castigates those who advocate income redistribution through prices and rejects the justification of non-equivalence by the fact that the equality of the totals of prices and values is preserved. He realizes fully that the optimum allocation of labour resources cannot be achieved once and for all and that the proper proportions of today may be the disproportions of tomorrow. Furthermore he envisages the consequences of this fact—including the need for a more flexible price policy which would enable the price structure to keep pace with basic changes in economic conditions as a whole. This point deserves stressing since it provides a good illustration of the difference between Strumilin's ideas and those of economists who treat money–commodity categories as primarily a recording device. The latter type of price is more efficient the less the unit of calculation changes . . .

Strumilin's solution is decided and consistent; there can be no question of opposition between the law of value and the plan; the law of value must be the basis of planned social activity if society wants to manage its economy effectively.

But is it correct? Is the whole problem of resource allocation in a socialist economy solved by recognizing the regulating role of the law of value? Is every deviation from the law of value really a symptom of irrationality in economic management or, in other words—waste?

These problems to which we shall proceed are considered in the light of Strumilin's work; not because I wish to scrutinize his views in particular, but because his decisive position makes it easier to clear up the misunderstandings which have accumulated round the problem of the law of value and the model of the functioning of a socialist economy.

His reasoning embraces two areas of the problem—a broader and a narrower one.

The narrower one deals with the law of value in socialism through reasoning identical to that of the first volume of *Capital*. This is

---

[1] 'Our plans at any given stage are determined, as we know, not only by the economic but also by the various political tasks of the moment. These tasks sometimes demand certain sacrifices from us at the cost of some secondary economic interests in order to achieve at a given moment more important political results. In such cases the law of value must obviously also be subordinated to the more general tasks of the plan' (*ibid.*, p. 128).

reasoning at a very high level of abstraction corresponding to the conditions of a simple commodity economy. Value—the basis on which the state of equilibrium rests—is determined exclusively by the socially indispensable outlays of living labour regardless of capital outlays (total fixed and turnover capital engaged in production). It follows from the argument that he always considers the average outlay within a whole branch of industry as the socially indispensable outlay. Thus in a socialist economy he ignores the possibility of applying elements similar to the Marxist concept of the value of agricultural products in Volume 3 of *Capital*—they allow for specific marginal magnitudes in certain circumstances.[1] And when he mentions the law of value in socialism and postulates patterns of output which guarantee the equivalence of exchange, he thinks of equivalence solely on the basis of values as defined in Volume 1 of *Capital*, rejecting all its modified forms.

The problem also has its broader aspects. For even when we abstract from a definition of the basic magnitude from which we shall measure the deviations (defined according to Volume 1 of *Capital* or according to production price, to average branch outlays or to marginal outlays) the basic problem remains. In a socialist economy is there an objective necessity for distributing the labour available to society so that the price ratio of goods corresponds to the relations between some basic magnitude? It will be observed that, despite important differences, all formulae for constructing the basic magnitude, which are considered in Marxist literature, necessarily have one common feature: it is determined by the conditions of production. Perhaps the above formulation may be treated as the most general form assumed by the problem of the operation of the law of value in a socialist economy.

This is the general level at which I intend to conduct the analysis. I shall use the concepts 'law of value' and 'value' without delving into the problem of the actual form in which value appears in socialism and how it is quantitatively determined. I will merely assume that we are faced with a norm derived from the conditions of production.

Such a broad approach enables clarification of several matters of the first importance and in particular the question of the relation between resource allocation by means of the law of value and the problem of economic growth. Strumilin never explicitly stated that his argument was limited to discussing the pattern of labour resource allocation in only one given productive apparatus. On the contrary,

---

[1] See W. Brus, 'Uwagi o problemie rachunku marginalnego w gospodarce socjalistycznej' ('Some remarks on the problem of marginal calculus in a socialist economy'), *Ekonomista*, no. 3, 1958.

H

if the plan can guarantee balanced development only through satisfying the requirements of the law of value, such development cannot be imagined without including investment processes—and therefore without capital allocations, according to criteria provided by that law. Apart from political factors and particular social preferences of consumption patterns Strumilin excludes only one kind of decision from the operation of the law of value. That is the division of the national income into savings accumulation and consumption, i.e. the determination of the rate of growth. The specific passage from his pamphlet, *The Law of Value and Planning*, runs as follows:[1]

> We are faced with the completely justified question: does not the need to comply with the requirements of the law of value, referred to above, mean going too far in limiting and diminishing the importance of planning in the Soviet economy? In my opinion there is not such danger and can be no danger. Primarily, it must be recalled that in the USSR the areas within which planning operates and the dimensions of the tasks undertaken are incomparably greater and more varied than in the areas in which the law of value operates. Our plans determine not only the proportions of *output*—in complete agreement with the law of value—but also the basic patterns of *distribution*—which lie well beyond the sphere regulated by the law. (Examples are the ratio between consumption and saving (v:m) or between investment and defence expenditures.) Moreover, the division of national income into given proportions also fixes the main proportions of production between the basic types of capital goods and consumption goods. This holds even if we ignore the third area— 'means of destruction'—so important in the area of imperialistic wars.

(He goes on to discuss the political aims of the plan which we refer to above.)

Strumilin never mentions the distribution of investment expendi-

---

[1] *Problems of Socialism and Communism*, p. 128, (italics in original). It is interesting that in the shorter version of the article 'The law of value and planning', the basic idea of this quotation is put rather differently. After noting that the plan covers a wider field of operation than the law of value we read: 'our plans determine the proportions of production and such basic proportions of *distribution* as the relation between consumption and accumulation ... etc.' (p. 128). The difference is clear. From the first formulation it follows that the plan establishes only the ratio v:m in accordance with the law and that the division between investment and defence expenditures 'lies outside the sphere regulated by the law of value.' However, here the impression is that the structure of outputs are also outside the sphere of the operation of the law of value.

ture between sectors that the plan establishes in accordance with the law of value and the ratio $v:m$ and the division into investment and defence expenditures lies outside the sphere regulated by the law of value. Here is undoubtedly a key point in the whole problem of the law's operation especially from the standpoint of the model of the functioning of a socialist economy.

Before proceeding to the relationship between investment and the law of value we must consider its role in allocating social labour on the basis of the existing productive equipment. It will probably be fruitful to conduct the analysis in two stages beginning with the least complicated:

1. First we will relate the law of value to the structure of current product on assuming the productive capacity to be given and normally utilized.[1] Here let us consider the problem given the output of objects of labour (raw materials, semi-manufactures). In other words we assume that transformations are possible only within the structure of the final output of consumer goods. Then we shall also go on to consider briefly the relationship of the law to the structure of output of the objects of labour.

2. Secondly we shall relate the law of value to the structure of investment. This analysis will be conducted on the assumption that the state sector of production is the only existing one and that the economy is closed except for a few clearly marked instances. Other simplifications will, necessarily, also appear and some of them will be briefly discussed later.[2]

The operation of the law of value with the given productive apparatus

Beginning the first phase of our analysis, we assume that we are faced with a given structure of final production of consumer goods, as well as given socially necessary outlays for the production of each good (i.e. of a given value). The total value of supply equals the sum of effective demand; but a given structure of production and the assumption of a free choice of consumption goods on the market, making demand equal with supply for each good, requires a

[1] I do not understand this assumption as identical with the complete constancy of output of consumer goods since changes in the size of output may also take place as a result of changes in the 'coefficient of efficiency' (the use of equipment, the productivity of 'living' labour, the use of raw materials, etc.) and hence without new investment or changes in the sources of supply.

[2] One of these simplifications is the use of the term 'the equivalence of price with value' or 'the deviation of price from value' since strictly one should speak of the equivalence or non-equivalence of price ratios with value ratios (cf. p. 91).

108   *The law of value in a socialist economy*

deviation of the structure of prices from value. This deviation results in above-normal profitability for some goods and below-normal profitability or even loss for others.

The functioning of the law of value should find expression in a tendency for the structure of production to move in the direction of equalizing profitability. Assuming that shifting production will not run into any difficulties either from the angle of the structure of the fixed means of production, or from the angle of the structure of the working force and material supply, then equilibrium should come about through an increased share of those goods which at the initial point were the most profitable and a decreased share of goods bringing a low profit or a loss. The structure of production should change in such a way as to make possible equilibrium of supply with demand for every good, with the price structure corresponding to the structure of value. In this way profitability would be made equal with the maintenance of the total value of supply and the sum total of effective demand.[1]

However, the question must be asked as to whether or not changes in the structure of production are in harmony with the interests of the society and the goals of the socialist economy. With the exception of the influence of various 'social preferences' the answer is a categorical 'Yes'. It is easy to prove, using the well-known 'indifference curves' (not necessarily in the form of a smooth even curve, but also in the form of broken convex curves), that when two

[1] Obviously, equilibrium conditions here are presented in a simplified way; for we have not taken account of the interdependence of the number of goods produced and the effects on cost of possible changes in the value of goods resulting from changes in the scale of output. As it is we assume unchanging value for each scale of output (or at least, for each level considered). Already such an assumption implies a certain shape of the cost curve: the constancy of total value with unquestionably inverse relation between the scale of output and the fixed cost per unit can only mean rising marginal costs. Hence it would ultimately be possible here to apply Lerner's formula of equilibrium at the point where marginal costs intersect with price. However, I do not wish to go into this type of problem especially in any attempt to pass to a somewhat lower level of abstraction. It would demand consideration of a number of variants for the cost curve, the nature of the flexibility of demand, and many other aspects of the theory of production which are not indispensable at this point in the analysis. I feel that the equilibrium conditions given above (prices corresponding to value, and the uniform profitability of different articles), may within the framework of the assumptions adopted, be considered as a simplified correspondent to the equalization of the rates of substitution.

Apart from this it must be noted that the example cited does not necessarily refer to any correction of a predetermined pattern of output (correction *ex post*). One might equally well assume that the original pattern of output is the first variant of the plan while the corrected structure constitutes a second variant. By this statement I mean to avoid any possible misunderstanding that the problem is treated exclusively on the assumption of market forms of economic relations.

structures of consumption are given, that structure which corresponds to equilibrium prices and unit outlays will require lower total outlays. Of course, if the broken line was an overall picture of equivalent structures of consumption the minimum sum total of outlays would be in all the possible points lying on the section of the curve with the same slope as the outlays line. In special cases when all the available structures of production of consumer goods would be placed on one straight segment with a slope equal to the line of outlays, solutions according to the criterion of the magnitude of the sum total of outlays would be equivalent.

Using the criteria formulated above, we can say that in the described situation, the law of value actually does work. There appears an objective necessity of arranging proportions of production and exchange in accordance with the principle of equivalence. The law of value does play here the role of the regulating force; it is the law of proportional distribution of a given amount of society's labour.

Does such a process of shaping the structure (proportions) of production by adapting them to the structure of demand constitute a recognition of the principles of 'consumer's sovereignty'? As usual, the answer largely depends on the way in which the latter is understood. If it is understood as the adaptation of the structure of output to the pattern of needs as manifested in effective demand *under given conditions, for a given distribution of the national income,* etc., then apart from particular social preferences, the answer would have to be in the affirmative. There is no reason why the principle of 'consumer's sovereignty' understood in this way should not be applied in complete accordance with socialist economic aims. What is more, it is precisely the socialist economy which theoretically creates the best circumstances for the adaptation of the structure of output to the pattern of the needs of the consumers. This is because it eliminates the existence of special interests deriving from private ownership which hampers the freedom of the processes of adaptation.[1]

If, however, the principle of 'consumer's sovereignty' is raised to the rank of a basic premise for the rational management of an economy in general; if the consumer is turned into a kind of king whose every whim changes the pattern of output almost as efficiently as an officer's word changes the ranks of His Majesty's guard;

[1] Changes in the structure of production which are socially advantageous may be entirely at variance with the interests of the owner of a given enterprise or group of enterprises. Hence the monopolistic practices of preventing shifts in production by means of price policy and artificial interference with the structure of demand. A significant picture of this type of phenomenon is given by J. K. Galbraith in *The Affluent Society* (Boston, 1958).

then we have entered a fictional world which has no concern with economic reality. For, in the first place, equilibrium is established in conditions determined by production value being determined by the socially indispensable labour outlay per unit of output. Thus, in the last analysis, production determines the volume of demand for a given good with a given income distribution.

If, for example, the socially necessary outlay of labour for manufacturing a particular good changes for the better, it becomes less scarce and cheaper, which obviously affects demand and brings about various changes in the decisions of the 'sovereign'. In the second place, the structure of demand is obviously also determined by the distribution of incomes. In the third place, the tastes of consumers do not fall from the skies, but are the product of a whole complex of economic and sociological factors.

Thus the principle of 'consumer sovereignty' is not fit to be the cornerstone of economic theory. On the contrary, only by analysing the social laws of production and distribution, while taking into account several non-economic factors, can one explain the behaviour of the consumer, not individually, of course, but as a regular mass phenomenon.

As we have seen, the regulating role of the law of value means that the structure of consumer goods output is adjusted to the pattern of demand given the conditions of production and the distribution of income. However, there are situations when even such 'consumer sovereignty' may be at odds with public interest. Two types of cases exist in which conflicts arise between the structure of consumer demand, based on the principle of conformity and social preferences: 1. When production and exchange patterns (proportions) consistent with the law of value lead to an excessive consumption of products which are socially detrimental (because of their physical properties) and to an unnecessary limitation of the consumption of socially desirable products. We can include in this category the classical example of liquor versus books, although the problem is far more complex; 2. When it is deemed advisable to correct the social structure of the distribution of money income by means of the price system.

To what extent is it desirable or permissible to include this type of preference in determining the proportions of production and exchange? This question is difficult to answer from a general theoretical point of view, although many authors invoke here the authority of the basic economic law of socialism.

The first type of case has non-economic justification. All we can say about it is that to some extent any civilized society probably has a right to shape the structure of production for its population by

means of special—and not only educational—measures. It is because 'sovereignty' does not automatically guarantee rationality of behaviour (this applies not only to the consumer).

A socialist society can claim an even stronger right to influence its structure of consumption because in principle it should be free from the private property interest. In capitalism, behind an increase in the price of commodity A above its value and a decrease in price of commodity B below its value, there are the individual interests of particular *entrepreneurs* and especially those of monopolists or oligopolists. Such interest does not play any part in analogous decisions taken by economic authorities in a socialist state. This is particularly apparent when price ratios of particular goods or groups of goods produced in state enterprises are changed, but the sum of prices (the whole mass of commodities) remains constant. The general level of income of the state may be attained at higher prices of shoes and lower prices of textiles or vice versa. *From this point of view*, price ratios are a matter of indifference and they can be established on the basis of purely social preferences which would not be true in the case of private ownership of shoe and textile factories. Hence in a socialist economy the scope for active price policy, i.e. deviations of prices from values, is greater. When the production of different types of goods is concentrated in the hands of one owner—the State—reduced profits or losses at one point are compensated by correspondingly increased profit at another.

The second case is of a different nature. The subject of social preferences here is not the material structure of consumption but the distribution of income among different social groups or categories of the employed. The most important case—especially in the period of transition from capitalism to socialism—is that of employing prices to correct the distribution of income between the urban and the rural populations. It is from this angle that the problem of equivalence or non-equivalence was often discussed by Soviet economists in the 1920s. Strictly speaking, this particular problem should be eliminated by our assumption limiting us to an economy with only state-ownership. But even within this framework the question of the function of prices in correcting income distribution does not completely lose its relevance. Although a socialist state has at its disposal many direct methods of influencing the distribution of income—such as wage policy—there are circumstances in which the use of price may be necessary, or more advisable than the use of direct methods. This applies primarily to situations in which conflicts arise between needs and actual possibilities of differentiating incomes for purposes of creating incentive. It is often considered advisable to solve this conflict by admitting relatively wide differences between

money earnings; their impact is then reduced by setting above-value prices for products consumed by people in higher income brackets and below-value prices for those purchased by lower income groups.[1]

Assuming in both cases that deviations of prices from value are not formal and hence that prices will balance demand and supply, active price policy leads to a division of labour different from that established by the law of value. In connection with what has been said above it must be clear, however, that satisfying social preferences by means of establishing the proportions deviating from the law of value results in a definite cost—in the form of surplus of total outlays above the minimum. Minimization of total outlays per given unit of final consumer output demands that conditions should be made precise—including or excluding autonomous social preferences. If these are included, the outlays minimization calculus is made only in the framework of alternatives satisfying the social preferences postulated. Beyond this optimizing procedure are, however, the appointment of aims and confrontation of gains and losses which result from accepting proportions different from those determined by the law of value. It is necessary to be aware of these consequences in decision-making. Therefore, the intended effects should be weighed against the adverse results of a decision conflicting with the law of value: deviations should take place only where justified by real needs, and then on a scale necessary to meet them. Gains and losses should be carefully weighed, particularly because a socialist state has wide possibilities of pursuing an active price policy. Owing to the existence of one common pool, the relative ease with which losses can be offset by surpluses may lead, and as experience indicates often does lead, to abuse of the redistributive function of price and to arbitrariness in economic policy. Attention should also be focused on methods of implementing a policy of setting prices at variance with values; methods should be used which result in the minimum side effects of the deviations.[2]

Even with all these reservations in mind there is no doubt that under certain conditions the exchange and output patterns which are optimal for public interest, are not identical with those corresponding

[1] In practice, an adverse situation may develop in which the differentiation of real incomes is greater than that of money incomes. In normal conditions, however, this is achieved not by price policy but by means of various kinds of free or subsidized benefits.

[2] It is worth noting that the deviations of prices from value in the final consumer product are of much less consequence than deviations in the prices of the means of production, because they have no effect on calculation in the following phases of manufacturing. It is true that they exercise some influence on the reproduction of the labour force, but this connection is certainly less direct, especially when deviations are not a rule.

to the law of value. Thus according to the criteria accepted above we can say, even at the first stage of the analysis, that the operation of the law of value in *a socialist economy is subject to certain limitations as a result of special social preferences regarding the physical structure of consumption and the social structure of the distribution of income.*

So far we have considered the problem of establishing production and exchange structures in the field of final consumer output. We have assumed that changes in production do not encounter difficulties either in the structure of productive capacity or in supplies of materials. This is obviously not a very realistic assumption. In fact the attainment of equilibrium at prices corresponding to value may not only be undesirable, but even impossible without appropriate adaptation in capacity or in the output of the objects of labour (raw materials etc.).[1]

Let us now consider the role of the law of value in forming the output structure for objects of labour while continuing to assume a given productive apparatus.

It is important to note that the output *structure for objects of labour* is linked with the output of 1. consumer goods 2. investment goods (including increased stocks). If we assume that the division of the national income into an accumulation fund and a consumption fund is decided *ex ante*, we must necessarily divide the total output of the objects of labour into broad classes: the supply of materials for the production of consumer goods and the supply of materials for the production of investment goods. Technically, it is not always easy to make this division, especially as a considerable part of such materials may serve both ends. However, let us assume that such a division was made and that it was protected from any further interference. Then it would be necessary to make separate analyses for the objects of labour used in producing investment goods and for those used for consumer goods. Taking into account that the structure of investment goods is closely connected with the determination of the direction of investments, we cannot deal with them at this point. Instead we shall limit ourselves to a short analysis of the output pattern of the objects of labour in the framework of the share earmarked for consumer goods.

Both the size and pattern of demand for the objects of labour within this group are established by the needs of consumer goods output. Equilibrium in the production of objects of labour can be

---

[1] A separate problem which cannot be considered here, because of several non-economic aspects, are labour difficulties encountered in consequence of shifts in production—the problem of an appropriate structure of supply of skilled labour, and its mobility.

attained only in relation to effective demand for consumer goods regardless of whether a given pattern of output fulfils the demands of the law of value. Therefore, the deviation of the prices of consumer goods from values not only causes certain changes in the structure of consumer demand but also in the structure of the demand for means of production. Hence it also leads to a tendency to change the output pattern of the means of production.

In principle the output pattern of objects of labour ought to adapt itself to the demand pattern of final producers. The optimum distribution of society's labour resources is reached when demand for the objects of labour is satisfied at prices corresponding to values, i.e. without needing direct allocation. The output pattern for the objects of labour may also be affected by special social preferences particularly concerning the use of substitutes. Here again arise problems similar to those with which we have already dealt. The effects of the resulting deviations of prices from values (or of a system of direct rationing in physical terms) may depend on the actual circumstances involved. Either they are confined to the relationships between producers of the objects of labour and the producers of consumer goods or they affect the output structure and consumer demand as well.

The first case is found in its pure form when social preferences affect only the choice of methods of satisfying a given demand and where the degree of that satisfaction is neglected or at least where consumer demand is not affected (e.g. substitution of one kind of raw material for another without altering the use-value of the product or the capacity of the market). The second case is found when social preferences between methods do affect the use properties of the product (or even only the consumers' subjective assessment of them), altering the pattern of demand and hence also those of output and exchange proportions.

Finally we have the situation in which the pattern of output of the objects of labour is other than optimal because of capacity bottle-necks. If bottle-necks cannot be eliminated by foreign trade, the only possibility is new investment. Given a productive apparatus, and given potential alterations in the actual output pattern of objects of labour by means of foreign trade, we run up against disproportions which will obviously affect the structure of output of consumer goods and the structure of demand.

Thus, it would seem, the operation of the law of value in the production of the objects of labour does not raise any new theoretical points apart from obvious complications to the process of adaptation caused by the mutual interaction of the spheres of consumer goods and the objects of labour. Of much greater importance is the problem

of time-lags in adapting the pattern of supply to a pattern of demand. These may result from the inflexibility of supply of many raw materials (especially agricultural and mineral ones). At the same time, however, the demand for the objects of labour is much more stable than the demand for final consumer goods, particularly with respect to manufactured goods.

The law of value and the choice of investment pattern

So far our argument seems to confirm the earlier discussion of Strumilin's approach to choosing the investment pattern as a basis for examining the operation of the law of value in a socialist economy. From our discussions it follows that the structure of capacity enables us to determine the structure of output in a way that bases exchange on the principle of equivalence. (Naturally, this assertion abstracts from certain social preferences in consumption and from correction by foreign trade.) When capacity utilization is very high, the question of overcoming disproportions between the structure of needs and that of production is pre-eminently connected with investments. As I have pointed out, Strumilin does not carry his argument to this conclusion, but it is quite clear that the possibilities of making shifts within the output of a given productive apparatus play a limited though important role. If the regulating role of the law of value was not extended to cover the structure of the allocation of investments, sooner or later the tendency to achieve equilibrium with prices corresponding to values would meet insuperable obstacles.

What is implied for investment choices by the regulating influence of the law of value? What criteria stem from the operation of the law in allocating investment resources among various competing ends? Let us try to answer these questions assuming that the rate of investment is determined autonomously by the central planning authority, which also determines the size of investment for social purposes, defence etc. Thus, the problem concerns allocating investment expenditures for strictly economic purposes for spheres in which no special extra-economic preferences are at play. How far such a distinction is possible will be discussed presently.

In our answer we shall deal mainly with the question of choosing the directions of investment, i.e. the fields in which capacity is to be increased and also the rate of any increase. We shall enter neither into the problem of choosing the methods of production nor into that of the methods of implementing investment projects.

Let us return to our starting point. There exists a disproportion between the structure of supply and the structure of demand for consumer goods, and all possibilities of eliminating it by shifts

within the existing apparatus have been exhausted. This disproportion manifests itself in that the margin of profit on a certain group of commodities is above normal, and for another group, below normal (possibly even involving a loss).[1]

According to the law of value, investment should be allotted so as to promote equalization of profit rates: to invest, first of all, in those sectors in which profitability is higher than normal while investing less, or not at all, or even allowing disinvestment in sectors where profits are lower or non-existent.

If this simple rule could be considered as exhausting the whole matter, those who regard market criteria as sufficient for the choice of the directions of investment would be right.[2] However, the whole problem is not so simple. Investments make a system dynamic; they change the data and alter equilibrium conditions. Hence, actual relationships among quantities do not provide sufficient indication for choosing the directions of investment in a socialist economy. Let us deal with this problem in greater detail.

We have to start with the problem of the marginal capital output ratio. It is not enough to say that the margin of profit on commodity *A* is higher than on commodity *B*, and to decide on this basis to increase the productive capacity of commodity *A*. The size of investment expenditures necessary for increasing production has to be taken into account. This marginal capital output ratio is not reflected in profit differentials calculated on the basis of value in its strict sense.

Strumilin, among others, makes this postulation without considering the amount of fixed and working capital used in production. On the other hand, it is manifested only by differences in profitability calculated on the basis of the 'prices of production' in the sense this term was given by Marx in vol. 3 of *Capital*. As a result the latter

---

[1] The cause of such deviations may be bottle-necks both in capacity for producing consumer goods directly and also in capacity for producing those objects of labour needed to produce consumer goods. The manner by which these disproportions are reflected through differences in profitability depends upon the principle adopted for determining prices of the objects of labour. When equilibrium prices are employed in the turnover of the objects of labour, disproportions in outlet are reflected in differences in profitability correspondingly placed at each level; otherwise the effects of disproportion at all levels will be concentrated in the differences of profitability of consumer goods.

[2] 'It is *only from the market* that enterprises and economic managements at all levels can receive indications on the actual state of social needs and the degree to which they are satisfied as well as on the correct and economically most effective area, character, structure, rate and location of production and *productive investments*'. J. Popkiewicz, 'Prawdziwa rentowność' ('True rentability') in the collection *Dyskusji o prawie wartości ciąg dalszy* (*Discussions about the Law of Value, continued*), Warsaw, 1957, pp. 35–6 (my italics—*W.B.*)

can better express long-term alternatives of choice. But even the production prices cannot be taken literally, because they reflect the capital coefficients of a previous period. Theoretically the production prices could be corrected by what might be termed a 'capital co-efficient of reproduction', but in practice it is not realistic. It follows that, with any formulations of the basic magnitude, more differences in profitability cannot be regarded as an automatic indication for investment priorities. To say this is no more than stating a truism, and it would not be worth mentioning were it not that difficulties involved in rigid implementation of the principle of equivalence are clearly illuminated. But this is not the most important thing.

The second problem is the influence of investment on conditions of production and thus on ratios between values. For example, the price of product A deviates from the value upwards (value 5, price 8) and that of product B deviates downwards (value 10, price 7). Assuming capital coefficients equal, the priority of investment in the production of A is clear against the background of the given value and price relations. Let us imagine, however, that no special progress took place in the technology of producing A, and therefore, that new equipment does not significantly change the amount of the socially necessary labour outlay per unit of the commodity. Further-more, new investment in the production of B allows a reduction in outlay per unit from 10 to 4. With this new ratio of values the price ratio $A:B = 8 : 7$ turns out to be closer to equilibrium conditions than the previously postulated one of 5 : 10. From an economic point of view, investing in production of B and achieving an equili-brium based on the relation $A : B = 5 : 4$ becomes a more justified solution than investing in A, and reducing capacity for producing B, as old equipment wears out and attaining equilibrium on the basis of value relation $A : B = 5 : 10$. Although this is an extremely simplified example, it illustrates the genuine potential for deep-seated change in per-unit labour input. Such relative changes for indifferent products can lead to profitability differentials, as a result of using new productive equipment.

Thus, we already have two factors which impose fundamental modifications on the choice of investment pattern which might be made on the basis of existing output and exchange patterns. We are not concerned here with the institutional aspect, i.e. whether in-vestments are made by autonomous enterprises, or by the central authority which is guided by market signals. And yet, the above-mentioned factors will suffice only when each investment decision is considered separately, as if in isolation from others. If, however, an investment project for a particular sector is considered as a component part of the total set of planned investment decisions,

then the scope of alterations involved in patterning investment is considerably extended. We can say that it acquires a new quality. Now we are not only concerned with the degree of capital intensity and how it affects the conditions of production in a given branch, but with more or less radical transformations in the general level of technique, in the magnitude and structure of the productive capacity of the country in the level and structure of income, of costs etc. If general investment decisions are made in a long-term plan, i.e. on the basis of what is called a broad time horizon, then clearly problems of equilibrium should be considered for a completely new set of conditions. Moreover, not only purely economic conditions must be considered, but also all those sociocultural conditions which affect the structure of demand.

Joan Robinson writes in one of her papers that 'profits obtainable from any particular commodity may serve as a useful guide to the planners in deciding priorities of expansion, and in so far as they follow this guidance they are acting upon the principle of the competitive model and tending to bring about an equalization of the expected rate of profit on investment in all lines of production of saleable commodities'.[1]

Generally speaking one can hardly deny the logical correctness of this statement, as indeed of any statement in which the principle of the equalization of marginal revenues is taken as the criterion for rational allocation of resources. As long as the next input to some branch of production brings greater returns than in other branches, it should be given priority. Neither does the concept of profit used by the author call for reservations; by profit she understands the whole surplus over cost included in price. Indeed, this is one of the indispensable yardsticks for measuring the effects of economic activities both under socialism, and in long-term choices. The effects cannot be measured without considering the intensity of the need satisfied by a given commodity—that is without evaluating the price that the buyer is prepared to pay. If with the same amount of means we can produce two kinds of goods, one of which can be sold at a higher price, then by producing it we achieve better results from a general economic point of view as well as from the point of view of the enterprise. If we disregard very subtle differences, the requirement that expected rates of profit should be equalized can, in fact, be considered identical to the requirement that price ratios should be equalized with the ratios of values. And this is the tendency to shape the structure of production and exchange in accordance with the law of value.

[1] J. Robinson, 'Some Reflections on the Philosophy of Prices', *Manchester School of Economic and Social Studies*, no. 2, 1958, p. 134.

However, one reservation of great consequence should be raised here: the requirement that equalization of profit rates should not be applied to the *initial structure*, but to the projected structure. In calculating 'expected profits' in a socialist economy, we must take into account all the new conditions which will be different in the final situation from their original state because of the fruition of a set of investment decisions. *The law of value acquires here a new specific sense, far different from its usual interpretation;* it works *in the perspective aspect* (a very important, though often forgotten aspect). From the point of view of optimal resource use, we must bear in mind that the structure of productive capacity should ultimately create the future conditions for adjusting the output structure to the then prevailing demand structure and in this sense the future production and exchange proportions should be based, as far as possible, on the principle of equivalence, consistent with the law of value. It is not, by any means, easy to meet this requirement for long-term planning since many component parts of the whole picture are very difficult to predict, especially in quantitative form. Nevertheless, it cannot be ignored that as the technique of planning improves, it should play an increasingly important role.

That this aspect of the law of value has been admitted, does not mean that the principle of the equalization of the rates of profit becomes a sufficient 'guide for planning authorities to determine development priorities', or that these authorities 'act according to the principles of a competitive model'.

In the first place, the equalization of profit rates cannot be treated as the guide for development, but rather as a supplementary, though very important, factor. It operates within the framework of a chosen pattern of development rather than in choosing that pattern. Equilibrium based on value is unequivocally determined only for a given productive apparatus and not at the moment when basic decisions concerning the future productive apparatus are to be made. The equalization of profit rates implying that the proportions of production and exchange correspond to the law of value can be achieved at different levels and for different levels and for different structures of capacity. Whether the principle of equivalence is satisfied with cheaper chemical and more expensive electrical goods or vice versa, cannot be deduced from the rule itself, regardless of the choice of general lines of development. If a relatively greater amount of resources is employed in the chemical industry, it is to be expected that chemical prices corresponding to values will drop in relation to those of electrical goods. This, of course, will have a bearing on demand. Equilibrium based on value, the equalization of the rates of profit etc., will be attained with different proportions than cases

in which investment decisions would relatively accelerate the development of the electrical equipment industry. Although choosing the direction of development is not an act of an arbitrary nature, the criteria for this choice cannot be reduced to the law of value even for a distant time horizon. Only within the broad framework of the target system, desired equally for the level and structural composition of its capacity, can and should we introduce criteria based on the law of value. Then, we can strive for a mutual adjustment of patterns of supply and demand, prices and incomes, etc. in which conditions of equivalence can be satisfied. (This assumes that they are not at odds with socially preferred patterns of consumption and income distribution or at odds with the requirements of further growth.) The scrutiny of these criteria will not be without influence on the original structure; sometimes certain corrections will probably be necessary because of a mutuality of dependence. However, this mutuality does not mean that the basic and dominating direction of influence cannot be detected. But what is dominant here is the dependent nature of equilibrium determined by the autonomous prospective system of general conditions.

Secondly, planning authorities cannot act according to the principles of a competitive model for investment projects which fix the general lines of an economy's development. This would mean not subordinating the direction of investment to the prospective situation, but primarily to signs and incentives coming from the market. Therefore, out of a given set of production and exchange proportions, arises a given system of prices and costs, a given structure of supply and demand etc. To act according to the rules of a competitive model is to act under the influence of the law of value for today, and perhaps for the relatively near future. Achieving the main directions of investment by means of these rules would shape the process of growth in the characteristic manner of a capitalist economy.

Two causes lead to the connection between the investment decisions made by private enterprises and the market. First, a given set of costs and prices largely determines investment possibilities, and they in turn always depend to some extent on the size of profits. Secondly, the existing set of market magnitudes is the most measurable element in the choice of investment. Capitalist enterprises include, of course, in their calculations such elements as the marginal capital coefficients, or of rationalization in methods of production; the effect of investment on technical coefficients and on the structure of supply and market capacity; and certain forecasts of general trends in economic activity.

However, general forecasts are not very reliable so that it is

difficult to stray far from the point of departure. Since there is nothing that one could describe as a specifically intended end result, and since any resulting situation is the accidental product of spontaneous, unco-ordinated, often contradictory individual decisions, there is no other choice but to found decisions on the existing economic situation in order to enable measurable profitability calculation. Leaving aside social-service investment which cannot be translated into the language of direct profitability, one can say that in capitalism the time horizon and the scale of related investment are limited not only by the supplies of capital available to individual enterprises, but generally also by the relations of production which exclude co-ordinated conscious activity aimed at the creation of a harmonious target situation. These factors make it impossible to get beyond current market conditions.

The degree to which the time horizon and scale of investment is limited may differ depending on a number of factors, above all, the degree of capital concentration. Where capital is divided among a great number of separate bodies, the time horizon and scale of investment are particularly limited, and investment decisions are taken under an immense pressure of existing conditions. The fiction of perfect competition is relatively close to reality. It assumes that the influence of individual decisions is infinitely small and hence that after any one of these decisions the existing situation stays constant. With the increasing concentration of capital, the problem of adjusting to given market conditions gives way to estimation of the possibilities of influencing the market in order to promote one's own economic interests. But even monopolies, or oligopolies, only push back the limitations, they cannot eliminate them. The motives governing private actions prevent utilization of the objective possibilities of progress, do not allow use of a wider time horizon, and constrain the scale of investment to that which merely permits calculation in terms of directly measurable profits. An attempt to escape these limitations is found in the increased public investment activity of modern capitalism. This is not the place for an appreciation of the effectiveness of this type of increased state intervention. But one thing is certain—in spite of the increasing part played by public investment, the development curve of contemporary capitalism is still, in the main, determined by private decisions.

Capitalistic production relations thus maintain that the transition from one set of proportions to another occurs through successive fractional changes, and that their direction is largely determined by the current set of actual market conditions. The difference between the curve (or rather the broken line) of capitalist development and the straight line of transition from the original position to the one

I

aimed at is well illustrated by the so called 'pursuit curve'.[1] True, the situation shown by means of the pursuit curve does not fully reflect the merits of planned development but from our point of view it is worth mentioning.

In the 1920s, among many interesting scientific discussions in the Soviet Union, there was controversy between the supporters of two different conceptions of the plan: the so-called genetic approach, and the teleological approach. Those in favour of the genetic approach stressed the importance of the original economic structure (proportions) from which the directions of further development were to follow. Those in favour of the teleological approach contended that planning should, first, concentrate on the target economic structure and only then on the paths of transition from the original to the future structure. Although it is difficult to review the entire dispute, which was affected by historical circumstances, it appears that the teleological approach has much in its favour because it emphasizes the active, transforming nature of the plan.

However, special care is needed to avoid the dangers of arbitrariness and of disregarding feasibility, especially in determining the magnitude of possible changes and their pace. To refuse to submit meekly to the conditions of today should not mean to ignore them. Thus, there is also some truth in the genetic approach. Although planned investment decisions cannot be subordinated primarily to adjusting the original economic structure toward an equilibrium based on the law of value, at the same time, this adjustment shuold not be disregarded. The need to eliminate disproportions existing in the original setting does not form sufficient criteria for choosing the directions of investment, but it is undoubtedly one of such criteria. *Ceteris paribus*, that solution will be closer to the optimum which, without harming the economy in the long-term, helps to eliminate current structural disproportions—the cause of non-equivalence. Moreover, one must remember that transition has an easier passage the closer it is to balanced growth (i.e. it is easier the more effectively structural disproportions, appearing at particular stages, are mitigated without simultaneously disturbing the main trend of development). Investment efforts in a socialist society cannot be one-sided and concentrated only on attaining the prescribed future regardless of what happens along the way. This kind of one-sidedness endangers both immediate and long-term objectives, and explains the importance of complementary investment projects designed to directly eliminate capacity bottle-necks. The allocation of resources for this kind of investment is subject to rules similar to those which

[1] See M. Dobb, *On Economic Theory and Socialism*, p. 40.

determine the output pattern in a given capacity structure. Apart from specific social preferences as to the structure of consumption, such allocation should be based on the law of value in its 'current' aspect, due to consideration given to the capital coefficients and their impact on the ratios of values.

Then the relationship between the role of the initial and of the target economic structure in determining investment allocation is one of hierarchy rather than of two exclusive alternatives. The decisive role belongs to the optimal target structure. Therefore, the role of the initial structure depends upon the degree of difference between target proportions and initial ones. Investment decisions based on the law of value are correct in a planned economy when the economically justified proportions of the target structure largely coincide with those of the initial one. When, however, the target structure differs radically from the initial one, the task of investment planning, far from attaining equivalence with the given ratios of value, may entail the opposite. It may mean shattering the existing structure and violating the conditions of equivalence if such occur. This is particularly true in periods of rapid industrialization with a profound transformation of social relations. I cannot agree with the view[1] that autonomous determination of the directions of investment is necessarily limited to this kind of special case of a more or less exceptional and shortlasting nature while in normal cases the general market indicator would be sufficient. Special conditions undoubtedly affect the sharpness of the 'bend', but they are not adequate to explain why the choice of the main directions of investment are so relatively independent of the requirements of the law of value. An explanation can only be found among the general properties of a planned, socialist economy for which macro-economic, long-term and dynamic points of view are supreme. True, previously under-developed socialist countries will attain a mature economic structure, the necessity of moving in leaps will gradually wane, and in planning target positions more attention will be given to ensuring current equilibrium. On the other hand, this does not mean that such economies will become less dynamic, less capable of rapid economic growth. With a growing rate of technical progress, any period of several years will induce essential changes in overall economic structures. If we grant a growth in the importance of long-term plans clearly the *ex ante* formation of target structures which differ substantially from initial ones are not exceptional and pertinent only

[1] A view of this kind is put forward by Ch. Bettelheim in *Les Problèmes théoriques et pratiques de la planification*. Similarly some Yugoslavian writers strongly emphasize this point (see for example Borivoje Jelič, 'Neki aspekti dejstva plana i trizista u nasoj privredi', *Ekonomist*, no. 1–2, 1958, Belgrade).

to the initial growth stages of underdeveloped socialist countries. Rather they are normal features of a planned socialist economy. Thus it is not only during rapid industrialization in general that the guidelines of the law of value are insufficient to fix the main directions of investment under socialism. At best, relying solely on the law of value would set the growth process on a slow and vastly circuitous route.

I think our discussions confirm the thesis, that the question of a rational choice of the directions of investment cannot be solved by accepting the simple formula which recommends expanding the capacity of goods whose market price is higher than value, in order to align price and value ratios.

Although the relative deviation of current price ratios from the ratios of socially necessary outlays should play some role in making decisions as to the structure of investment, it is nevertheless difficult to assume that this deviation might become the primary indication for allocating investment outlays based on the deviation of prices from costs in a given moment. As a criterion for decisions dealing with the basic investment decisions (which in turn determine the direction of economic development and the final structure of consumption) the deviation of prices from costs at a given moment is definitely inadequate. Dependence on this deviation as a criterion with the optimum choice of future consumption might lead to completely mistaken conclusions.

Planning investment does not reject criteria stemming from the law of value, but (to paraphrase Marx in *The Introduction to the Critique of Political Economy*) it absorbs them as elements subordinated to a more developed proposition. The result is a wider range of criteria peculiar to an economy in which conscious macrodecisions determine the distances and movements of all components of the economic process, at least in general.

The plan defines, to some extent autonomously—i.e not on the basis of current market indications, a general set of proportions. But now in this framework, if in the final analysis different structures of final consumer output fulfilling appointed aims are possible, the rule of harmony between equilibrium price ratios and outlay ratios (in condition of target situation—the law of value in perspective aspect) comes to the fore again. And only the appearance of social preferences in the target situation will give a basis for the deviations of equilibrium price ratios from value ratios.

Socialist planning achieves socio-economic rationality of the production and distribution processes. As such it demands subordinating some objectives for individual sectors to the objectives of society's entire productive and distributive endeavour, it demands

the integration of sectoral objectives towards the common goal by which society is guided in its economic activities.[1]

This common end is not, of course, the sum of autonomous ends. The need for the integration of individual aims into common social goals arises because the latter is not a simple collection of the objectives attained by separate economic units. This is evidenced through the process of choosing the direction of investment flows and thus determining the general trends of development. When Marxist economists stress centralization of basic investment decisions, the cause is not merely a desire to have the central authority behave (though in a different form) in the image of the market. In actual fact, it might realize a market structure of the economy better than the market itself, since frictions are avoided. If only because of the broad social interest, the central authority wants to ensure economic patterns different from even those in the most perfect markets.

Can socio-economic criteria of rationality be expressed in a quantitative way similar to those of private economic rationality, which is based on relating money outlays to profits? Some authors think so. One of them is Oskar Lange who believes that rational economic activity is possible only when the ends and means are expressed in a quantitative way in uniform units of measurement.[2] I entertain some doubts about the accuracy of his view. It seems that to express the purposes of socialist economic activity in a uniform quantitative index (e.g. the size of national income) can only serve as a general guide. In my opinion, this holds because the line of distinction between economic and non-economic factors cannot be clearly distinguished if viewed from a sufficient distance. After all, the whole of economic activity under socialism serves to achieve definite social ends, and it is difficult to distinguish strictly economic elements from those of a broadly social nature. I am disregarding the steady increase in the long-term economic importance attached to factors traditionally treated as non-economic (the whole problem of investing in man).

Differences of opinion on this subject are of rather secondary importance. In particular on the choice of the major trend of investment, they appear to be conducted on the common basis of accepting the superiority of social objectives. Viewing criteria based on the law of value as insufficient is not tantamount to abnegating quantitative calculation. It does, however, imply that the latter are to be constantly weighed against criteria of a rather qualitative nature (those which concern broad social benefits).

At this point I want to refer briefly to criticism of the centralized

[1] See O. Lange, *Political Economy*, p. 179.
[2] *Ibid.*, p. 181.

model found at the end of the previous chapter. It was asserted that if the law of value was disturbed in this model and the resulting price structure was faulty, the choice of the main flow of investment was necessarily irrational.[1] It is difficult to agree with this, though, of course, it does not exclude the existence of other causes of error. The central authority in a planned economy is in a contrary situation to that occupied by individual capitalist enterprises for which all the elements of the economic situation are given from without. Prices (including the price of capital) constitute the tangible indicators whilst concealing the economic perspectives. For a central planning body, particularly on a long-term basis, many of these elements should be treated as variables dependent on decisions dictated by broad global criteria. The central body, unlike an individual enterprise, can adjust prices for its own purposes on the basis of its knowledge of the economy's general prospect for expansion. The choice of long-term investment trends by the central authority are not restricted to the range of assumptions which must satisfy an entrepreneur. That is not to say that the central authority is different to a proper price structure in making investment decisions. But where long-term decisions are involved, the role of prices is much greater in selecting methods for executing planned investment projects, than in determining the aims themselves. This is understandable since the choice of means affects chiefly the existing supply of labour, whose cost should correspond to the prevailing economic conditions. Finally, the price system is basic to freeing the central authority from the responsibility for every investment decision. It is a condition of decentralizing a portion of investment decisions that there exists a correct price system since it is an indispensable form of reflecting alternatives of choice. When the price system is incorrect, even small decisions must be taken centrally; this certainly would not favour rational choice.[2]

Conclusions

The most general conclusion to be drawn from this chapter is probably that Strumilin's view of the law of value (with its useful elements) does not fully allow for the tremendous complexity of the problem. Whether the law, strictly interpreted as equivalence of exchange, operates under socialism unfortunately defies a simple

[1] See p. 88 above.
[2] See the very interesting statement of L. Kantorovich in the discussion in the Economic Institute of the Academy of Sciences of the USSR (*Soviet Papers on the Law of Value* no. 1, pp. 289–95).

answer. Though the reader might prefer it, in my opinion the answer is not clear-cut.

Operation of the law of value cannot be separated from attempts to control the output structure so that supply and demand balance at price ratios which correspond to value ratios. To attain this type of equilibrium requires that the regulating role of the law of value be consistently observed in the realm of investment decisions. We know, however, that subordination of main investment flows to the law cannot be accepted as an objective necessity. The chief investment decisions made by central authorities should be autonomous. This does not imply that by definition the choice of solutions must differ from any that would follow from the law of value. It is essential to examine economic results on the direction of development, on the target structure of capacity, and as the transition from the initial to the target position, which would follow from applying the law. The autonomous character of investment decisions means that central authorities need not be constrained to maintain any structure which uses the law of value as a prime criterion of rationality. For in line with the basic objective regularities of a socialist economy, the above decisions may also go in other directions, without causing losses and with results closer to the social optimum.

The law of value, then, is not an absolute, general regulator of output and exchange proportions. It retains this role only within limits determined by autonomous decisions at the level of the central authority and primarily by decisions on investments and on certain current preferences. Within these bounds, the allocation of the available labour resources is the more rational, the better the proportions of production and exchange conform to conditions of equivalence. Consequently, using our concepts strictly, we must say that the law of value operates under socialism within certain limits. Thus defined, it would be erroneous to treat the law's role as being of little significance merely because of its largely static nature. The dynamic aspect hardly eliminates problems of resource allocation under given conditions. They are included as subordinate, but significant, elements.

Does the law of value, as defined here, pre-determine to any extent the structure of the mechanism of functioning of a socialist economy? Certainly not directly and not in the traditional sense which identifies the area of operation of the law of value with that of using the money–commodity forms. Our analysis of the factors regulating the socialist division of labour leads rather to revelation of specific conditions which ought to be fulfilled by an efficient economic mechanism. This mechanism ought to make it possible to transcend the law of value while simultaneously enabling us to conform with the law's

requirements in all situations where the law of value retains its quality as a regulating factor of the division of labour in a socialist society.

These are the criteria which should be applied when evaluating the assumptions of models of the functioning of a socialist economy.

5   **A model of a planned economy
with a built-in market mechanism
('a decentralized model')**

Thus far we have rigorously confined ourselves to a generalized analysis of the working of the law of value. We wanted to study the relationship that exists between the optimal proportions of the division of society's labour resources under socialism and the proportions of that division determined by the law of value. This was exclusively an analysis of what could be called the essence of the allocation problem in a socialist economy, completely excluding the actual form of the allocation. In particular, our discussion did not include the role of money–commodity forms of resources allocation and their relation to the law of value. Only one general thesis has been formulated in this respect: the existence of money–commodity categories itself does not necessarily mean that the law is in operation. In this chapter we shall elaborate this thesis and draw various conclusions relevant to the theory of models of the functioning of a socialist economy.

Definition of the market mechanism

Money–commodity categories, or value categories, such as commodity, money, price, trade, credit etc. in a socialist economy may have different meanings and in varying degrees may be connected with the problem of resource allocation. For instance under 'war communism' price as a money–commodity category was used to express the aggregate output of individual establishments and of the whole state economy. Yet in the government sector the form of purchase and sale did not appear at all, and goods produced were transferred from producer to consumer by means of direct, non-monetary distribution. Price in this case fulfilled the function of a conventional, accounting magnitude used primarily for recording and statistical purposes. Similar in character are the so-called constant prices long used as basic units for measuring the degree of plan fulfilment in enterprises or industries. In principle a purely recording role can also be played by any other price system (including current price) provided it is not related to any acts of purchase and sale or to the flow of money from the recipient to the

supplier. An interesting problem arises concerning the relationship between price as applied in this way and real money–commodity relations; it seems that some relationship, even if only genetic, does always exist here; this among others, justifies the use of the term 'price' rather than another term.

The institution of *khozraschot* in a centralized model enlarges the area of applicability of money–commodity categories and partially increases their role in the allocation process. There is no need to describe the institution itself, or to explain how this role is increased at this time. I would only like to stress that in the case of an enterprise operating on the principle of *khozraschot*, the volume of resources that are at its disposal is related to the process of selling and thus to that of commodity exchange. In the *khozraschot* system resources allocation cannot occur without money; the movements of material resources are accompanied by those of money. This partially justifies the common expression that under a *khozraschot* system, the allocation of live and embodied labour is accomplished through money–commodity forms. However, in a centralized model among enterprises or between them and the centre, money is not an active tool for influencing movements of material components in the reproduction process; it plays, in principle, a passive part.[1] Magnitudes expressed in money terms do not constitute a basis for choice; they only express inputs and outputs on the basis of given objectives and methods of production. That under this system we use a type of money–commodity form in allocation, helps to control implementation of the decisions of central authorities and also provides its own economic incentives, not to mention a record of inputs and outputs. However, we must distinguish between the conditions under which the money–commodity forms of allocation play a passive auxiliary role, and those under which they are basic, active instruments for influencing the distribution of resources.

Even in a centralized model, money is active on the labour market and on the consumer goods market in so far as it expresses economic magnitudes, wages and prices, and these affect the choices of decision-makers, employees and consumers. Central influence on these choices is exerted by utilizing money–commodity categories, i.e. by means of money–commodity forms. If these forms are used similarly as instruments for influencing enterprise decisions (within the domain of state ownership) in the full sense of this word this is allocation by money–commodity forms.

Therefore, to speak of applying money–commodity forms in a socialist economy, we need more precise definition of the scope and role of those forms. To avoid misunderstandings, henceforth, I

[1] See pp. 75–80 above.

shall use the phrase: the employment of the market mechanism in a socialist economy, when speaking of the situation in which money–commodity forms are a basic, active tool of resource allocation. Thus market mechanism is used in a centralized model for distributing both labour and consumer goods. In accordance with the above definition, one cannot speak of a market mechanism in a centralized model; *khozraschot* and the market mechanism are not synonymous, although in both cases money–commodity forms are used.[1] Of course, the market mechanism appears in a socialist economy of the Yugoslav type.

Khozraschot does not deprive methods of planned allocation of their direct, imperative nature, in spite of the fact that it is connected with the specific use of money–commodity categories. For this reason, when we refer below to direct, imperative and thus administrative methods of achieving given patterns of output and exchange, bear in mind that these methods may also comprise *khozraschot* meant strictly as an institution of the centralized model.

Once the market mechanism is introduced, planned allocation is implemented by influencing the decisions of autonomous economic units in an indirect way, by providing alternatives of choice. In keeping with our terminology, these practices will be referred to as economic methods.

The distinction between the law of value and money–commodity forms including the market mechanism

Following these introductory explanations, let us turn to the problem. As before, let us commence with final production of consumer goods when, from a general social standpoint, there are no obstacles to shaping the output structure in order to ensure equivalence of exchange. In other words, we will begin from the point where economic proportions regulated by the law of value correspond to social preferences and secure the optimum resource allocation given the structure of capacity.

The structure of output which enables the equalization of price-and-value relations, can at least in principle be achieved either by means of the market mechanism or by direct action of the central authority.

1. *The market mechanism.* Enterprises have freedom of choice, and in order to maximize profits, they can react to differences in profitability.[2]

---

[1] In practice certain elements of the market mechanism may be bound up with the institution of *khozraschot*.

[2] I am ignoring the question of whether an incentive system is connected with profitability, and if so, what kind. Strictly speaking, in order to determine the

Assuming that consumer goods prices balance supply and demand, disproportions in output will be reflected by higher or lower profits. Output shifts caused by these differences should lead to an equilibrium based on value.

Within the framework of the market allocation, two cases may be distinguished:

a. State authorities do not interfere with market processes; prices develop freely on the market according to actual demand and supply relationship. This case we shall term 'free market mechanism', but one should bear in mind an essential difference distinguishing it from the classic mechanism of a competitive market under capitalism. Here everything works within a general framework established by the central authority, particularly with regard to the volume and pattern of distribution of the income consumed.

b. State authorities interfere with market processes. The rules of behaviour of the enterprises do not change, but enterprises no longer fix prices themselves according to spontaneous changes in the market situation. Instead they are fixed by independent state authorities directly, or by special measures of economic policy. This case we shall call 'regulated market mechanism'.

In our assumed case, both the free and regulated market mechanism should theoretically achieve the same result—an approach to the economic proportions which agree with the law of value. It may be questioned whether state intervention is at all sensible if price-fixing authorities are to observe the principle of market equilibrium. However, we must appreciate the danger that large enterprises may exploit their monopoly position in the market. Prevention of such tendencies provides the chief justification for instituting the regulated market mechanism where the compliance with the law of value is consistent with social optimum. This phenomenon, at the first glance, looks like a paradox; the activities of state authorities are directed

---

maximized profit magnitude (amount, rate, amount per employee, etc.) we must study the nature of reaction to changes in prices and costs alongside changes in the volume of output. See my article 'Koncepcje bodźców opartych na zysku' ('Incentives based on profit'), *Życie Gospodarcze*, no. 25, 1957; this is also dealt with by Aleksy Wakar in the second of his *Ekonomia socjalizmu, Wybrane zagadnienia* (*The Economics of Socialism, Selected Problems*), Warsaw, 1958, pp. 209–11. Benjamin Ward made some interesting remarks on this subject in 'The firm in Illyria', *The American Economic Review*, vol. 45, no. 4, September, 1958. He feels that where workers share in the profits, Lerner's rule about increasing output until marginal cost equals price should be modified; equilibrium is reached when the marginal income per employee is equal to the marginal cost of employing a worker.

But this type of discussion lies outside the scope of this book. For our purposes, it is sufficient to assume that enterprises react to differences in profitability judged relative to an accepted standard.

not against the market, but in defence of its 'perfection'. However, the paradox is only apparent in this case; what conflicts with the social interest is not the market process itself, but obstacles in its course. Apart from preventing monopoly, the regulated market mechanism is also helpful in making prices resistant to the temporary business fluctuations which sometimes mislead the producers. The negative side of the regulated market mechanism could be insufficient price flexibility producing delayed responses to changed economic conditions.

2. *Direct influence by administrative measures.* The enterprises have no freedom in choosing the volume of output since choice is reserved to the central authority (or appropriate agents at a lower level acting on its behalf). However, it does not necessarily mean that it will be impossible to reach an equilibrium based on value. Appropriate reckoning by the central authority and the issuing to enterprises of quantitatively determined instructions changing output volume may bring price ratios in line with those of value.

At this time I will not touch on the advisability of using either of the methods in the actual conditions under which a socialist economy functions. All I want to show is that the pattern of labour allocation may be accomplished in harmony with the law of value both by applying the market mechanism (free or regulated) and by using administrative measures or planners' fiats.

Let us now turn to the situation where the structure of consumer goods output which corresponds to the law of value is opposed to the optimum structure because there exist certain social preferences (see chapter 4). We will assume that these preferences are reflected not by that structure of supply which satisfies the conditions of equivalence, but by the original structure at which equilibrium prices were not equal to values. This means that the prices which balance supply and demand should be at a level different from values, and similarly those changes *must be avoided* in the supply structure which tends to arise in such a state of relative prices and profitabilities.

How can this be achieved?

In this case, the free market mechanism would be useless since it would work towards increasing the output and consumption of the profitable product (until price equals value) and decreasing the output and consumption of the unprofitable (less profitable) product (again until price equals value). Thus, it becomes necessary for the appropriate authorities to intervene either by economic or administrative measures.

Intervention by economic measures means employing the regulated market mechanism for influencing independent enterprise decisions. E.g. when value $= 5$, the price of A is fixed at 8 with the simultaneous

imposition of a tax on the producers, amounting to 3 per unit of commodity A. The price of B (value $= 10$) is set at 7, but at the same time a subsidy is assigned to the producers, amounting to 3 per unit of commodity B. Profitability continues to guide enterprises following principles discussed already, but the equalization of profitabilities is achieved at different levels of output than before.

Thus two price systems are created insulated from one another by tax (or subsidy). The purchaser's price system which balances supply with demand at prices deviating from values, and the producer's which corresponds to value, ensures equilibrium. It is, however, a peculiar type of equilibrium; actually the more expensive product is cheaper to the purchaser, and vice versa. Thus, we have a portion of income redistributed—through the budget—between the buyers of products A and B and also between the producers of A and B.

Naturally, this method is not the only feasible one. In certain cases it may be sufficient to set the tax (or subsidy) without directly fixing the purchase price, but leaving it to find its own level. Other possibilities are a minimum or maximum price, more or less complex taxation systems etc. There is no need here to probe any deeper into this kind of problem, but it is essential for us to remember that regardless of detailed technical solutions, we are dealing with the market mechanism working against, and not in accordance with the law of value.

The same position of supply, demand and prices could be achieved through administrative measures by direct orders to limit the production of A and to increase the production of B, regardless of the high profitability of A and the lack of profit of B.

By this reasoning, in spite of the crude nature of the example, we can arrive at important conclusions, rather removed from the almost generally accepted view. The specialist literature often assumes that in a planned economy there is a strict relationship between the scope of the law of value and that of the utilization of money–commodity forms. But it appears that the law may work when direct, imperative forms of allocation are used. On the other hand, the market mechanism (regulated) may be used for attaining output and exchange patterns different from those that would develop spontaneously under the influence of that law. In this situation, the central planning authority achieves its aims through the market mechanism by appropriately formulating the alternatives for autonomous economic units.

Such possibilities are related not solely to producing consumer goods, but also to producing the means of production. Adapting the supply structure of the latter to its demand structure (itself a function of the structure of both final production of consumer and

investment goods as well as a function of techniques) may be accomplished either by administrative or economic measures. Either measure can apply both when final demand is affected by the law of value, and when it is influenced by social preferences which require different proportions. Of course, using the market mechanism for planning the supply structure of the means of production presumes fulfilment of a number of conditions to which a centralized planning authority is unaccustomed. Primarily, prices of the means of production (in inter-enterprise transactions) should reflect not only the conditions of production (costs), but also the conditions of exchange. Briefly, the latter amounts to the relative scarcity of individual kinds of producer goods, because of authorized plan targets (both current and long term). Thus, using the market mechanism requires that prices of the means of production are *sui generis* equilibrium prices balancing supply with demand. Furthermore, they must constitute correct indices (for producer and consumer) in selecting alternatives under conditions which are engendered by the more general planning decisions. In essence, prices must deviate from value wherever supply is not balanced with demand at prices corresponding to values. In such a position there are deficiencies or surpluses and thus prices of inter-enterprise trade must be treated as instruments of economic *policy* and not merely as units of measurement. As a form of executing the planned preferences of society, the market mechanism aids both the selection of the manner of realizing an investment project and of the direction which supplementary investment should follow. The latter, as previously noted, is designed to remove currently certain bottle-necks in the production apparatus. Such investment projects are usually included in the category of decentralized investment and are largely undertaken in the framework of the existing conditions of production and exchange. Therefore, it seems feasible to influence them by means of money–commodity forms (in this case mainly by the rate of interest).

However, the market mechanism (as was noted in chapter 2— Dobb–Lange controversy—and chapter 4) is not suitable for determining the basic lines of an economy's development. The choice of general and long-term *directions* of investment must be of a direct character in a planned economy. Such decisions form the framework within which all the economic units act. They provide top-level criteria which aid in assessing the relative importance of each element in the production process.

Assuming that both framework and criteria are established by direct central decisions, the market mechanism may then be used as an instrument of planned management. It is a serious misapprehension to treat the mechanism as suitable only for situations

where spontaneous forces are at work. It is not merely a synonym for an economy in which macro-economic processes derive only from a base of micro-economic activities. The (regulated) market mechanism should be treated as one of the theoretically possible forms of achieving socio-economic rationality—as a form that satisfies the need for integrating sectoral objectives with the common goal which guides society in its economic activities.

In chapter 2, (esp. the section on the Preobrazhenski–Bukharin discussions) I tried to show instances in which Marxist literature attempts to distinguish between the operation of the law of value and the application of money–commodity forms. In the late 1930s, a formulation of this distinction appears to have been used to justify the following thesis: although the law of value would be entirely eliminated after the transition period (an incorrect supposition), nevertheless money–commodity forms would be preserved. Instances are the market mechanism for allocating consumer goods and labour power, and *khozraschot* in the domain of state ownership, not to mention commodity relations stemming from the existence of co-operative ownership.

In spite of this, the problem was far from receiving a clear and consistent solution. Marxist theoretical thought never fully freed itself from the belief that applying the market mechanism in socialism would lead to an irrevocable subordination to the law of value and thus open the door to spontaneity in economic activity. For the nature of planning, direct imperative forms of allocation are most suitable. In this belief can be found the roots of various requests once offered to justify purging all money–commodity forms from the Soviet economy following subjection of the law of value. An extension of this argument is the 'theoretical revolution' which Stalin[1] initiated in 1941 when he rejected the thesis that the law of value should be surmounted in socialism. If the elimination of money–commodity forms is considered unreal and incorrect, then the law of value must be 'resuscitated'. He saw this, but never clearly defined its content or its sphere of operation. From that moment misunderstandings multiplied, the more so as attempts at clarifying the situation tended to be taken not as independent analysis, but as exegeses of the texts. And, the author of these felt himself less and less bound by scientific accuracy and consistency. Even after 1953 and after the 20th Party Congress of the CPSU, the confused relationship between the law of value and the market mechanism could be seen. A good example is the criticism levelled against excessive centralization in a planned economy. The postulated

[1] See J. Stalin, *Report to the Seventeenth Congress of the CPSU (B) on the Work of the Central Committee* (Moscow, 1951), pp. 82–5.

abandonment of hyper-centralization and utilization of the market mechanism was formulated as the attempt to give increased scope to the law of value.[1] By now, it should be clear that these postulates are not identical: the first pertains to the form and the second to the substance of society's labour resource allocation. When planning the socialist economic structure within defined limits, we should allow for the operation of the objective law of value. If we want to avoid losses or non-optimum results, we should observe the principle of equivalence. The second postulate fixes the scope for making use of the market mechanism on a different level in a socialist economy. The scope of operation of the law of value and the potential scope for using the market mechanism are not the same thing. The market mechanism may be used not only when we want to attain the proportions corresponding to the law of value, but also when we want to achieve different proportions—proportions consistent with both society's overall preferences and scale and the predominant principles of socio-economic rationality in a socialist system.

This is not an answer to the advisability of using in a planned economy one or the other—market or command mechanism. Neither does it mean that in reality the choice of mechanism is a matter of indifference, nor that both can fulfil the dual requirement which an efficient mechanism of a socialist economy ought to satisfy (i.e. the ability to operate outside the terms of the law of value and at the same time to realize its requirement within the bounds of its operation). Our hitherto highly abstract reasoning does not yet allow us to draw conclusions of this kind. We shall attempt to draw them later on at least in a general form, when the outlines of a centralized model described in chapter 3, find expression in the detailed description of a planned economy with a built-in market mechanism, and when, therefore, certain comparisons will be possible.

One already well-established conclusion emerges from our analysis of the differences between the substance of proportions and forms of their realization. *In theory* none of these forms can be recognized *a priori* as *basically* consistent or *basically* inconsistent with a socialist planned economy. There are no theoretical foundations for worshipping administrative directives as a synonym for planning, or for idealizing the market mechanism as a synonym for harmony with the requirements of objective economic laws, particularly of the law of value. There are no theoretical grounds for denying that requirements of objective economic laws can be achieved through direct

---

[1] This theoretical premise is one I have frequently used in my own work. See for example *Prawo wartości a problematyka bodźców ekonomicznych* (*The Law of Value and the Problem of Economic Incentives*), pp. 58–9, 61; 'O roli prawa wartości w gospodarce socjalistycznej' ('The role of the law of value in a socialist economy'), *Ekonomista*, no. 5, 1956, pp. 75–7, 79,

K

commands, or for denying that planned targets can be reached through the market mechanism. *In particular the theory of a regulated market mechanism—strongly attacked on doctrinal grounds—in itself contains nothing that would make it alien to socialism or basically inconsistent with the premises of a socialist economy.*

Disputes over the role of economic and administrative measures and their mutual relationship in a management system are and will continue to be of fundamental importance. They will be decided not at the level where the essence of socialism is investigated, but on the realistic plane where the advisability and usefulness of one form or the other is appraised or of their combination.

A description of the decentralized model

Chapter 3 outlined the functioning of a planned economy which employs mainly direct administrative forms of allocation (the centralized model). Some features of the market mechanism as it operates in a socialist economy were noted in the course of that discussion. These were insufficient for conducting a comparative analysis of the suitability of such a mechanism. They need to be supplemented by an outline of the operation of a planned economy which makes use of the market mechanism. As in chapter 3, we are not going to describe any concrete management system, as it never is and cannot be homogeneous or free from practical compromise. Instead we shall present a picture of the principles of operation in their pure form and thus describe a model of a planned economy with a *built-in market mechanism*—what is commonly, although perhaps not very accurately, called a *decentralized model*.[1]

[1] Among the known organization forms of the socialist economy it is the Yugoslav system which makes the greatest use of the market mechanism. I would like, however, to make quite clear that the abstract outline given here is by no means a picture of the Yugoslav system. As in my description of the centralized model, I do not allow for the existence of socio-economic sectors other than the state sector. I have also ignored every practical 'defection' from the market mechanism and all the specific factors connected with the origins and development of the Yugoslav system, and, as well, the attendant ideological problems. Among other things, no consideration is taken of the role played by local authorities, which is a basic element in concretely analysing the Yugoslav system.

Detailed descriptions of the actual functioning of that system can be found in the rich material on this subject in Polish as well as other languages. Czesław Bobrowski gives an analysis of the Yugoslav economic system together with the circumstances of its initiation and development, *Jugosławia socjalistyczna (Socialist Yugoslavia)*, Warsaw, 1957. See also a collection of papers by Yugoslav writers, *Ekonomika ip olityka Jugoslawii (The Economy and Policy of Yugoslavia)*, Warsaw, 1957, and the more popular *System jugosłowiański z bliska (A close-up of the Yugoslav System)*, Warsaw, 1957, by W. Brus and S. Jakubowicz.

The main characteristic of a *decentralized model*[1] is that *economic decisions are taken at various levels*. For simplicity, we shall ignore several levels which appear in practice and deal with two levels: A. the central authority and B. the socialized enterprise or enterprise associations.

The *central authority* constructs the national economic plan as a whole on the basis of a general social preference scale by using long-term socio-economic criteria of rationality. Here there is no basic difference between the central plan in a centralized model and in a decentralized one. The *range* of problems covered by planning is also similar, although some indices in a decentralized model are less detailed, especially for output assortments. The central plan in a decentralized model handles problems such as the rate of growth of output and national income; division of national income between accumulation and consumption; the distribution of accumulation between fixed capital investment and stock increases; determination of the main investment trends for branches of industry and regions; the division of that consumption between collective and individual consumption; the determination of changes in the income structure (again at branch and regional levels); the branch and regional structures of production; determination of the output of the most important products in physical units; employment and labour productivity; the size and structure of foreign trade, and so on.

Basic differences do exist in the way the plan is executed and in the type of connection between the central plan and enterprise plans. In the centralized model, to introduce an index into the plan is the same as to make a direct decision issued as planning order. In a decentralized model, the overwhelming majority of centrally planned indices are not obligatory and are not identical with a direct decision. The central authority takes direct decisions only in the following areas:

1. In dividing national income, by determining:
   a. the share of individual incomes and the basic outline of the earnings structure for wage and salary earners;[2]

[1] I shall use this term as an abbreviation for a planned economy with built-in market mechanism.

[2] Central decision to divide national income roughly into wages and profits and also to fix the earnings structure of employees may take various forms. Some examples are limitations on the wages fund, establishment of wage rates differentiated by industrial branch and the level of qualification etc. But, apart from the form which is adopted, the very principle of centrally deciding these problems cannot be violated in a socialist economy. We refer to the main elements of distribution which, as we shall see later, are not intended to eliminate the possibility of allowing enterprises to take their own decisions on some problems in this area, since these decisions are influenced centrally by indirect methods.

    b. the division of enterprises, net incomes between centralized funds and funds which are controlled by enterprises themselves;

    c. the division of the centralized funds between collective consumption and accumulation (particularly the size of the central investment fund).

2. In choosing main investment trends, which is accomplished by allocating the central investment fund among branches and by prescribing increments to capacity and saying specifically how they are to be achieved. Connected with this are direct decisions in the choice of the best method for achieving a desired capacity (methods of investment) without the necessity, however, of taking direct decisions about detailed problems in this field.

Areas which call for direct decisions are of basic significance in determining the main economic patterns. However, they do not encompass the whole problem of dividing national income and of choosing investment areas (and the more so—methods of investment) since some decisions in these matters are left to the enterprise. This leads to the problem of how the central authority can indirectly affect the decisions made at the lower level.

A specific type of direct decision taken by the central authority is the creation or liquidation of enterprises. The function of initiation in the socialist system cannot be assigned to individual enterprises; this must be the prerogative of organs which receive the mandate of social ownership.

Except for the above, other economic decisions in a decentralized model are taken *at the level of the enterprise.*

At the moment of its establishment, the enterprise is equipped with the necessary fixed and working capital and *it organizes in itself the reproduction process* (capital replacement). Its most important tasks are selecting the current production goals, the size and structure of output, the methods of production, and the structure of inputs. It appears on the market as the purchaser of the means of production and autonomously chooses its sources of supply; it also appears as the seller of finished goods, autonomously choosing the areas in which it disposes of them. The enterprise also decides how to divide income (after taxation) and the size and trends of its investments. Enterprise decisions to create or to expand capacity find additional financial support in the amortization fund or in credit facilities available to it. Even in the case of projects initiated centrally, an enterprise may have some scope for making its own decisions, such as when it must choose the actual methods for carrying out a given investment project. Finally, it is clear that in a decentralized model, the questions of internal organization, the wage system

within the rules which have been established centrally, the structure of employment, and so on, all belong to the area of autonomous decision-making. The problem of the right of an enterprise to determine the selling prices is treated separately.

The criteria used as a basis for autonomous enterprise decisions derive from the *profitability principle*. It is the sole possible principle for operating those enterprises which have a genuine right of choice, especially as to the aims and methods of production. In the centralized model where economic decisions are made outside the enterprise, only the volume of output of a given assortment may be maximized. Productive technique, particularly normed input co-efficients, are determined and reflected by physical and financial constraints on an enterprise. Conversely, where the task is one of minimizing inputs, then the effect is given in the shape of a pre-determined volume of output. Any comparison of inputs with product is centrally made where the decision is taken. When the choice of ends and techniques is developed to the enterprise level it would be entirely illogical to use one-sided standards to express separately either end products or inputs. In this situation the standard for judging enterprise activity can only be a synthetic magnitude which compares final results and inputs in money form. The principle of profitability can take many forms. For example, if we assume that the sum of labour payments is fixed *a priori*, then what is maximized may be the value of net output (total value added). However, in the end all the concrete forms can be reduced to the profit maximization or the difference between revenue and all expenditures needed to achieve it.[1]

From a theoretical point of view the profitability principle should

[1] Profit maximization in a decentralized socialist enterprise should not be identified with profit maximization in a capitalist enterprise. The difference is basic, not merely because of the different social nature of profit, but also because of the part profit plays in the economy. Profit maximization is the ultimate goal of the capitalist enterprise since there is no integration of the ends of individual enterprises into a common goal established in the society's economic plan (see O. Lange, *Political Economy*, vol. 1 ch. 5, pp. 179–81). On the other hand, in a socialist economy an enterprise goal is always subordinate and auxiliary to the primary goals (or group thereof) which are elaborated in the general economic plan. As an example, profit as the goal of a decentralized socialist enterprise does not differ from the maximization of either gross output or the volume of output, and these are normally the established goals of enterprises in a centralized model. In both cases the problem is to achieve the social ends by appropriately selecting the ends of activity of lower levels. Whether profit as the aim of socialist enterprises adequately fulfils its purpose in achieving general social goals is obviously open to dispute. (Similarly, the question of whether the principle of maximizing output is an effective solution to enterprise management is also open to dispute). Answers are to be sought within the framework of the usefulness of a market mechanism (economic means) in a socialist economy.

not be identified with the use of a system of incentives based on profit. It is quite possible that profit may serve as the standard for measuring the efficiency of an enterprise without wages being relatively or absolutely connected to the size of profit. However, in general we may assume that where material incentives are employed, employees' personal incomes will somehow be connected with the main efficiency standard of the enterprise. It is also logical to make expanded reproduction (economic growth) within an enterprise to some degree dependent on economic results. This is of basic importance for rationally allocating labour resources. Therefore, we shall assume further that when an enterprise obtains good results, it improves its prospects for expansion raising the level of employee incomes. Conversely, when results are unfavourable, and it loses a part of its funds, the employees' incomes decline (possibly to a legal minimum) and in extreme cases, it may even go bankrupt. The use of profitability as the main efficiency criterion and the basis of incentives is intended to foster rational management in production and exchange.

That the decentralized socialist enterprises are guided by profitability explains why they may not set up new enterprises. If directors and employees provided such capital and, thereby, acquired title to share its profits (personal interest), this would obviously contravene the socialist nature of productive relations. As an incentive, the profit motive may affect only the results of an enterprise's own efforts towards effective use of the factors entrusted to it for undertaking a given sphere of productive or service activity. Likewise, it is impossible to admit free direct flow of capital between enterprises or branches. This is basic to the nature of competition in a planned market economy and to the processes of adjustment evoked by market-derived indicators and incentives.

The elaboration of this model indicates that unlike the centralized model which centralizes current economic decisions (the 'third group' of decisions in the scheme outlined on page 63) the decentralized model resolves the problem of the 'controversial' type of decisions in favour of decentralization. The role of money–commodity forms in the state sector is accordingly transformed from a passive to an active one.

In a decentralized model, we are faced with plans independently constructed at different levels (in our simplified case at two). The plan of the central level, although it covers many problems which are included in the plans of individual enterprises is no mere summary of enterprises' plans or a passive anticipation of micro-economic decisions. It is an autonomous plan constructed with national interest in mind and considering both economic and non-economic factors.

It is also true that enterprises' plans do not formally constitute parts of the central plan. This is so, not only because they contain elements which are too detailed to be included in the central plan, but chiefly because they are independently elaborated and may not formally and unconditionally be brought into conformity with the central plan.

Nevertheless, though there is no formal hierarchical relationship between the plans of the different levels, *the principle of central plan primacy*, and hence the primacy of national economy interests as a whole *is preserved in the decentralized model*.

The primacy is a product of the nature of the direct decisions at the centre. The choice of an income distribution determines the extent of consumer demand and also its structure in so far as that is dependent on the pattern of income distribution. This central choice is also the major element in determining the magnitude of investment goods demand. The choice of major investment trends determines the basic elements of change in the size and structure of an economy's productive capacity. In determining the growth rate and the general structure of the economy, the central authority simultaneously fixes the main guidelines for enterprises' choice, and in the last analysis, creates the framework within which profit-guided enterprises make their autonomous choices.

Given that there are no social special preferences in consumption, and in income distribution,[1] and that there is no danger of monopolistic action, and no serious time-lags in the adjustment of the supply structure to demand after relative price movements; then the free market mechanism ought to lead to an equilibrium which corresponds to that economic structure desired by the central authority. This situation would closely resemble Lange's model with one important difference. The central authority directly fixes the main investment trends whereas a uniform interest rate performs this function à la Lange.

However, even at a high level of abstraction, it is difficult to regard these assumptions as realistic. Moreover, we must bear in mind that direct decisions emanating from central authority do not entirely exhaust the problem of dividing national income into accumulation and consumption. In a certain area the enterprises may independently decide whether a given part of their profit should be assigned to accumulation or to consumption. As a result, investment trends and income distribution are also only partly prescribed. The point at issue is that general direct decisions do not guarantee the primacy of the central over the enterprise plan, if other specific decisions are left to the operation of a free market mechanism.

[1] In relation to the structure of nominal incomes, see pp. 110–13.

As previously stated, in a decentralized model, the central authority must make some use of the *regulated market mechanism*. In this way, the framework created by general direct decisions is filled out by a number of indirect decisions.

Thus, in the second place, the primacy of the central plan is dependent on a number of indirect decisions taken at the centre. They are directed towards arranging economic conditions in order that an enterprise's profit-guided decisions conform with the basic aims of the plan, and thereby to assist society in achieving its overall social goal.[1]

In general, indirect decisions deal with factors which affect the size of an enterprise's profit by means of both costs and revenues. On the cost side, these may be decisions determining the amortization rates, depreciation allowances, interest rates on short-term and investment credits or, above all, the prices of the means of production and wages. On the revenue side, these are largely decisions determining enterprise obligations to the state and to local authorities or decisions on an enterprise's selling prices. Differentials in applying policies in the fields of taxes and credits and tariffs and exchange affect costs and incomes of industrial branches and types of output. In this way, they become instruments for influencing the volume of output and the degree to which capacity is utilized. Secondarily, they also affect the structure of output, the choice of technique, the manner of dividing profit between accumulation and employees' incomes, and broad investment trends in so far as enterprises deploy their own means.

I do not want to dwell on the technical aspects of how the central authority influences enterprise decision-making, especially since this problem has received a great deal of attention (with reference to Yugoslavia). What is quite clear is that in the decentralized model, the market mechanism is not a means of subordinating production and exchange proportions to spontaneous processes, but an instrument which serves to adjust individual enterprise activities to overall social preferences as expressed in the plan. Money plays an active role, not only in the consumer good and labour markets, but also in the state sector; this role is exploited in order to reach the same type of goals for which the centralized model uses direct imperative

---

[1] By direct decisions of the central authority I mean direct establishment of a certain group of aims and the appropriate allocation of available means. By indirect decisions, I mean decisions which influence the choice of aims and the allocation of means in enterprises by appropriately shaping economic conditions. Obviously, direct decisions of the central authority have also an indirect significance since they determine the overall conditions within which enterprises operate.

planning in physical terms.[1] Having resources allocated by means of active money does not exclude physical-term balancing in the decentralized model. As I tried to show in an earlier chapter, the role of use-value is fundamental to socialism. Balancing in physical units is indispensable to a planned economy which—because of the nature of the macro-economic problem and the normally high rate of capacity utilization—finds aggregate magnitudes inadequate. Therefore, in the planning process of every model of the socialist economy, the central authority must also draw up physical balances for a large number of basic products. In this way, it can detect the bottle-necks and take measures necessary for eliminating them by influencing either supply or demand or both. Nevertheless, balancing in physical terms should not be confused with the administrative distribution of products. Unlike the centralized model, where the use of the balance method of planning is closely connected with physical distribution, in the decentralized model the confrontation of demands with the possibility of their meeting is expressed in a set of economic magnitudes. Chiefly these are prices which by their effect on suppliers and purchasers become the instrument for obtaining the equilibrium desired by planners. By constraining the use of physical balancing to macro-economic analysis of the central level, the decentralized model does not need to create a complicated system of physical allocation, or to use very detailed balances for every level of the economy.

This type of solution has important consequences for the horizontal relationships between enterprises. In a centralized model, these merely constitute the executive stage of processes which are entirely determined by direct central decision. In a decentralized model, they are an active factor in shaping the reproduction process within the framework of planning preferences. This holds not only for the turnover of the means of production, but also for the means of consumption among the state-owned enterprises (industry-trade).

Applying the market mechanism of allocation makes many complex demands both on the structure of prices and on the system of price formation.

I have previously elaborated on the basic requirements of a price system. To recapitulate briefly, the prices of both consumer goods and the means of production in inter-enterprise transactions should

---

[1] The nature of the relationship between the centre and enterprises in a de-centralized model completely justifies using the term enterprise *autonomy* instead of enterprise *independence*. The term *autonomy* is a more apt description of the state of affairs in which 1, the sphere of decision of the enterprises is limited and 2, the decisions of the enterprises are taken on the basis of indices of choice alternatives determined centrally so as consciously to assist in realizing the primary social goals.

reflect not only production conditions but also those of exchange. (They should reflect the relationship between output volume and need, as well as socially necessary inputs per unit of output.)[1] In general, this means that it is necessary strictly to preserve correspondence between the price system and overall economic conditions, which includes the degree of scarcity of a good. Divergence between the structure of prices and economic conditions in a decentralized model cannot be allowed.

The basic requirement for a system price formation is that prices be made independent parameters for the enterprises.

Prices are one of the basic instruments for influencing enterprise decisions, making them conform to the plan's objectives. Taking this for granted, they should reflect social preferences as accurately as possible, while constituting *given* indices for choosing among various alternatives (independent of an enterprise's own interests). This concept of a decentralized model includes the principles that prices are independent of the will of the enterprise. This is not the same as state authorities directly fixing all prices. Wherever the market for a given product has real features of a competitive market, when it is impossible for enterprises to exercise a monopolistic influence on price, and when there are no special social preferences demanding different prices for the consumer and for the supplier, the formation of prices may be left to the action of free markets.

This is the situation in which the convergence of price and value ratios promotes social preference within the outlines of central decisions. In all other cases (either certain preferences or the danger of a monopolistic interference with prices), special methods are necessary in a decentralized model to safeguard the parametric character of prices. Indirect methods (e.g. a flexible rate of turnover tax) are permissible if they guarantee the independence of prices of the particular interest of enterprises. If not, then direct methods must be used. It must be remembered that the high degree of concentration and specialization of production, together with the high level of capacity utilization found in socialism favours the emergence of monopolistic tendencies. (There are factors working against this, such as derive from the awareness of the general interest.) To counteract these tendencies by artificial stimulation of competition (e.g. by deconcentrating production) would obviously be irrational, hence it becomes still more important to ensure that state organs have effective influence on price formation. Effective influence enables exploitation of concentration and specialization in produc-

---

[1] This does not eliminate the possibility of differentiating supply prices and consumer prices.

tion, and yet allows the productive apparatus to be fully employed without the adverse effects of market monopolies.

This problem illustrates the central position occupied by society's overall point of view in the decentralized model. (The same could be said of wages.) The criterion for selecting concrete forms of the market mechanism is their efficiency as instruments for obtaining the goals establishment in the plan.

Analysis of the arguments for the decentralized model

Closer scrutiny of the assumptions for a decentralized model confirms that application of the market mechanism is not intended to supplant the plan, but to create an instrument for implementing it. However, in itself it fails to answer the question whether, and to what extent, the market mechanism is really a better instrument of planning than the direct commands of the centralized model. On this subject, Polish and foreign discussion of the model have recently produced a series of interesting arguments both for and against applying a market mechanism to a planned economy.

Chief among arguments favouring application of the market mechanism is the one which raises the *problem of the elasticity of adjustment by which supply responds to demand*. A high degree of supply flexibility is particularly important in consumer goods, for which demand is very difficult to predict in detail because of its complexity and variability. Yet, in the supply of the means of production, the importance of flexibility should not be neglected; excessive stability in demand patterns for the means of production would be akin to a conservative attitude towards technical progress and product innovation.

Insufficient elasticity in the adaptation of supply to demand means a waste of resources. Some products cannot be sold and others vanish from the market, and the consumer is forced to buy products other than those which he wanted, and which could be offered to him. It is difficult to measure such waste, but it is important to the ends of a socialist economy.

Within the plan's outlines the advantage of the market mechanism in this case is that the adaptation of the supply structure to the demand structure is left to direct relationships between the supplier and the buyer. Thus, it requires no detailed formulations or constant approval by the central authority. In the centralized model the processes by which supply is adapted are made rather rigidly. It is impossible to expect the central authority to make accurate judgments on an enormous number of elements which compose the structure of supply and demand. At the same time, the hierarchical arrangement

of plans (and the resulting criteria for evaluating efficiency at lower levels) implies that where conflicts arise, genuine consumer satisfaction must always yield to fulfilment of plan targets. Furthermore, it is of little consequence whether these targets actually reflect the social effects of economic activity.

Where the market mechanism is applied, it can be assumed that profit-oriented enterprise will compose an output pattern which is motivated by actual market conditions. Differences in the profitability of products may become a factor in choosing output assortment and only saleable goods will be produced. Assuming that the price structure corresponds to economic conditions and that social preferences are taken into account, a shift in output to more profitable items should be justified on the grounds that it serves society's needs better, since resources are used more effectively. Supply elasticity is increased the wider the scope granted to the market mechanism. This is the case in which the use of the market mechanism is not limited exclusively to current production decisions within a given capacity structure, but also contains the choice of investment trends (mainly for decentralized investment). The accrued advantages seem beyond dispute, since an enterprise which better adapts itself to consumer needs has better chances of expansion, of somewhat increasing its productive capacity, and of improving its technique and the use properties of its product. When there is a general equilibrium of supply and demand and a normal buyer's market exists, the enterprise tends to become interested in certain developmental possibilities as a way of strengthening its competitive position. This must also be considered advantageous. Assuming a well-structured incentive system based on profits, this interest may widen the time horizon in an enterprise's 'strategy', another feature which is extremely difficult to achieve in the centralized model.

In connection with overall equilibrium, it is worth noting the importance of flexible adjustments of the supply structure to the demand structure. Nobody would any longer think that an excess of aggregate effective demand over total supply is a normal feature of a socialist economy. On the contrary, the preservation of equilibrium between purchasing power and the supply of goods is rightly considered one of the basic elements in the plan and a prerequisite for harmonious economic development. At the same time, the possibility of relatively precise balancing of both these magnitudes, without incurring over-production and under-utilization of capacity, must be reckoned as one of the most important elements of superiority of socialism over capitalism. This is one of the reasons why the buyer's market cannot and ought not to be as extensive as it is in capitalism, where it is a symptom of waste and of the inability to

utilize fully the society's productive forces. A slight excess of supply over demand, and hence the creation of a limited buyer's market, is useful for stimulating supply, but it would be nonsense to increase this margin and to relinquish the chance to increase output and incomes. Thus, in a socialist economy, surpluses in the balance of income and expenditure are normally rather quickly dispersed and rigorous efforts made to maintain reserves at an economically justified minimum. Maintenance of minimum reserves attaches special importance to the process by which supply adjusts to demand. Where the margin is large, divergences of the supply structure from the demand structure have very little effect on general market equilibrium. With small margins, relatively minor divergences may disturb the market equilibrium. For these reasons, it is of basic importance to study the flexibility of supply adjustment in evaluating the mechanism of functioning of a planned economy.

In understanding this adjustment process, it should not be presumed that production has a passive role in relation to consumer tastes. Production shapes demand by supplying new ways of satisfying needs, and at the same time it creates needs. In evaluating the mechanism of the functioning of an economic model, it is extremely important to know whether and to what extent it favours the introduction of new products and the improvement of existing ones. However, these problems are implied in the idea of the process by which the supply structure adjusts to the demand structure. They are questions not of launching any form of new or improved products, but those which in given circumstances are accepted by consumers and hence, in this sense, get approval from the market.

The second group of arguments favouring the application of a market mechanism touches problems associated with *rational utilization of the factors of production with the minimization of inputs in order to achieve planned goals*. When an enterprise seeks profit maximization, *ceteris paribus*, a continual tendency to lower production costs appears. It seems very important again that, in a decentralized model, enterprise efficiency should not be evaluated by comparing its results with indices of a hierarchically constructed plan whose indices tend to be established at the lowest possible level. Hierarchical indices are more or less precise but always contain an element of the subjective. In our model, evaluative standards are in a certain sense absolute and relate to the amount of profit (or changes of this amount) which is dependent on reducing outlays. Thus, the model may be expected not to 'conceal reserves', but to tend to create incentives for their full utilization. Such expectation is justified by the following reasons:

1. It is in the interest of the enterprise to diminish physical labour

inputs (both 'living' and 'embodied') per unit of output, and hence systematically to improve the internal organization of its production process, to make its technology more efficient and so on. Moreover, the enterprise is able to do it by being free to select its own internal organization and by having certain means at its own disposal (including some investment funds).

2. It is in the interest of the enterprise to find the most economical combination of factors of production as expressed in money terms. This is no less important than reducing physical outlays per unit. Assuming that the social importance of individual factors of production is reflected in a parametric set of prices and wages, proper factor substitution is advantageous to the entire economy. This is because it yields lower inputs in money terms, even without reducing the physical norms of outlay of individual factors (or increasing the physical outlay of some of these factors). An enterprise can aim at the most economical combination of productive factors because of its freedom to determine the structure of its inputs, to select its supply sources, and to partially finance projects which are prerequisites for introducing more rational operation. Production techniques in this situation can more easily be evaluated for their economic worth.[1] This is because the choice of technique is not limited to the central authority alone, but extends down to the enterprise level. Efficiency calculations for techniques of production, when made centrally, are always somewhat abstract and cannot encompass all the actual circumstances which may vitally affect the results. Hence, if all decisions are made centrally and passed directly to enterprises in an obligatory form, there is always a great danger of making serious errors. Mindful of this, a two-level procedure seems very attractive, In the first place, all the basic cost considerations of introducing and applying new technical processes can be assessed socially by means of factor prices and the conditions of credit. In the second place, these elements are 'filtered' through enterprise calculations. That unit is interested in economic results and is able to compare the general assumptions with the concrete needs, organizational methods, alternative production costs, and so on. This does not pertain to the solution of larger crucial problems

[1] The problem of economically evaluating production techniques in a socialist economy has been dealt with recently by Aleksy Wakar in his paper 'The Place of Economic Calculation in the Political Economy of Socialism', *Zycie Gospodarcze*, no. 9, 1960. Although Wakar's general belief that in its existing form, the socialist economy provides no solution to the problem of economically evaluating production techniques is obviously hasty and unjustified, his stress on the importance of indirect calculation, i.e. through prices, costs, and profits, is a valid concept. We shall deal with this problem somewhat more closely in our section on the role of prices of the means of production (pp. 173 ff. infra).

which lie outside an enterprise's scale of calculation and time horizon; in these cases, the one-level central type of decision is quite justified.

3. The enterprise is concerned with the mutual relationship between outlays and results. This is because a decentralized enterprise's activity is motivated by profitability, or the synthetic net result of inputs and receipts which allows it to make a full-scale assessment of the results of its own activity. In the centralized model input and product are compared centrally, which means that the function of the enterprise is only an executive one. Even in principle, it is to be doubted whether this favours a rational management of the economy, since it may involve both rigidity and inability to assess actual circumstances. In practice, it is impossible to eliminate completely the active role of the enterprise. It would reveal the damaging effects of employing one-sided indices, and it would separate standards for evaluating efficiency based on gross production from those based on cost. It is evident that mere cost reduction does not provide sufficient grounds to judge an enterprise's performance, if output has declined in quantity or quality. Conversely, an increase in output unrelated to changes in inputs is equally inadequate as a criterion. The use of one-sided criteria in judging output or inputs leads to an irrational use of means (even when outputs are assessed by more sophisticated methods than the so-called 'index of gross output' which included outlays in results). As we have seen, the situation is not much improved by using more complex criteria, applied in the form of separate indices. Apart even from the task of gauging the relative importance of the positive and negative aspects of each of the criteria, wherever many indices are applied, one always emerges predominate which again leads to a one-sided evaluation.

Where the possibility exists for autonomously determining output structure and technique, profitability calculations ought to enable better assignment of the productive programme to enterprises within an industrial branch. This possibility arises because the sum of branch outlays is reduced for the whole output, and given the selling price, there should be a tendency to produce each item in those enterprises at lower costs. By seeking profitability, enterprises whose costs cannot be covered by the price (which expresses the social scale of preferences)[1] will tend to discontinue the production of a given article.

[1] This does not deny the possibility of differentiating the prices for suppliers. In such a situation, however, the organizational unit immediately above the enterprise (e.g. the association of enterprises) ought to receive a uniform price. Differentiated prices to individual enterprises are then internal policies of the association within the framework of the actual sale price. The association is then concerned with the size of the difference between its receipts (selling prices)

It must be noted that the advantages to be derived from applying the market mechanism depend on correctly reflecting the true ratios of social costs in an enterprise's calculations. This presents many difficult postulates for the calculation of costs.

The third group of arguments favouring the market mechanism in planned economy emphasizes the importance of *balancing the process of expanded reproduction called 'balanced growth'*. One aspect of this was examined in the chapter devoted to the operation of the law of value in a socialist economy. There we indicated that the main investment trends in socialism are not inescapably fixed by the need to eliminate disproportions in the initial economic conditions. Nevertheless, the possibility of eliminating or diminishing such disproportions, without unfavourably affecting the growth rate or the lines of development adopted, is obviously of extreme importance. The same holds for the possibility of eliminating any disproportions which might appear in the transition from the initial to the target position. The potential for achieving this depends largely on whether and to what degree those responsible for economic decisions respect the indications and incentives provided by the regulated market. Those many relatively small but annoying disproportions actually do appear in a centralized economy. It occurs not only and not primarily because of an objective need to secure crucial priorities but rather because of rigidity which is caused by the lack of effective links between the market and production. In a decentralized model, such connections do exist. The individual parts of the national economy have a chance for self-development and this is important in eliminating the kind of disproportions under consideration. It also aids in mobilizing reserves which are usually invisible to the central authority. The extent of the self-development process depends on what economic results are achieved by enterprises. This factor in turn should guarantee a proper allocation of the means available to enterprises, as well as ensure that they are employed in the right directions.

In the decentralized model one important factor favouring the market mechanism and interconnected with enterprise self-development concerns the development of initiative 'from below'. Understood in the broadest terms of technical and organizational progress, it aids the application of better production methods, the improvement of existing products and the introduction of new ones. One of

---

and the sum of its payments in terms of differentiated accounting prices. See W. Brus, 'Zysk, ceny i zjednoczenia' ('Profit, prices and associations'), *Zycie Gospodarcze*, no. 9, 1958, and H. Fiszel, 'Ceny rozliczeniowe, system podatkowy, rola zjednoczeń' ('Clearing prices, the tax system and the role of associations'), *Zycie Gospodarcze*, nos. 51 and 52, 1959.

the most important criticisms of the centralized model is that the initiative in these areas lies almost exclusively in the realm of the central authority. Not only is the lower level unable to act, but because of the system of efficiency standards and incentives, it is far more interested in maintaining the *status quo* than in progressing through technical and organizational innovations. Since these would disturb the fulfilment of current output targets, especially the quantitative ones, in a centralized model there arise economic and political pressures on enterprises from above. The latter arises from the attempts of superior organs to break down enterprise conservatism and result not so much from human nature, but from the accepted rules of the game. Here innovation, which one might expect to be the first concern of every enterprise, is introduced from without —most frequently in the form of short-lived campaigns.

The decentralized model can be expected to give better results in this field for a number of reasons: the freedom which an enterprise has in determining the aims and methods of production; the part played by horizontal inter-enterprise links; the correlation between the achieved results and the possibilities of expansion; as well as the standards of efficiency evaluation (the principle of profitability); and the resulting form of incentives. The decentralized model does not exclude using certain elements of competition among socialist enterprises, and creates a situation in which systematic progress is necessary or at least desirable for the interests of both enterprise and employee. The idea of achieving social goals through enterprise self-interest and not in spite of it and the idea of influencing enterprise progress by appropriately moulding economic conditions is the hallmark of solutions to the model which employ market mechanism.

A fourth group of arguments favouring the use of the market mechanism in a planned economy derives from the problems of *providing appropriate conditions for the planning activity of the central authority*. This argument is founded on the assumption that if the lower levels have a greater degree of autonomy, the central authority need not take an enormous number of detailed day-to-day decisions. It follows that it will be able to concentrate on the basic problems, especially long-term ones and to undertake more profound analyses of economic processes. This is a very important argument, especially in view of obvious informational limitations on the central authority. If we assume that, when the central authority is so freed, better basic decisions can be made, then we can expect to find here a cumulative effect. The better the decisions dealing with the main trends of expansion, the greater the precision in their mutual co-ordination and synchronization, the less will be the need for emergency intervention, and this in turn will again create better conditions for basic

L

work on the plan. The accrued advantages are difficult to measure, but on the other hand, centralism has little to show to its credit in this area. For these reasons decentralization proposals were intended 'to improve central planning and to raise it to a higher level', as one 'of the main conditions for proper economic development.' 'Planning is improved not by introducing a multiplicity of indices, by making extremely detailed projects, and by formal balancing, but by securing a more profound economic analysis and well-founded estimates of economic developments in those areas where precise economic calculation is impossible.[1]

Here it seems that decentralization would have a particularly favourable effect by increasing the importance of the long-term plans in the broad system of planning. The shift of emphasis to long-term plans is one of the most important factors in improving the effectiveness of planning in general and thus the possibility of guiding expansion by long-term aims becomes the great opportunity for socialism. A centralized system of management does not favour full exploitation of this potential.

Our problem here ties in with yet another element of rationalizing the operations of the central authority, and that is the strengthening of criteria for checking central decisions and forecasts. For example, in the centralized model, choosing the output-mix automatically sets in motion the marketing mechanism regardless of the degree to which the planned output structure meets the actual needs of purchasers. Often the only chance of judging a decision is found in the consumer goods market where free choice exists within the framework established by the planned distribution of the national income. Poor decisions result in surpluses or shortages of goods and hence in a waste of a certain amount of society's labour. In a decentralized model whose basic conditions are centrally established, independent enterprise expedites the process of economic adjustment. The compliance or non-compliance of these adjustments with the central plan is an important check on both the accuracy of the forecasts and the effectiveness of the means used to obtain them. At the same time, deviations from the plan are not automatically identical with disproportions. If, for example, the demand for a consumer good is different from what was predicated, in spite of the fact that general proportions (including the pattern of the distribution of national income) are as intended, the disproportion would be compounded by maintaining the supply pattern predicted *a priori* instead of changing it to correspond to the actual demand structure. Thus the

[1] Theses of the Economic Council on some directions of change in the economic model. From the text given in *Dyskusja o polskim modelu gospodarczym* (*A Discussion of the Polish Economic Model*), Warsaw, 1957, pp. 271 ff.

active role of the horizontal links between enterprises, all of which are interested in the economic results of their activity, becomes a factor for control and correction of the plan's assumptions.

Finally, there is the problem of a price system. The decentralized model, as we know, demands that the price system corresponds closely to the whole of existing economic conditions. Without such correspondence, enterprise decisions would not be based on accurate alternatives of choice which express social preferences. But the part played by such a price system is not limited to formulating choice alternatives for enterprises. It is generally true that the current price system does not supply sufficient data for broad central decision-making, especially when this process involves determination of the main areas of expansion. Nevertheless, in some decisions, investment decisions included, a price system which reflects the economic situation in accordance with the planned lines of development is a basic instrument of calculation. Given a set of prices derived from a series of central decisions as to fundamental economic proportions, that set must be upheld as an instrument for calculation, not only in enterprises but also at the centre. Therefore, in connection with the plan's assumptions, this instrument of calculation becomes something objective and premises for secondary decisions can be directly derived from the original decisions.

Hitherto, these arguments in favour of applying a market mechanism to a planned economy have chiefly emphasized the purely economic aspects. It is, however, quite clear that the functioning of a socialist economy does not only involve economic problems. *The criteria for assessing the accuracy of a model solution must also include the social aspect.* First to be considered here is the influence of these solutions on the position of man in economic activity, on the possibilities of developing the creative initiative of the masses, and on the way in which the interests of individuals and social groups are brought into relationship with those of the whole economy. In this respect, the superiority of the decentralized model seems beyond doubt. Centralization of all acts of choice means that it is only possible to influence economic decisions from the most general political level. Even if we ignore those cases where the structure of political institutions is unfavourable to this kind of central action, actually effecting it is hindered because ability to judge a very broad range of problems is required. Such is not and cannot be very common. For all its dispersion of choice-making, a decentralized model does not in any way limit the possibility of exerting a democratic influence on central decisions; rather the reverse would be true. Simultaneously, it allows the appearance of low-level initiative which secures direct participation of the masses in economic manage-

ment and forms a ground for training certain groups or individuals to assume higher levels of responsibility. So viewed, the position of the enterprise in a decentralized model is of special importance. In a situation where the enterprise role is not purely an executive function, and where the enterprise is to some extent a centre of autonomous decision, the creative elements in the working class and the intelligentsia find genuine scope for action and development. Bearing in mind that a multi-level decision network is related to a system of indices and incentives (which encourages technical and organizational innovations and fuses the interests of the particular with the general) then the connection between the decentralized model and the system of the *workers' councils* becomes quite clear. Employees' participation in socialized management (frequently an element in programmes of the revolutionary workers' movement)[1] finds an economic basis for its implementation in a system of management where some freedom of decision is left to the enterprise.

A system of workers' councils raises many complicated problems. It constitutes an attempt, if not to eliminate, at least to lessen the distinction between those who give instructions and those who execute them. Although an analysis of this problem lies outside the scope of this book and even of economics in general, it is a very important constituent part of the general problem in overcoming certain contradictions of the socialist socio-economic system. It is particularly important in overcoming the contradiction between the need for centralization and the need for democratization of economic life. These two tendencies (mentioned in chapter 1) are parallel results of the development of productive forces, particularly in the socialist system.

Thus, the problem of the mechanism of functioning of a socialist economy involves basic philosophical and sociological ideas of Marxism; it involves the Marxist idea of the liberation of the individual by suppressing the alienation of the individual from his work, the means and the results of production. Socialist production relations form the basic premise for eliminating alienation. However, in order to achieve it, a certain system of control of production and distribution must be adopted. It would need to promote the difficult process of transforming the working man into a conscious participant in the economic management of society, so that he would have a full grasp of society's aims and of his own role in their realization.

Naturally these few remarks have done little more than touch on the problem of the relationship between a solution to the model and the complex of factors which determine the social position of an

[1] See for example the statements made in the programme of the Russian Communist Party at the 8th Congress in 1919.

individual in the economy. But it is an aspect which must be considered in assessing the advantages of the decentralized model.

Arguments against the decentralized model

Generally arguments hostile to decentralization concentrate on dangers implied in the market mechanism for some of the most important features of a planned economy. Another group of arguments points to the problem of creating the necessary conditions for the efficient functioning of the market mechanism.

Criticisms of the first type question *whether the use of the market mechanism permits a precise determination of the basic economic structure (proportion) of development.* As is essential for a socialist planned economy, these constitute the chief field of independent decisions of the central authority.

In a decentralized model, low levels are assigned a degree of autonomy in distributing net output. The central authority does not distribute all of the national income, but leaves some scope to enterprise associations or local authorities. This involves the following questions:

1. There is a certain margin of freedom for dividing national income between accumulation and consumption, since enterprises have a portion of their profits to devote either to the expansion of production or to consumption.

2. The situation is similar for dividing national income consumed between collective and individual consumption. (These are respectively outlays for social and cultural purposes and those for individual worker incomes.) In principle the central authority makes the division; however, depending on the size of the relevant part of the profit, part of this distribution is made autonomously at lower levels.

The points made under 1 and 2 obviously have a bearing on the precision of the centrally-determined income structure, and that in turn affects the demand structure.

3. Lower levels have some voice in allocating investment resources between productive and non-productive investment, and in the choice of the general investment trends.

4. Lastly, the amortization fund poses two important problems: a. the problem of relating the overall amortization rate and the actual restitution requirements of different parts of the economy in any given period; b. the question of gathering the amortization fund together, and establishing criteria for withdrawals. We must remember that for practical purposes the fund is largely a part of the fund for economic growth.

All these points greatly aid an appraisal of the usefulness of a decentralized model. For, without a measure of low-level freedom in the division of the national income the advantages of a flexible responsiveness of supply, minimization of inputs coefficients, a potential for self-development, and others will be absent. Within the constraints of central decisions a certain autonomy in income distribution is also enormously important for a system of workers' councils constituting the material basis for the direct employee participation in management. However, such autonomy at the lower levels may permit deviations from the plan in the income distribution and hence disturb general equilibrium. Experience shows that the danger lies not only in the tendency to excessive increases in consumption at the expense of accumulation (which results from distributing the surpluses among employees), but also in a strong tendency to increase the decentralized investment. Especially if the increase is in non-productive investment, the whole investment may be threatened due to an excessive absorption of labour and supplies.

Does this mean, however, an *ad limine* impossibility of maintaining the proportions laid down in the plan? I feel such a conclusion would be unjustified since in a decentralized model, the central authority has many means of indirectly affecting enterprise decisions. These are a. influencing enterprise revenues through central price policy; b. influencing the distribution of profits through a differential tax policy (e.g. progressive taxation on profit-derived individual incomes and certain tax exemptions for that part of profit used for productive purposes, differentiated according to various aims); c. influencing the choice of decentralized investment trends by a credit policy (one effective method is to lay down appropriately constructed conditions for allocating central funds which are such an important complement to an enterprise's own funds); d. influencing the manner in which enterprises use any funds at their disposal (including the amortization fund) by means of interest rate policy.

It is clear that economic policy faces difficult problems in avoiding the Scylla of excessively limiting enterprises' powers of distribution and the Charybdis of uncontrolled disturbances to the planned structure of the economy. The central authority without becoming too obsessed with detail must have full control over the distributive processes. And this, in itself is one more of a series of reasons which require that particular attention be paid to the parametric nature of any price system.

Recognizing the major importance of purely economic measures in affecting distribution, which are not the subject of direct decisions of the central authority, it is difficult to conceive of optimum macro-economic proportions guaranteed only by this kind of

measure. Practically, it is impossible to avoid entirely the use of administrative measures (e.g. fixing a ceiling for certain kinds of inputs and blocking part of the amortization fund). This is doubly true in those periods when there is as yet insufficient experience in the precise use of economic measures. It is also important to create an overall system of controlling enterprise activities including those where the enterprise has a free hand. For the first time we confront the problems of combining economic and the administrative measures, a problem which we shall touch upon more than once.

But, apart from strictly economic and administrative measures, a planned socialist economy has also at its disposal specific measures for influencing different economic units. We might call them *'the measures for co-ordination'*. By this I mean the various forms of action based on that feature (at least potentially) of a socialist economy which Dickinson so strongly emphasized—the complete openness of economic life, the 'glass walls' of the socialist economic system.[1]

Undoubtedly, well-organized flows of information in themselves constitute a factor which co-ordinates economic activity. Information about technical innovations, new production designs, and above all a full knowledge of both planned development trends and the state economic policy contribute immensely in determining the structure and technique of current production and, most importantly, in determining investment. When we also consider institutionalized forms of co-ordination and co-operation at the branch and national level, it is evident that even when highly decentralized, a socialist economy operates in a framework entirely different from that of a capitalist economy. Individual units are not (or at least need not be) condemned to predict the results of the blind interaction of market forces, but can (roughly) determine their place in the whole of the economic structure, both for the present and for the future. This is the more so when long-term plans are accorded their proper place and really constitute the main guide lines for the enterprises.

Favourable conditions for co-ordination should not be confused with automatic achievement of full co-ordination; from the context, it ought to follow that exclusive reliance on the 'measures of co-ordination' would be absurd. Thus arises the problem of assigning roles to economic as opposed to administrative measures. Its solution should take note of the benefits of 'glass walls', clearly outlined prospects in the plan, the abolition of trade secrets, and so on.

Now we shall pass from the question of the planned income distribution to considering the second group of objections against

[1] See H. D. Dickinson, 'Price formation in a socialist community', *The Economic Journal*, no. 6, 1933.

the decentralized model. These *doubts about effectiveness of economic control over production* are related to the previous question, since the structure of distribution in terms of value must correspond to the physical structure of society's final output.

The problem of effectively regulating output by means of a market mechanism has been a subject of more lively discussion than any other in the socialist countries, especially in Poland. A verbatim reiteration of the many objections to the efficiency of the market mechanism is impossible, although they can be reduced to several basic ones.[1]

1. Regulating output through the market mechanism is *ex post* regulation, while that which employs planning directives occurs *ex ante*. The latter is more advantageous since it avoids destabilizing an equilibrium while corrections after the event do not.

2. Market regulation of output occurs at two levels: first, planners decide to alter the output structure, then they alter the set of prices whose purpose is appropriately to affect the decisions of producers. Critics hold this procedure improper, since a. it aims at obtaining indirectly what can be more quickly obtained by a directive to alter the output structure; b. it contains a dual possibility of error (one in planning, the other in the interpreting plan decisions in the language of prices); c. it is based on the reaction of producers to changes in the price structure—reaction which cannot be accurately predicted—instead of on quantitatively precise and directly addressed production targets.

3. Regulating output through the market mechanism, sets impracticable requirements for the price system. In particular, it requires a very high degree of price flexibility because of the perpetual need for adjustments to the level of each product's profitability; otherwise, 'convenient' and 'inconvenient' items would emerge in production. Such a requirement can only be fulfilled where the principle of a free determination of market prices is observed. But, as a principle, it is inconsistent with the assumption that a price system is a fundamental tool of the central authority and that it is parametric for enterprise decision-making. Moreover, the free determination of prices on the market opens the door for monopolistic practices. On the other hand, prices fixed by the state do not

---

[1] The following is drawn mainly from articles contained in *Ekonomici dyskutuja o prawie wartości* (*Economists Discuss the Law of Value*), Warsaw, 1958; M. Pohorille, 'Na marginesie dyskusji o roli prawa wartości w ustroj socjalistycznym' ('Some comments on the discussion about the role of the law of value in the socialist system'); B. Gliński, 'W sprawie koncepcji szerszego wykorzystania prawa wartości w godspodarce sojalistycznej' (On the more extensive use of the law of value in a socialist economy'); J. Pajestka, 'W kleszczach prawa wartości' ('In the grip of the law of value').

guarantee the necessary price flexibility. Another insurmountable difficulty is that of establishing equilibrium prices for the means of production, which are not sold on a market *sensu stricto*.

4. Connected with the difficulties of price setting is that of profit maximization as the direct goal of producers and as the basis of the incentive system. Its efficiency in aiding society to obtain the overriding aim of economic activity (commonly maximization of *per capita* national income) depends largely on the accuracy of prices for final goods and factors.

Let us now consider the justification of each of these criticisms even though it is not always possible to analyse each separately, since they are frequently linked.

The first criticism, *ex post* regulation by means of the market mechanism, *ex ante* regulation by means of administrative measures, seems to result from a misunderstanding. *Ex post* regulation is actually a feature of an uncontrolled economy, deprived of a central body which would undertake to pursue the social ends expressed in a plan. It would not be a feature of the *planned* economy where the market mechanism is used as a *means for consciously influencing* economic processes. For the moment let us assume that every change in the output structure of a decentralized model requires changes in the structure of prices. Let us assume further that the central authority after analysing economic trends concludes that in the next planning period the structure of output must be changed. The desired proportions are determined *in natura* or in value, as the situation demands; the appropriate decisions are cast in the field directly controlled by the central authority (income distribution, division of income, investment trends etc.); and the necessary changes are made in the price system. Now if these later changes assist in achieving the desired structure of supply and demand, why should this kind of procedure be described as *ex post* regulation? Thus, though the differences between the market and the use of planning orders obviously go very deep and though the example given is not meant to conceal them, it nevertheless seems that there are no grounds for describing one as a method of *ex post* regulation and the other as the only possible way of achieving *ex ante* regulation. *From this viewpoint* there are no differences between the two. The case is stronger still if we recall that the economic instruments available to the central authority in the decentralized model are not limited to price manipulation and that the package of instruments are an integral element of the plan which is elaborated together with other elements.

The root of the complaint that the decentralized model is by nature incapable of *ex ante* economic regulation is again to be

found in identifying the market mechanism in a planned economy
with that in freely competitive capitalism. The very word 'market'
seems to set up a chain of unpleasant associations.

We should note at this point an additional important factor for
estimating the efficiency of an economic system. Clearly—regardless
of the model—it is never possible to assume absolute infallibility on
the part of the central authority especially in adapting the supply
pattern to that of needs. This operation is always derived by trial
and error so that problems of verifying decisions and creating a
system for detecting and correcting errors are always apparent.
Therefore, a planned economy cannot discard *ex post* regulation,
for the accuracy of decisions can only be seen when their results are
compared with actual needs. This is particularly clear in the market
for consumer goods, but it is of no less importance for producer
goods, especially when the detailed structure of production and its
synchronization in time is concerned.

Then the system for checking decisions in a decentralized model
seems to be far superior to that found in the centralized model. In
the latter, as we have seen the, dominant links are vertical lines
dependent on a hierarchical arrangement of lower-level plans to
those of the superior level. If the postulates of the plan prove false
during the period for which it was intended, it is difficult to correct
the situation. The purchasing enterprise gives notice to its superiors
that a change is needed; these must obtain a decision from the
supplier's superiors; from there the appropriate order goes vertically
downward to the supplying enterprise. It happens quite frequently
that it is impossible to obtain a decision to amend the original plan
except at the highest level. This is especially acute when the adjustment cannot be localized at one point, but affects a number of
mutually connected elements of the economy and demands some
reallocation of the factors of production. In principle, the logic of
the centralized model excludes possible adjustments by way of direct
horizontal links between the supplier and the purchaser. It is unusual
to circumvent the central authority (or a lower level of the economic
administration in matters of minor importance) mainly because the
basic standard of enterprise efficiency and the criterion for material
incentives is the degree to which planning orders are fulfilled and
not the degree to which actual needs expressed as effective demand
are satisfied. As we have frequently pointed out here, it is one of the
main causes of rigidity in the centralized adjustment mechanism,
and one which makes output perpetually lag behind needs, especially
where tastes are subject to frequent change. As the economy grows
and the living standard rises, this inadequacy is felt more and more
strongly since the scope of demands made on production becomes

more varied. The harmful effects of insufficient flexibility are found not only in the feelings of the final consumer (which cannot be measured) but also in the very real figures of unsaleable stocks.

In the decentralized model, the supplier can react directly to consumer demand. Enterprise dependence on the market as a product of profit motivated efficiency standards and incentives and the full freedom to pattern output and regulate its size, produces a sensitivity of supply to demand when enterprises' programmes are elaborated and executed. The plethora of detailed problems left untouched by the central authority are unaffected by special social preferences, and thus there is no reason to counteract the preferences expressed in effective demand. If in such cases adjustments can be made directly, without waiting for high level decisions, it helps not only to secure more speed and accuracy but also to relieve the central authority of the burden of petty detail.[1]

Any analysis of the adjustment mechanism in a decentralized model is closely connected with the second criticism above, and especially with the problem of whether adjustment should be direct or indirect. This criticism is the result of assuming that every shift in production must have central approval as in the centralized model, and that every change in the structure of production means that prices must be altered. Were this assumption correct, then indeed the market mechanism would be much more complicated than the mechanism of orders. Two decisions would be required instead of one (one merely to make the change and one to alter prices appropriately). It should be recalled that even in this case the market mechanism would have a distinct advantage over the mechanism of orders since it can operate through the economic self-interest of the enterprise and not in spite of it. An order to produce at a less advantageous price, with no change in price relationships, leads to a conflict of enterprise self-interest and the social interest as expressed in the central authority's decision. The result is that the latter is often resisted, sometimes effectively. Like using other economic instruments, using prices recognizes the need to integrate as far as possible the enterprise self-interest and social interest at every level.

[1] In passing, however, we should note several conditions for, or limitations on, such a mechanism of adjustment: 1. the existence of a buyer's market (hence the problem of prices balancing supply with demand); 2. the determination of the boundaries within which the processes of adjustment may take place without disturbing general social preferences (this is a question of ensuring that the priority targets of the central plan can be achieved; i.e. among other things that the supply of the means of production and labour for priority purposes is adequate); 3. the question of the efficiency (especially relevant to the time factor) of the market's adjustment mechanism in the case of adaptations comprising a few large changes related to top priorities rather than to many small changes (see pp. 38–9).

This is an extremely important difference for an economy's efficiency although obviously its significance is not limited to this point alone.

Thus, even if it were true that the use of a market mechanism would always demand two sets of decisions, a glance at other aspects of the problem would make us pause before discarding it. In reality, however, the problem of the two sets of decisions looks quite different. Obviously, it is difficult to establish a quantitative scale, but there is little doubt that in any given period a considerable number of output shifts can be decentralized without the participation of the central authority and without endangering the system of social preferences. Once again it is necessary to remember that we are talking about an economy in which the basic factors governing market conditions are determined in a general outline by the direct central decisions. The general structure of supply is determined by earlier investment decisions; the general structure of demand is determined by decisions on income distribution between accumulation and consumption, with the structure of individual incomes, and with the direction of investment; and the general structure of prices is adjusted to other elements of the plan for the period in question. Hence the majority of adjustments made in the course of the planning period are basically movements within a framework set up *ex ante* by the central authority. In these conditions detailed adaptation of the supply structure to the demand structure can be founded on direct transactions between suppliers and purchasers. In principle there is no need for day-to-day intervention by the central authority (although in some cases it may be necessary) and yet there is no danger that the market will transform itself into the uncontrolled mechanism of competitive capitalism.

It is fair to ask, however, whether the adaptation of supply to demand will not require permanent adjustments in the profitability of individual products, and primarily through alterations in prices. Will it not, in fact, confront us with the necessity of choosing one of two alternatives: either spontaneous price changes made by enterprises or constant interference of the state authorities to take the appropriate measures? (At this point I will not elaborate on the question of how far the state authorities are able to ensure such a flexibility in their price policy.) Some critics of the decentralized model imagine that the relationship between changes in the output structure and the price system on the one hand and profitability on the other is a totally mechanical one. It is quite clear that when an enterprise finds it as easy to sell a more profitable product as a less profitable one, then it will prefer the more profitable one. But, assuming the existence of a buyer's market, if the chances of selling the more profitable product are limited, then the enterprise willy-

nilly will be forced to turn to less profitable products which it can sell.[1] Thus, changes of supply structure in response to market conditions do not necessarily require price changes in order to equalize profit margins. If the price structure is accurate (above all, if it has a proper influence on demand), a great deal of adjustment will be accomplished without price changes corresponding to the demand situation. Obviously a producer will try to improve the profitability of the most saleable products by lowering costs or modernizing his equipment and will try to influence the market so as to increase the sale of more profitable products, etc., but this does not contradict the concept we outlined above.

Examining demand's direct influence on production also helps to show that it is difficult to determine the strength of producer reaction to market conditions. This is by no means an easy problem, but as experience grows and methods of analysis are improved, the accuracy of forecasts increases. However, in many problems of detail the difficulty is not that central forecasts should be as accurate as possible, but that they should create economic conditions in which the buyer will effectively determine the exact quantitative proportions.

The market mechanism requires, as can be seen from our arguments, a much more flexible system of prices than the system of directives. The reasoning outlined here does not undermine this obvious truth. We are trying to show, however, that not every change in supply requires a price manipulation and that certain limited adjustments can take place without corresponding price changes and the concomitant central intervention, for example by the equalization of prices with costs. There is a definite limit to occasions when adjustments can be made without an alteration in prices. Thus, an enterprise, in maximizing profit, can produce less profitable goods if those more profitable cannot be sold, but it will not produce unprofitable goods. Therefore, when definite social preferences exist, changes in the price structure may prove necessary to make it particularly profitable to produce a certain group of commodities. Moreover any requirements of far-reaching changes in the structure of output may make it imperative fundamentally to change the price structure. The extreme case arises when *ad hoc* alterations are insufficient and long-term changes demand new investment. While such price changes can and ought to be related

---

[1] M. Pohorille touches on this in the article mentioned above when discussing the capitalist economy. This is even more true in the decentralized model of a planned economy where there are far greater possibilities for long-term forecasting and determination of the demand structure and for organizing the links between supplier and consumer. A particularly important role is played by what we have called measures of co-ordination and especially by the knowledge of the general lines of an economy's development.

to basic planning decisions, a solution—as far as our argument is concerned—offers less difficulty; at the same time the other means available for influencing the economic interest of enterprises should be borne in mind. Notwithstanding these qualifications, it remains true that here the role of price policy and the need for a greater flexibility in its application are far more important than in the centralized model. The difference is so significant that it is of degree as well as of kind; it could not be otherwise when money plays an active role in an economy.

In order to consider the remaining arguments against the use of the market mechanism in a planned economy, a somewhat wider examination of the problems is needed. Rather than attempt a full-scale study of prices, I wish merely to look at some problems connected with the general principles of functioning of the socialist economy.

Some price problems in a decentralized model

The decentralized model involves multiple levels of decision-taking which implies some method of integrating decisions for the social good. It implies that the set of economic magnitudes guides decisions made at lower levels in order to achieve the principle 'what is good for the national economy is equally good for the enterprise'. Assuming enterprises are profit motivated, realization of this principle to any extent may depend on how far price ratios reflect the real alternatives of choice (rates of substitution) in the whole of the economy. For the enterprise prices must accurately indicate alternatives in selecting the structures of both output and input. Hence, in a planned economy, the market mechanism makes special demands on the price system, such as can be found neither in the capitalist economy nor in a centralized socialist economy. In the former the price system is not consciously subordinated *ex ante* to accepted social and economic goals; in the latter, prices in principle are not even an active instrument for influencing enterprise decisions. Given the difficulty or even impossibility of meeting these demands on the price system, certain reservations about using the market mechanism are in order.

The reservations derive chiefly from three difficulties:

1. The problem of determining the so-called basic (normal) prices which might be said to represent a concretization of value in a given system of productive relations.

2. The problem of whether, and according to what rules, the current price ratios should deviate from basic price ratios; this affects particularly the price of the means of production.

3. The problem of the technique used in pricing in order to ensure a sufficient degree of flexibility and the parametric nature of prices in relation to the enterprises.

The first difficulty reduces to establishing which elements should be considered in a socialist economy as constituent parts of socially necessary labour per unit of product. We have already touched on this problem in our discussion of Strumilin's views (chapter 4) and the disputed points are numerous. I shall restrict myself here to the more important ones:

a. Whether the basic price ratios should be founded on average costs or on marginal costs defined as the average variable cost in a group of higher-cost producers and assuming that this group produces an important portion of the total output of a given article.[1]

b. Whether basic prices ratios should be founded on the ratios of direct inputs (including amortization) or in a broader definition of costs which includes a charge for the use of fixed and working capital and for land. This is the problem of an interest rate and a rent charge for land in the calculation of basic prices in a socialist economy, which has been considered at length in Soviet discussions on prices and the law of value. Those who favour a capital charge base their concept of basic price on a magnitude similar to the Marxist production price. Their views have many energetic opponents.[2] Recently L. Kantorovich presented a general justification for including charges for such factors as productive equipment and

---

[1] W. Brus, 'Niektóre problemy teorii cen w gospodarce socjalistycznej', ('Some Problems of price theory in a socialist economy') in *Zagadnienia ekonomii politycznej socjalizmu* (*Problems of the Political Economy of Socialism*), 2nd ed., p. 303. A whole series of important contributions to the discussion of basic price is to be found in the collection *Spór o ceny* (*The Controversy about Prices*), Warsaw, 1958, pt. 1. Among other things, this contains proposals for pricing principles published by one of the committees of the Economic Council, the paper which originated the discussion. A valuable attempt to justify the rationality of basing price relations on marginal costs is to be found in Jan Lipiński, 'Ceny a koszty' ('Prices and costs'), *Ekonomista*, no. 4, 1958.

[2] See *Soviet Papers on the Law of Value*, nos. 1 and 2. A number of important contributions to this problem are to be found in the collection of articles *Dyskusja o prawie wartości i cenach w ZSRR* (*The Discussion of the Law of Value and Prices in the USSR*), Warsaw, 1958. It should be noted that Maurice Dobb supports the 'production price' approach in two articles: 'Uwagi o roli prawa wartości w gospodarce socjalistycznej i systemie cen' ('Some notes on the role of the law of value in a socialist economy and the price system'), *Gospodarka Planowa*, No. 10, 1956, reprinted in 'Teoria ekonomii a socjalizm' ('Economic theory and socialism'), Warsaw, 1959 and in an expanded form, in 'A comment on the "Discussion about price policy"', *Soviet Studies*, vol. 9, no. 2. An extended case for the 'production price' approach in a socialist economy can also be found in the first edition of Charles Bettelheim, *Les problèmes théoretiques et pratiques de la planification*, 1945.

land in cost calculations. He has even coined a special term *prokatnaya otsenka* (literally: rent estimate). 'We use the expression *prokatnaya otsenka*', writes Kantorovich, 'because it is an estimate of the price which would have to be paid were the machine to be hired out for a certain time. It may also be considered as the rent of equipment for which we need not pay but need account for. In our opinion this should also be included in *khozraschot*'.[1]

c. Whether the cost calculations (and basic prices) should embrace only the money costs paid out by an enterprise or also the costs incurred by social funds. This is mainly a question of the so-called social benefits, expenditures for all kinds of social services subsidizing the consumption of some goods, and so on. Strumilin stresses the necessity for reckoning this type of outlay in costs,[2] and some Yugoslav economists hold similar views.[3]

All these questions are extremely important. Their solution is essential for creating a price system which would reflect the whole of society's real economic alternatives of choice—hence the attention devoted to them by socialist price theory.

Unfortunately, the difficulties of employing prices as an instrument for guiding decisions are not limited to the basic pricing process itself. The basic price is a reflection of the conditions of production; basic price ratios express the ratios of society's indispensable outlays per unit of output. They do not, on the other hand, express the ratio between the quantity of units produced and the demand for them (at basic prices) and hence do not express what are usually called scarcity ratios. Nor do they reflect the social preferences in the consumption of certain products. Experience in using prices as the chief tool of guiding consumer preferences shows that in principle success is achieved only when they correspond to the conditions of market equilibrium. If a price differs from the equilibrium level, it ceases wholly or in part to fulfil its function as an instrument for affecting consumer decisions. Thereafter it is necessary to use direct controls, i.e. various forms of rationing.

A similar situation arises when prices are used as an instrument to influence autonomous producer decisions, especially in the demand for the means of production but also with regard to supply.

[1] L. Kantorovich, *Ekonomicheski ruschot nayllchshego ispolzovanya resursov*, Academy of Sciences of the USSR (Moscow, 1959).

[2] See for example S. Strumilin, 'The law of value and the recognizing of the social cost of production in a socialist economy', *Planovoe Khozyaystvo*, no. 2, 1957.

[3] See for example Bogdan Pilič, 'Ekonomski razvoy i politika cena', at the Third Congress of the Union of Economic Societies of Yugoslavia in 1958. *Ekonomist*, Belgrade, nos. 1–2, 1958, pp. 227–49. In Yugoslavia various methods for including social benefits in cost calculation have been employed for some time.

We now come to *the second group of problems*, that of the deviation of actual sale prices from the basic prices. The key point here is price deviation in the means of production. One aspect of the difficulty is the need to reflect scarcity of the means of production in the structure of prices in the decentralized model. Many economists feel the contrary, that unlike the consumer goods prices, the prices of the means of production should not diverge from these given by the conditions of production. This view shared by Bettelheim[1] distinguishes the so-called internal value, determined by the conditions of production (i.e. value in our terminology) from the so-called external value determined by what he calls the conditions of consumption. (External value is nothing else than the market equilibrium price.) He asserts that one of the basic aims of planning is to create circumstances in which internal value equals external value, i.e. the situation where the structure of supply exactly corresponds to the structure of society's needs. Bettelheim nevertheless feels that changes in external value ought to affect the conditions under which goods are released to the final consumer (i.e. the structure of prices of the means of consumption) and ought not to affect the means of production. This is a matter of principle: the deviation of the prices of the means of production from their internal values would distort economic calculation. The costs of production at later stages of manufacture would be somewhat distorted since elements of the inputs of embodied labour would be reckoned according to prices which imprecisely reflect socially indispensable labour outlays. In that situation equal prices of various cost components might express different quantities of socially indispensable labour time, while different prices might express equal quantities. Bettelheim is not explicit, but it is implicit in his choice of context that he does not mean the absolute price level of the means of production, but price ratios which ought to correspond to the ratios of value.

Bettelheim's view is typical of those which oppose using prices of the means of production which deviate from their productive basis. Price ratios corresponding to the ratios of socially indispensable labour outlays are regarded as the proper index of alternatives of choice for intermediate goods and as the accurate reflection of opportunity cost for the buyers of the means of production. No allowance is made for deviations which are meant to reflect the ratios between the available quantities of producer goods and the demand for them. And this is no fictitious deviation, but reflects real economic conditions. The outcome is that when there are two

[1] Ch. Bettelheim, *Les problèmes théoretiques et pratiques de la planification*, chapter 3.

M

types of means of production which require the same labour input per unit one may be 'scarcer' in relation to demand while the other may be less sought after, or more 'abundant'. Any difficulty arising here cannot be bypassed even if we remain aware of the importance of value, as determined by the conditions of production. It was Marx who wrote the often quoted words that:[1]

> Every individual article, or every definite quantity of a commodity may, indeed, contain no more than the social labour required for its production, and from this point of view the market-value of this entire commodity represents only necessary labour, but if this commodity has been produced in excess of the existing social needs, then so much of the social labour-time is squandered and the mass of the commodity comes to represent a much smaller quantity of social labour in the market than is actually incorporated in it . . . The reverse applies if the quantity of social labour employed in the production of a certain kind of commodity is too small to meet the social demand for that commodity.

This should, of course, not be interpreted as an identification of 'internal value' with 'external value'. Marx goes on to emphasize that 'the exchange—or sale—of goods according to their value is here a rational principle, the natural law of their equilibrium; taking this law as a starting point there are the divergences which must be explained and not the other way round, deducing the law itself from the divergences.'[2] No such real divergences can be ignored, particularly in a socialist economy because the ratio of supply and demand of a producer good is generally fixed by planned macro-economic decisions based on social rationality.

Bettelheim's concept of the distortion of economic calculation holds only where the disproportion between supply and demand is a temporary result of short time lags in the adaptation of the output structure to the structure of needs. It would be useless and even harmful to reflect this kind of disproportion in the prices of the means of production since that might lead producers to engage in adjustments which would quickly prove unnecessary. But the problem looks quite different where divergences are more extensive and last longer, and especially where they are related to the capacity structure of industry or to particular social preferences for employing certain goods in production (e.g. internal rather than foreign sources of supply in an exchange crisis). Here it is even difficult to apply the word 'disproportion' in its usual sense to the non-agreement of output volume and the demand for particular producer

---

[1] K. Marx, *Capital*, (Moscow, 1959), vol. 3, pp. 183–4.
[2] *Ibid.*, p. 184.

goods. What are found are quantitative ratios accepted in the plan and meant to realize long-term social aims. Assuming accurate basic decisions in the central plan, then the 'scarcities' and 'gluts' are objective in character, and economic calculations are distorted, not by taking them into consideration but by leaving them out. Although it is often said that to permit allowance for scarcities is to admit alien capitalistic laws to a socialist economy, quite the reverse is true. In competitive capitalism, while the divergence of prices from their productive basis is a common phenomenon for individual goods, these divergences, especially the more marked ones, do not last long. The appearance of divergences sets in motion a levelling mechanism. There is a flow of capital to the more profitable lines of production; a withdrawal of capital from the less rentable ones; shifts within industries and so on. These divergences are not the result of consciously established long-range goals which require means to be concentrated in priority sectors. Instead they are caused by spontaneous disproportions which give rise to spontaneous tendencies to overcome them. In an anarchistic capitalist economy, founded on the exploitation of the direct producers, this spontaneity continually leads to new disproportions. In a socialist economy the plan, which reflects social preferences, determines the main areas of expansion for at least five years (and, as planning methods are improved, for even longer spans). It also fixes the structure of capacity, the basic productive conditions in individual lines of production, and hence the degree of scarcity of various products (including the means of production). Therefore, the degree of scarcity of individual producer goods must be accepted as given and not subject to change in any major aspect, and certainly not spontaneously.[1] It is not market spontaneity, but the plan which determines the size and basic elements in the output structure for the means of production together with the size and basic elements of the structure of the demand for them. In order to obtain optimum fulfilment of the plan it is absolutely necessary to take these elements into account.[2]

[1] This does not mean that the degree of scarcity is always identical throughout the whole planning period. At different phases of the planning period, the degree of scarcity of a good may vary. These changes, however, are (or theoretically ought to be) determined *ex ante* by macro-economic decisions and taken into account in balancing.

[2] Here it is interesting to note that such an approach has recently received increasing sympathy among economists in the socialist countries. L. Kantorovich in his book *The Economic Calculation of the Optimum Use of Resources* strongly emphasizes the necessity of accounting for scarcity. Some of his critics are opposed (in principle, legitimately) to attaching excessive importance to the scarcity problem for solving dynamic problems, since the degree of scarcity is dependent on the general lines of investment pursued. But even these critics recognize that it is rational to account for scarcity on the basis of a predetermined

Objections on principle thus become unjustified. Within the framework of the productive conditions established by general planning decisions the degree of scarcity should be reflected in socialist economic calculation. One method of doing this is by reflecting the scarcity in the structure of selling price for the means of production.

Alternatively allowance for this factor can be made in central calculations without utilizing the deviations of prices from their productive basis (basic price). In that case the central authority will make a decision on the basis of the ratio between the availabilities of individual producer goods and related demands on the basis of existing potentials for substitution versus the cost of their production and so on. It can even invent a special system of computation prices (objectively determined evaluations in Kantorovich's language) by weighing the various deficits and surpluses. However, these evaluations will not be reflected in enterprise calculations. There the only prices used will derive from the conditions of production (the socially indispensable per unit outlays). Allocation of the means of production will be made by direct central decisions and physical distribution will be employed. Physical allocation becomes then an instrument for equating demand with supply and products identical in price are in fact evaluated differently (according to the degree of difficulty in obtaining an allocation order for them). In this situation the central authority performs many tasks. It must directly fix productive technique at all levels, persuade enterprises to use substitutes without compensation in costs, instruct the producers of the means of production to produce at deficit prices and so on. Only in this way can the inconsistency between centrally-made calculations and low-level calculations be resolved in some degree. Otherwise premises of the former will not be known when the latter make money computations—computations which in turn cannot be considered accurate unless verified individually at the centre. At first glance this seems paradoxical, but here the objective necessity of allowing for scarcity is confirmed. Only by including this element is it possible to say whether an expenditure of 10 zlotys in the product X is really worth a half of an expenditure of 20 zlotys in product Y, or would it be perhaps preferable to spend 20 zlotys on product Y instead of spending 10 zlotys on X.

---

or planned pattern of development. These are the same assumptions which we adopt. Thus, for example, A. Katz, in 'O nepravilnoy koncepcii ekonomicheskikh raschotov', writes: 'If productive conditions are given and are constant in a particular period then to allow for "scarcity" in calculations may involve a particular optimum variant of total outlays which differs somewhat from the minimal outlays for each kind of production', *Voprosy Ekonomiki*, no. 5, 1960, p. 117.

Hence to reflect scarcity of the means of production is not to change the criteria of economic calculation in a socialist economy, it is merely a way of integrating central and operative reckoning. A price which deviates from unit value because of a relative deficit or surplus is a *sui generis* translation of social preferences into a language which can be understood by the enterprise. The scarcity of an individual item of means of production thereby ceases to be a secret of the central authority and is intelligible to all. The result is of basic importance for the effective operation of the economy. In the first place, a clearly formulated index of what is cheaper and what more expensive, is important in itself, in counteracting erroneous solutions. In the second place, expressing alternative choices by means of prices as we have shown above, enables social interest and enterprise self-interest to be united and, thus alleviates tensions without disturbing the economy's basic structure. If the price of a scarce raw material X equals that of an easily available substitute Y on the basis of equal production costs, there is no incentive to make use of Y rather than X. Moreover, if as usually occurs, X is preferred to Y because of its use properties or even for historical reasons, then it will be in the enterprise's interest to use X. There are often strong pressures on distributive organs to grant the largest possible quota including a safety margin. Therefore, merely introducing physical distribution sometimes becomes an additional factor in increasing the shortages. At all events it is difficult in such a case to expect from the enterprise any active attempt to reduce tension.

If, however, prices are appropriately differentiated, and enterprises are made truly interested in their own economic results, it becomes profitable for them to find ways of conserving X. They can both substitute Y in current production and utilize their own investment funds. Concomitantly, such price differentiation should tend to produce as much of the scarce material as possible. Obviously the degree to which the deviations in selling prices are passed on to the producers can and ought to be regulated by state economic policy (through the tax system).

Where the basic structural elements of an economy's capacity are determined by autonomous macro-economic decisions, the possibility of shifting demand and supply is limited. The possibility should not, however, be disregarded. It forms an important factor in optimally allocating society's supply of labour within the plan's framework of the general targets. We referred to this whole subject in chapter 4, which discusses the role of the law of value in a socialist economy; in a sense allowing for scarcity in establishing prices for means of production is connected with the same subject.

Even theoretically, it is hard to believe that equilibrium prices for the means of production are sufficient for the operation of a socialist economy. Indeed, in some circumstances this method of allocation may prove to be inferior to direct distribution. Where there is a serious shortage of the basic means of production, the advantages of direct distribution (especially with a strictly determined hierarchy of users) may be greater than its disadvantages. But even the need for direct central decisions to distribute scarce means of production should not involve rejecting the importance of prices. On the contrary, there should be an attempt to use the price structure to underpin direct decisions by making prices reflect true scarcity ratios as accurately as possible. In that way a basis is created for appropriate computation at every level. The effect should lead enterprises to lessen the strain.[1]

Ample justification seems to exist to allow for scarcity in the prices of the means of production and the next difficulty is its compatibility with the planned nature of a socialist economy. Now the degree of scarcity is determined only for given technical coefficients which are in turn determined for a given set of prices. Given a particular set of technical coefficients, if deficits and surpluses appear and prices are adjusted appropriately, the latter may lead to changes in the technical coefficients and consequently scarcity ratios may change as well. Additionally, even if difficulties in determining the degree of scarcity are overcome, there still remains the problem of transposing deficits and surpluses into the structure of prices. To effectively accomplish this takes a knowledge of the complicated network of mutually interdependent coefficients of the flexibility of demand for producer goods.

Much has been written about these problems. They have received most consideration from those economists who deny rational economic behaviour in a socialist economy and who find the only solution is to allow spontaneous market operations to fix the prices of the means of production. Recently also the scarcity problem has

[1] Cf. M. Kalecki, 'Rady robotnicze a centralne planowanie' ('Worker's councils and central planning'), *Nowe Drogi*, nos. 11–12, 1956, reprinted in *Dyskusja, o polskim modelu gospodarczym* (*The Discussion on the Polish Economic Model*), p. 39. In the Economic Council's *W sprawie zasad ksztattowania cen* (The Principles of Price Determination) can be found the proposition that in cases where a rapid shift in production is impossible (as a result, for example, of bottlenecks in the productive apparatus), the price ratios of the means of production ought to allow for the scarcity factor (cf. *Spór o ceny*, p. 14). See also W. Brus, 'Niektóre problemy teorii cen w gospodarce socjalistycznej' ('Some problems of price theory in socialist economy') in *Zagadnienia Ekonomii Politycznej Socjalizmu* (*Problems of the Political Economy of Socialism*), 2nd ed., pp. 328–31 and 342–4.

arisen in connection with the alleged lack of economic criteria for evaluating production techniques.[1]

Without a doubt, the lack of these criteria poses difficulties which it would be unwise to underestimate. At the same time, there is in my opinion no need for excessive pessimism. A socialist economy enables a choice of rational methods of production. Moreover, only in socialism is it possible to choose production techniques which are rational in the broad (and strict) sense of the word—that is from the position of society's overall interests. Despite the usual criticism, the issue here relates to the potential for direct (i.e. physical) calculation of macro-economic decisions. These, as we have frequently pointed out, establish a framework and points of reference for all secondary economic decisions.

Generally to hold that an inherent weakness of direct calculation is its lack of means to evaluate technical coefficients (techniques)[2] shows a confusion of socialist conditions and rationality criteria with those of capitalism. Where no overriding goals are given for the general social interest, the sole possible mode of procedure lies in direct calculation. There the data for those engaged in economic activity are prices which distinguish choices of the trends in production and techniques used. Selection among alternatives is guided by a given set of prices with certain corrections for expected changes. The alternatives chosen affect the ratio of demand to supply and so lead to price changes and in turn to changed trends in production and technique. Such general equilibrium, spontaneously evolved and continuously unsettled, results from the unco-ordinated microeconomic activities of individual economic units who are guided by their own 'calculation of rationality'. Under these circumstances, the degree of scarcity as expressed in the divergence of price from value implements changes in outputs and techniques.

As frequently emphasized, especially in chapter 4, rationality of decision-making cannot be so understood under socialism. Choices involving the chief types of output cannot be deduced from the market, or from the reaction to relative scarcities reflected in the current set of prices and profits. In reality, it is not scarcity which determines the choice areas of expansion; on the contrary, the latter, which are directly selected on the basis of general social criteria, determine the relative scarcity of the basic groups of production factors.

[1] See A. Wakar, 'Miejsce rachunku ekonomicznego w ekonomii politycznej socjalizmu' ('The place of economic calculation in the political economy of socialism'), *Życie Gospodarcze*, no. 19, 1960.

[2] See J. G. Zieliński, *Bezpośredni rachunek ekonomiczny* (*Direct Economic Calculation*).

But is this reasoning also true in choosing productive techniques? Thus far, this aspect has been secondary and we have concentrated mainly on demonstrating the rationality of directly choosing the *chief areas of expansion* at the central level. As far as the basic *difficulties associated with technique* are concerned, the matter seems rather similar in a socialist economy; it is both possible and necessary to select basic forms of technique by employing criteria of overall social rationality. There is no reason to suppose that major problems of technical method, like that of selecting the labour-intensity (more strictly—the problem of determining the degree of labour intensity in production methods) of a process or even, for example, the relative share of hydro- and thermal power stations in electricity generation, can be properly resolved only by using indirect market criteria. On the contrary, to depend on market criteria, 'indirect' economic calculation would be wrong in approaching these problems, or at best would mean that achieving the goals would be as roundabout as in the case of deducing basic economic goals from the market. The central authority, in making its direct assessment of the resources and of the basic factors of production and in comparing these resources with demand in physical quantities, is roughly able to assess trends in the development of processes in order to yield a greater degree of rationality in macro-economic choice terms than any kind of indirect calculation. Furthermore, it is of special importance that the choice of a process be synchronized *ex ante*. If, for example, it is reckoned that there will be a labour shortage in the first period of the plan and a considerable rise in the supply in the next period, then it is possible to plan special measures to develop labour-saving methods in the first period and concentrate on efforts in other directions (e.g. the saving of materials) for the next period. Is such a direct choice of technique any less rational than, for example, to wait until the labour costs rise in the first period (as a result of wage increases) and then to wait for these costs to fall in the following period and only then to make the appropriate technical decisions? Notwithstanding the question of whether conditions of labour supply would be adequately reflected in costs, it is safe to describe the above question as theoretical in socialism (or even in capitalism with well-organized labour unions). Where *basic problems* are concerned, there are no grounds whatsoever for maintaining that only indirect calculation can attest the wisdom of using a certain process. If it came to a choice between the forms of calculation in a planned economy, indirect forms would necessarily be rejected in making the broad choices of technology. For one thing, macro-economic justification of techniques is possible on the basis of direct calculation. Its accuracy, tested by the

procedure of successive approximations, obviously depends on the precision of the instruments used. This is an important reason for broad utilization of input–output analysis in a socialist economy.

We see that not only the choice of the basic ends of production but also the choice of the basic methods of production may and must be made through direct calculation in physical terms. The main priorities are also defined in this way and become criteria of economic rationality. From our point of view the most important fact is that direct macro-economic calculation of basic production targets reckons simultaneously general ratios between supply and demand of the more important inputs. Hence it determines, at least broadly, scarcity ratios for individual factors. Naturally, these ratios are neither absolute nor derived from subjective 'feelings', but are determined in conjunction with society's overall rationality criteria as elaborated in the plan. This procedure breaks the vicious circle whereby prices which reflect scarcity ratios can be determined only by given technical coefficients which in turn can only be determined at given prices. The circle is broken when the basic proportions (including the choice of basic technical coefficients) are derived from direct macro-economic calculation independently of the current set of market magnitudes.[1] Proportions determined in this way constitute a reference system establishing pricing and for indirect calculation at *lower levels of decision.*

The advantage of using indirect calculation at lower levels derives from the magnitude of detailed alternatives from which a choice must be made and from the complexity of factors affecting a decision's rationality. Here, in fact validation of the economic merit of a process usually becomes impossible, or at least very difficult, without using indirect calculation (calculation which deals with magnitudes expressed in money terms and reflecting also the degree of scarcity of the factors of production). It is, from this point of view, that I previously underlined the advantages of the decentralized model; thus I emphasized the element of truth in the views of those economists (i.e. Aleksy Wakar) who emphasize the importance of indirect calculation in enterprises and who call upon prices, costs and profits to justify technical methods of production.[2]

In my opinion it is easy to see the basic difference between this characterization of the role of indirect calculation and the view which sees such calculation as the sole possible instrument for choosing economically rational production processes. I cannot agree that indirect calculation plays the role of a 'demiurge' which fixes the

[1] This is one of the reasons why the method of balances contains certain elements of optimization calculation. See pp. 66–7 above.

[2] See p. 149 above.

general lines of expansion and technology. I regard it as a derivative of the fundamental macro-economic choices made by direct calculation. At the same time I see indirect calculation as a very important element in making detailed decisions, especially as it is connected with other advantages of using the market mechanism in a planned economy.

Thus the point of reference is given, at least for the basic factors of production; their relative scarcity or abundance over the planning period is laid down by the direct central decision on areas of expansion and types of technology used. Physical scarcities may be variously transposed into a price structure. Often the central authority, starting with the desired structure of final production, the known availabilities of the basic productive factors, a general assessment of expected technical possibilities etc. can make a direct analysis of substitution ratios and express them as price ratios. For example, the central authority can compare the cost of producing a scarce raw material and the cost of producing a substitute on the one hand, with the effects of using each of these materials in the planned production of a given final product on the other. On this basis, it can set bounds within which the price of the scarce raw material may diverge from the cost of producing it. If the input of a scarce raw material, as measured in the production costs needed to produce a unit of the finished good, is 10, and the input of the substitute measured in the same way is 15, then the price of the scarce raw material should not be lower than 15. A similar calculation can compare the cost of obtaining additional export goods to balance the importation of additional quantities of raw materials from abroad. Kantorovich gives the following example of 'an objectively determined evaluation': in order to meet the demand for metal, it would be necessary to use the production of technically backward enterprises producing at 750 roubles per ton while the average cost of production is 505 roubles per ton. If the metal produced by marginal enterprises is not used, then in some kinds of construction it will be necessary to replace the metal by reinforced concrete which would mean raising the cost of building by 300 roubles for each ton of the metal saved. In view of this, the price of metal may be set between 750 and 800 roubles.[1]

What we have presented are obviously only crude examples and serve as no more than illustrations of the general line of reasoning. In practice the interrelations are far more complicated, especially as any solution will tend to have a counter-effect on the original

[1] L. Kantorovich, *The Economic Calculation of the Optional Utilization of Resources*, p. 242, section 8 of chapter 2 contains some general remarks on this problem.

data (hence successive approximation). This effect must be considered, not only in planning the final output structure and the input mix, but also in planning prices to reflect relative factor scarcities. Even if difficult, because of the attainments of econometrics, it is hard to regard this and related problems as insoluble; the more so when basic proportions are involved. In the future, with development of mathematical methods in planning and economic analysis, the problems will be even easier to resolve.

For years Barone's attempt to solve the problem of economic calculation in socialism by means of an equations system was of no more than theoretical importance because it was impossible in practice to construct and solve such an enormous set of equations with so many highly fluid variables. Today econometrics, cybernetics and computing equipment cause some economists to revise this view, where the future is concerned.[1]

It is difficult to evaluate fully how far this new wave of optimism is justified. More doubts spring up because of the difficulties of perfecting an information system capable of supplying central authorities with all the economic data necessary for making prompt decisions. Hopes for the development of mathematical methods in a planned economy may rest on somewhat different grounds. Barone's idea was an attempt to solve (or to reduce to absurdity) the problem of economic calculation in socialism assuming completely centralized decision-making. For many reasons (which have already been discussed many times in this book and elsewhere), the complete centralization of economic decisions cannot be regarded as the only adequate arrangement for a socialist economy. Moreover, it never was and never could be fully achieved in its extreme form. It is sufficient to draw attention to the market for consumer goods and the labour market in the centralized model. Recently, despite important differences of opinion concerning the extent of autonomy permissible at lower levels, the conviction is growing that the extent of concentration of decision-making in the centralized model has serious disadvantages. Crucial in the hesitancy which some economists exhibit towards decentralization is the fear that indices of choice cannot be formulated precisely enough in prices by central authority. Hence they feel that it will be impossible to maintain the needed co-ordination between the plan's social preferences and low level decisions made on the basis of the given indices of alternatives of choice. Here is the very point where it becomes possible and advisable to seek help from mathematics. It is unreal to expect the creation of a supercentralized decision-making body by means of advanced

[1] See Adolf Nussbaumer, 'Zur Frage der Wirtschaftsrechnung in der Zentralverwaltungswirtschaft', *Zeitung für Nationalökonomie*, vol. 19, no. 3.

mathematics, and to expect the remaining levels to be automated executive units in the hierarchy. Moreover such a situation would not be desirable for the efficient operation of a socialist economy or for the fulfilment of its broadly conceived aims. It is much more realistic and desirable to use mathematical tools for specifying basic macro-economic proportions and for formulating a closely related price system. The latter would serve as accurate indices for choice-making at lower levels and thus enable them to initiate action and, at the same time, relate that action to other decisions being undertaken and to social preferences.

Thus, it would be incorrect to see in the development of mathematical methods the basis for the development of an ever more strict centralization of economic decisions in socialism. Rather the reverse would be true. Increased precision in macro-economic programming and co-ordination should create more and more favourable conditions for the planned economy in which the centrally established trends will be matched by extensive decentralization of particular decisions.

To return to our main subject, the possibility of pricing the means of production in line with the ratios of their scarcity—the question arises whether this can be accomplished through centrally-made computations. This question is even more pertinent when, as in the present and foreseeable circumstances, mathematical methods of planning in general and of price planning in particular are neither sufficiently accepted nor sufficiently accurate. Without delving into an assessment of future developments in this field, we can say that at present a complete price structure for the means of production (fulfilling the conditions discussed above) would be doomed to failure if based solely on a central analysis of ratios of substitution. What may be possible for a certain number of highly aggregated basic factors ceases to be so when one considers the vast variety of machinery, equipment, raw materials, semi-manufactures and the immense diversity of the ways in which they can be employed. Useful methods for deriving basic price ratios of the factor of production prove to be useless in composing a complete price system.

This, however, does not mean that the idea as such is wrong or that it is generally impossible to reflect scarcity ratios for the individual factors in a price system. This is possible, providing direct methods of deriving price ratios are supplemented, especially in detailed questions, by the indirect methods associated with the market. We see that the decentralized model not only creates the need for considering scarcity in any system pricing the means of production, but it also opens the possibilities for satisfying it. In the

decentralized model where enterprises are to a certain extent autonomous and guided by profit maximization and where no factor of production is assigned to the enterprises without payment, a market for the means of production is created. Ratios between supply and demand for particular producer goods appear on it not just as hypothetical figures for purposes of reckoning but as concrete, tangible forms which can be translated into the language of prices.

Undoubtedly, this is a peculiar market in which productive capacity and the output structure as well as aggregate demand and the basic elements of its structure are determined by central planning decisions. Moreover, either directly or by means of economic instruments, the market is structured to guarantee a necessary coherence between the activities of independent enterprises and planned development. In the decentralized model one of the chief elements external to the market is the set of prices on basic factors of production which may be determined by calculation carried out centrally.

Despite such limitations, it is a real enough market to disclose actual, detailed substitution rates within the framework of central planning decisions. There are sellers and purchasers of the means of production who make independent decisions on the basis of their reckoning of profitability. Prices, when compared with expected results from a specific means of production, figure in the equilibrium of supply and demand for producer goods. This holds for producer goods destined as current production and for investment goods. One source of the demand for investment goods derives from the enterprise's own means which are expended for the most profitable outputs. In the second place, centrally provided means for productive investment are also included in the calculation of enterprises; they are distributed, in principle, on credit terms with minimal attempts to control the physical structure of investment inputs. Hence, in this case also, price influences choice. By contrast in the centralized model, in which the input-mix is determined by in-kind distribution, price becomes merely a book-keeping device. If an investor is assigned 100 tons of X at a price 200, he is accordingly assigned a financial subsidy of 20,000; if he obtains a consignment of 100 tons of Y at a price of 220, his financial subsidy becomes 22,000.

The market for means of production in a decentralized model thus makes it possible to form equilibrium prices for producer goods; stated more cautiously and heeding the planned framework within which the market mechanism operates, it is better to speak of *sui generis* equilibrium prices. This does not mean that the function of pricing producer goods must wholly be left to the market, even in the area of detailed price relations in the framework laid down by

central decisions which we are considering here. The central authority may take active measures to intervene in the effects of the operation of the market mechanism, it may introduce alterations into the price structure, and so on. The market, however, is always an important source of information. It makes clear the actual rates of substitution and the flexibility of reaction to changes in the indices of choice alternatives. Thus it provides an indispensable basis for planned pricing (at least at present levels of economic sophistication).

Considerable space has been devoted to studying criteria and potentialities for differences in actual price and basic price ratios for means of production, both in demand and in supply, and so an indispensable (at least in the present stage of development of the methods for studying economic relations) basis has been laid down for the planned determination of the prices of the means of production, taking into account the scarcity ratios. Perhaps the importance of the problem justifies the space, particularly since it gave us some opportunity to touch upon a number of other questions, primarily the connection between 'direct' and 'indirect' economic calculation in socialism. Moreover, it seems that the place and role of the market in the decentralized model can be seen more clearly against such a background.

Only one more problem remains to be considered in appraising how far the requirements for a price system in the decentralized model are realistic. This is the problem of reconciling fire and water—of securing sufficient price flexibility while preserving prices as parameters for enterprises. There is no need to return to the importance of a simultaneous realization of both these postulates; it has been made quite clear in the course of our argument. The problem now is whether the state organs of price policy are technically able to adjust the price system to changing circumstances in a sufficiently flexible way.

It seems impossible to give a general answer to this question. Too many specific factors, including organizational and personal ones, are involved. What it is possible to do on a theoretical basis is to draw attention to some problems which have to be taken into consideration in any case.

In the first place, the price flexibility required by a decentralized model is not identical with continually changing prices. We have already discussed this. In a planned economy a relatively high degree of price stability by no means hinders the inclusion of a market mechanism. In a decentralized model the planning authority also has at its disposal adequate means for counteracting any price variations resulting from temporary causes; one might say accidental in relation to the fundamental trends in the economy. Not every change in

supply or demand patterns demands changed prices, and it is not always necessary to change prices in order to bring about changes in the structure of supply or demand. Market equilibrium must not be treated as a situation quantitatively defined with such absolute precision that it can appear only in given circumstances and only for a unique set of prices. In general, equilibrium is attainable within certain limits for different prices. It is disturbed only after overstepping these limits.[1] The problem is not how to adjust prices to all changes in conditions, but only to the essential ones. Moreover, when the direction or scale of price changes are undesirable from the point of view of social preferences, price adjustments should only be made when all other ways of maintaining equilibrium have been exhausted (e.g. the price of articles of primary need should only be raised when all the available means for increasing their supply have been exhausted).

In the second place, maintaining the pricing function apart from enterprises is not identical with the localization of this function in special state bodies which would unilaterally determine prices directly. For the problem is not that of depriving the enterprise of all initiative in this matter, but of making it impossible to manoeuvre prices in order to achieve unjustified advantages, especially those afforded by a monopolistic position. Protection against such a threat does not demand that these special organs be given the exclusive right to establish and alter prices in every case or for every item.

Sometimes it is sufficient to check the reasoning behind requests made by enterprises themselves, sensitive as they are to changes in economic circumstance. In other cases it may prove sufficiently effective to establish maximum or minimum prices, to set up the rates of turnover tax, and so on. As already indicated there may even be cases when the conditions of competition in some fields will itself eliminate the possibility of a monopolistic influence on price; in that case there is no need at all for the application of any special forms of control. At the same time, it is quite clear that in many cases it is only the direct establishment of prices by the state which can guarantee that prices will be independent of the enterprises; this is especially true of basic consumer and producer goods. Generally, however, the state's range of instruments for controlling the price system and movements within it, is rather wide. Careful selection of methods increases the chances of obtaining the required flexibility of prices without affecting their parametric nature in relation to enterprises.

[1] See M. Pohorille, 'Ceny produktów rolnych' ('The prices of agricultural products') in *Zagadnienia ekonomii politycznej socjalizmu* (*Problems of the Political Economy of Socialism*), 2nd ed., p. 411.

Finally, we should refer here to a question on which we have already touched in another context. This is the question of assessing price ratios and their movements in close relation to all the other problems of the plan and in particular to balancing. If, in determining both short and long range proportions of output and distribution, prices are appropriately utilized, then one source of the many difficulties facing price setting organs disappears. For, on the one hand, initially we can eliminate any solutions to the problems of balance which unnecessarily undermine the stability of the price system. Furthermore, changes in prices which are expected are included in the plan from the beginning and synchronized with the expected changes in the structure of supply and demand in consumer and producer goods. It is to be noted that the great importance of full-scale inclusion of price planning in the whole system of planning cannot be limited to the problems discussed here.[1]

In conclusion we can say there are no grounds for supposing that it is theoretically impossible to obtain a flexible system of prices which is at the same time parametric. It is, however, something which may be difficult to achieve in certain cases; so that even here the necessity of certain compromises is not excluded.

Pure and mixed solutions

Given our earlier description of the centralized model, our present consideration of the pros and cons of the decentralized model implies which is more suitable for properly dividing society's labour in socialism. As a rule, the principles of the decentralized model are not inconsistent with the need for the control authority to establish independently lines and rates of development on the basis of its long-term preferences. Since the instruments for influencing operative decisions are purely economic (employing enterprise self-interest) we can assume that output proportions based on central preferences will frequently be achieved more accurately and more efficiently than in the centralized model. Similarly the decentralized model makes possible fuller achievement of the demands of the law of value within a centrally established frame of reference. This is so primarily because of greater flexibility in the adjustment of mixes of both outputs and inputs by the enterprises themselves. They can respond to signs deduced from the market without waiting for the initiative of the central authority. Moreover, there exists what we have called the 'opportunity for self-development' by virtue of ensuring a

---

[1] The main importance of the use of 'objectively determined evaluations in the process of planning lies in the organic correspondence between the physical and value approach'. L. Kantorovich, p. 251.

correlation between the results achieved and the prospects for expansion. This should mean that the decentralized model can guarantee more fully balanced growth by bringing the output and exchange proportions as near as possible to those of the law of value without upsetting planned priorities.

Nevertheless if the desired model of a planned economy with a built-in market mechanism is adopted, that does not exclude all administrative methods. I have already made this reservation in emphasizing at various points the need for 'compromise' in mixed solutions.

It is obviously difficult to give an exhaustive list of the situations in which the market mechanism ought to be supported or even replaced by administrative measures. It is, however, tempting to give at least some idea of the factors which prompt us to caution in adopting a purist attitude toward using the market mechanism.

The grounds for allowing a conditional use of administrative measures are composed of several layers. Nearest the surface lie what we might call the subjective factors. The market mechanism is not to be a connection between independent capitalist enterprises, but a means for the realization of the primary aims of the plan. It demands a high degree of precision and a strict correlation between 1. the type of instruments employed and the quantitative solutions adopted, and 2. the goals of economic activity. In an economy lacking primary social aims there is no criterion for assessing whether, for example, the structure of prices is correct or incorrect. A price structure which yields a greater supply of the good A is no better and no worse than a price structure which gives an increased supply of the good B. A planned economy, however, always possesses a point of reference, which means that while one set of prices may serve for the realization of the planning aims, another may not. Thus, if we are unable to construct instruments whose influence on the enterprise decisions is sufficiently precise, then we must make direct decisions and use administrative methods to ensure their execution.

The precision of economic instruments (hence the rational range of applicability of the market mechanism, the degree of enterprise autonomy and so on) depends on the ability and experience of the managerial personnel at different levels. It also depends on the development of information services, techniques of programming and many other similar factors. These factors obviously change over time; both purely deductive reasoning and the observation of the actual process of socialist economic evolution allow us to state that these changes are progressive—the ability to construct and apply economic instruments of precision is increased. Simultaneously, it is quite apparent that the technical know-how in using the market

N

mechanism has not yet reached a level which would allow us to neglect those subjective factors which necessitate using administrative methods. Moreover, in an absolute sense such a level will never be attained. The complex incentive system needed to fulfil planned tasks by means of purely economic measures will always contain gaps of some kind. There, use of administrative methods will prove unavoidable.

The second layer is laid by those economic circumstances which necessitate rapid far-reaching changes in a country's economic structure. I do not share the opinion that rapid industrialization requires unlimited centralization of decision-making (and hence that everything which was done in this respect was reasonable), even in its initial phases. However, there is no doubt that violent changes in the economic structure create the type of strains, and on such a scale, which make the use of purely economic measures insufficiently effective in some sectors and quite impossible in others. A large number of painful bottle-necks produce a very sharp need for using highly selective central measures. In that case planning orders expressed in physical terms are sometimes more useful than the market mechanism which, by the nature of things, involves larger or smaller aggregates.[1]

One result of disproportions produced by heavy strains on the economy is the difficulty and, in some periods, the impossibility, of securing the basic conditions for the efficient functioning of the market mechanism—a buyer's market. Many of the above arguments used to refute the criticisms of the market mechanism then partially or even wholly lose their validity.

Finally there is the problem of the third layer, perhaps the most important theoretically. There are factors which in part justify using administrative measures even in conditions which might be termed normal when contrasted with those prevailing at a period of 'an industrialization leap'. Here we must assume that central authority will avoid errors which could create unnecessary strains in the economy.

Sometimes one encounters the view that the need to supplement the market mechanism by administrative measures is caused solely (apart from subjective factors) by structural disproportions and hence that it should not be ascribed to the socialist economy as such. This was my impression from reading some Yugoslav studies[2] and

[1] The connection between the strains which characterize the initial stage of industrialization and the usefulness of some of the methods peculiar to the centralized model were discussed in chapter 3 (see pp. 83–4 and p. 70).

[2] See for example B. Jelič, 'Neki aspekti dejstva plana tržišta u nasoj privredi', *Ekonomist*, Belgrade, No. 1–2, 1958.

other discussions. In my opinion such a view amounts to unjustified faith in the unconditional value of the market mechanism. It is unjustified from the same standpoint as the view excludes all market elements in the initial stage of industrialization. The latter position shows an unjustified faith in the absolute value of administrative methods.

To me, certain basic features of a socialist economy exhibit theoretical justification for the view that the market mechanism cannot be applied in a pure form. The socialist economy provides for a rapid growth rate which is closely connected with a high degree of capacity utilization (given the level of technology and organization) and usually with full employment. At the same time personal incomes grow continually in line with increases in the supply of goods and services. The total of these factors is that even when much care is taken to obtain general equilibrium, sectional and temporary bottle-necks cannot be avoided. These in turn lead to a certain rigidity and limit the possibilities for substitution for flexible reactions to market stimuli. In these cases the criticisms of the market mechanism made by Dobb and Baran are directly opposed.[1]

The bottle-necks referred to above obviously should not be confused with the result of overstraining the economy because of violent changes in its structure. However, even in the most normal circumstances, the socialist economy cannot be deprived of those highly selective instruments that are administrative measures, especially when they are employed with moderation. Simultaneously it should be recalled that charges of rigidity against centralized management are justified only when its methods are used as a rule. Then the consequence involves an enormous number of detailed relationships and alternatives. Furthermore, in specific cases involving those major shifts in the economy which are best viewed centrally, the use of planning directives may prove useful and even indispensable if speed is a factor.

Finally, there arises the question of counteracting dangerous monopolistic practices by enterprises. The factors we have just touched on add to the importance of this problem. If it is impossible to remove completely all rigidities hampering adjustment in a centralized system, it may also be impossible to eliminate monopolistic practices by economic means. This is doubly true if such factors as the lack of a buyer's market are involved. And it is not mitigated even if we assume that these weaknesses are limited to certain sectors and certain periods, and that economic instruments are wisely constructed and applied. Moreover, the position of an

[1] See p. 35, *supra*.

enterprise must be paired with a socialist economy's characteristically high concentration of production and its planned specialization. Obviously, the basic counterforce to the threat of monopolistic practices is contained in the principle of 'prices independent of the enterprise' (pricing and strict price control are thought by some economists to be administrative procedures). However, this is not always enough. It may happen that an enterprise will exploit its monopolistic position and exert pressure on the state pricing organs. It can do this by failing to increase the supply of a given product in order to avoid a fall in price. In such cases, beyond the economic instruments for producing a socially optimum utilization of capacities, it may prove necessary to apply obligatory indices for the volume of output. This could apply to either total output, the output of particular goods, assortments, or both.

In conclusion, factors which we have described amply support the assertion that every concrete system or organization of a socialist economy ought to make some provision for using administrative methods.

We are at once faced with the question as to whether this is equivalent to saying that a concrete system of functioning of a socialist economy must be a mixture of market elements and of a system of orders. I would like to stress that I reject such an interpretation. Perhaps the worst of many possibilities is to try to unite mechanically elements which are organically connected with different models. Every model has its own internal logic and it is, in general, more dangerous to disturb this logic than to adopt a poorer solution but in a consistent manner.

To preserve the internal logic of a model is not, however, to purge the system of management of every form coming from outside. The system which prevailed uninterruptedly for a quarter of a century in the socialist countries—roughly until 1955—cannot be blamed for being inconsistent, even though it contained certain elements of decentralization and markets. The logic of the centralized model was not disturbed, since these 'foreign' elements played a secondary role, subordinate to the fundamental principles on which the system was based. It is clear that the introduction of even such limited external elements, although necessary and advantageous, resulted in various kinds of conflicts.

According to our reasoning, the place occupied and part played by administrative methods should be seen in a similar way, but inversely. They are to perform auxiliary functions in a system based on the rules of a decentralized model.

To phrase it thus, is to suggest that the application of administrative measures should be limited, but limitation should not be thought

of as strict. The problem is not to determine in advance the areas and scope in which administrative measures may be applied (specifically the permissible number of imperative indices) but mainly to regard economic instruments as the rule and the use of administrative measures as the exception. As an exception they should be resorted to only in the case of empirically justified necessity. *The Theses of the Economic Council*, 1957, wisely interpret it thus: 'In order to carry out the planned control of development and of the activity of industry, the planning authorities should employ in the first place economic instruments, and then, if indispensable, administrative measures: wherever possible, these ought to be direct contacts and not administrative orders'.[1]

The second principle is closely related and states that economic measures should not be discarded where they are in themselves inadequate, without administrative measures. We have already discussed one situation of this kind. Merely because central allocation of scarce factors in physical units is needed, this should not exclude reflecting the scarcity in prices.[2] The same is true of other similar problems, e.g. a planning order to produce a particular assortment of goods ought to be linked as closely as possible with an appropriate arrangement of economic incentives. Failure to observe this principle over a period of time leads to a failure of the economic conditions in which enterprises operate to correspond to the general needs of the economy. Then an unnecessary conflict arises between the interest of the enterprises (the personal interest of their employees) and the interest of the national economy. As a result, the importance of administrative measures is increased not because of objective economic needs, but because of the failure of the economic circumstances to be adjusted to these needs. A divergence between actual economic proportions and the economic measures for affecting low-level activity has a damaging effect. Not only does it result in immediate economic losses and distortions, but it also harms the sense of a common interest and of harmonious operation at all levels. In a socialist economy these should be constantly reinforced.

The importance of the question of organization

We have elaborated a system of the functioning of a socialist economy based on the decentralized model and supplemented by administrative measures. Yet as a system it is not free from those conflicts inherent in a centralized model which contains certain

[1] See *Dyskusja o polskim modelu gospodarczym*, (Warsaw, 1957), p. 264.
[2] See p. 168 above.

elements of the market mechanism. To eliminate or alleviate these conflicts requires that a number of complicated problems be solved, including questions of organization. These questions have not yet had much consideration, and indeed, detailed consideration is, at best, difficult. However, attention must be drawn to at least one factor—the part played by organizational units superior to the enterprise.

For the purposes of argument, we used a simplified system of two levels; these were: the central authority and the enterprise. In practice, an intermediate level must be added in order to satisfy inherent tendencies towards concentration in modern production, tendencies which are particularly strong in a socialist economy. In a centralized model, the intermediate level is an administrative one; it is an extended arm of the central authority, a link in the system which serves to allocate the tasks and specify constraints determined by the higher authority; a cog in the mechanism which executes these orders. In a decentralized model the intermediate levels, where they are indispensable, should be economic organisms seeking solutions for the common problems of the enterprises of a given branch of production (horizontal organization) or for a group of enterprises which are vertically integrated. Within an association of enterprises sample questions covered are investment policy, specialization, co-operation and the optimum division of the output programme among enterprises. If it is assumed that when an enterprise joins an association, it has a vested interest in the economic success of the whole organization, then it follows that a number of interconnections thus far categorized as relations between the central authority and the enterprise are to be found in the relations of the central authority and associations of enterprises. In other words, what we have called in our analysis of the decentralized model, 'an enterprise', should not always be understood as an individual enterprise in the usual sense, but in a broader way so as to embrace the higher oganization form—the association of enterprises. The size and manner of organizing these enterprises may vary, but one fundamental feature of basic importance for the application of the market mechanism must be common to all. For the market mechanism to apply they must be economic and not administrative bodies. They ought to be units which make their own calculation of inputs and outputs and aim at the profit maximization within the framework of central decisions.

Assigning a major role to enterprise associations in the decentralized model involves a number of dangers, chief of which is that of monopolistic tendencies. At the same time, the smaller the number of these organizations, the easier they are to control. It is much

easier to employ both economic measures and co-ordinating measures. Its usefulness is enhanced when some special combination of economic and administrative measures is needed. Thus it is easier to use different methods in controlling the relations between the central authority and the associations on the one hand and between the association and the enterprises on the other.[1]

The questions facing these groups of enterprises—their structure and principles of operation—are only a fragment of the complex organizational matters which must be solved if a system based on the decentralized model is to function properly. Besides these, there are the problems of organizing central planning and policy-making bodies of control and co-ordination at the branch level, at the regional level, and so on. It would be a serious error to suppose that the transition from a centralized to a decentralized planned economy eradicates organizational dilemma or that the organizational apparatus is replaced by the market mechanism. The management of socialist economy, guided by a social scale of preference, is by no means an easy task. It cannot be performed without an appropriate apparatus whose maintenance is *sui generis* the price paid by society for the general advantages of the planned economic management. The market existence in a planned economy does not obviate this necessity, and although it is perhaps true that the required apparatus is smaller than that required in a centralized model, it has at the same time to be a qualitatively superior one.

Thus, it is not true, as appearances might suggest, that the main difference between the decentralized and the centralized model is the degree of complexity. In some cases using economic measures may prove more complicated because of the greater precision of the mechanism. Then we see that justification for the market mechanism in a planned economy lies first in the assessment of its results.

[1] The importance of associations to flexible operation and proper adaptation to actual conditions is emphasized by Kalecki. 'If enterprises were grouped in concerns still employing *khozraschot* the body immediately superior to an enterprise would itself be a gigantic enterprise. Incentives and orders issuing from the central authorities would then affect in the first case the concern as a whole . . . On the other hand incentives and orders issued by the management of the concern to the enterprises belonging to it could be, but would not necessarily have to be, of the same type. It is not impossible that individual concerns would evolve other systems for their internal use which would be more suitable to the specific requirements of a particular productive branch', M. Kalecki, 'Schemat nowego systemu bodźców i nakazów' ('The outline of a new system of incentives and orders') *Zycie Gospodarcze*, no. 29, 1957. Here we should remember the above remarks concerning price differentiation between enterprises on the basis of unified price obtained by the association (see p. 151 n.).

Conclusions

The conclusions to be drawn from our study may be summarized as follows:

1. For the fullest exploitation of the possibilities of the socialist economic system, the problems of its functioning must be solved. As a system it creates the basis for a conscious, planned determination of economic processes in the social interest. There are no reasons to believe that there is only one definite model of operation appropriate to a socialist economy. On the contrary, within the bounds of socialist production relations, a variety of solutions are acceptable and they may differ not only in detail but also in their basic conceptions. This justifies the use of the expression 'models of functioning of a socialist economy' and the inclusion of the theory of such models in the political economy of socialism.

2. The operation of the law of value in socialism is, and will continue to be, an important field of study for economic theory. However, the relationship between the law of value in its strict sense, and the mechanism of functioning of a socialist economy is by no means, as has been supposed, a direct one. By delineating the operation of the law of value and the application of money–commodity forms, we place our problem on a more suitable theoretical plane.

3. An analysis of the objective factors which regulate the division of labour in socialism (one of which is the law of value) does not *a priori* rule out either of the two basic models of functioning of socialist economy—the centralized model and the model of a planned economy with a built-in market mechanism ('the decentralized model'). The analysis does provide a number of basic criteria for assessing the desirability of using either model as a basis.

4. In my opinion, comparing the chief assumptions of either model given these criteria demonstrates the advantages of basing actual systems of the functioning of a socialist economy on the decentralized model.

I hope this last point, doubtless the most controversial, will not be interpreted to mean that I hold the decentralized model to be superior in an absolute sense. And when viewed against the whole work, I

hope it will not be said that I have ignored the difficulties of practically applying its rules. Finally, three points which I have emphasized ought to make such an interpretation impossible. In the first place, no system of functioning can be considered in isolation from the nature of economic tasks of a given period. Specifically I refer to the connection between the degree of centralization and the strains of the period when the socio-economic structure is rapidly reshaped. In the second place, and apart from the initial circumstances of rapid industrialization, decentralized rules of operation cannot be put into practice in their pure form without being supplemented by some kind of centralistic 'admixtures'. In the third place, for a really effective functioning of a decentralized model, more effective than a system constructed on a centralistic model, a series of conditions must be met. They are compelling even at the general level of this analysis, but would be more so with more detailed studies of prices and pricing, inter-enterprise and inter-level contacts, incentive arrangements, etc.

The point to emphasize is that, in so far as possible, the system of functioning of a socialist economy should be based on the principles of the decentralized model. In given conditions how far such a course of action can proceed lies outside the sphere of theoretical considerations.

The advantages of the decentralized model are to be found in a number of factors which I have attempted to present, especially in chapter 5. Each of these factors taken separately is important for a general evaluation. But, they are of greatest importance when taken together as parts of a unified concept and with such a global concept two aspects of the situation seem to be particularly important.

The first is that the whole conception is imbued with the spirit of democratic centralism. As a term unfortunately too often abused in describing practical forms of economic organization, its principle is a classic example of the dialectical unity of opposites. It reflects the real contradiction between two equally objective needs of a socialist economy—the need for centralism and the need for democracy in its methods of control. The conception of a decentralized model originates from a recognition of this contradiction and constitutes the way in which it may be resolved.

Critics of the decentralized model have often objected that it represents ideas retrograde to the objective tendencies of economic progress. They say these tendencies are accompanied by a growing centralization of resource allocation and support their argument by pointing to the experience of capitalist countries. It ought to be quite clear from our analysis of the decentralized model why this objection is off target. Even in a decentralized model the extent to

which decision-making is concentrated and the potential for centrally influencing the whole of economic processes is incomparably greater than in any capitalist economy however strongly it claims to be a 'mixed' one. The differences are of a qualitative character and derive from differences in the socio-economic order and its specific laws.

At the same time the decentralized model also allows for the other side of the objective conditions of economic progress. This is the democratization of the forms of economic management. Its principles limit the area of centralization to an indispensable minimum leaving as wide an area of autonomy as possible to lower levels. As chief instruments for influencing low-level decisions, the ones selected are those which harmonize the activities of different economic planes and which favour development of the creative initiative of each other.

The second main feature of a generalized approach to a decentralized model is that it fully recognizes the necessity to express effectively the social interest in terms of the self-interest of groups, e.g. the staff of the enterprises, and individuals. This boils down to the problem of economic incentives.

The place assigned to economic incentives is still a frequent source of misunderstandings. They often find expression in the criticism of what is called 'fetishization' of material incentives. It is difficult to deny the truth of the assertion that incentives are not everything, and that apart from them it is necessary to take into account a broad variety of non-economic motives of human activity and make use of them. However merely because a particular factor is not sufficient by itself to obtain a given effect does not mean that it automatically ceases to be indispensable. This is particularly true of the complex of motivating attitudes governing men in the economic process. Criticism of the 'fetishization' of material incentives sometimes seems to overlook this aspect of the matter.

Economic incentives do not in themselves solve all the problems to be found in the relation of man to his work. However, as long as the social interest is not directly identified with the group or personal interest, an appropriate solution in the field of economic incentives has to be considered as a basic factor influencing human behaviour in the economic process.

We know from experience that an enormous effort—political, educational, organizational—is often necessary to eliminate or alleviate the effects of badly established economic 'rules of the game'. At best these expensive brakes exert their effect for only a short period. It is necessary to demonstrate how much more effective it is considering both current economic interests and long-term aims of the social education of man to create conditions in which political,

educational and organizational factors are consonant with the factors of material interest. The tendency to shift the emphasis to non-economic factors is particularly unfortunate in a situation where the system of material incentives contains errors. Any objective difficulties in overcoming these errors are then made worse due to the subjective factor diminishing the importance of the problem itself.

The decentralized model is realistic in its evaluation of the relation between economic and non-economic motives of human activity in a socialist society. If groups and individuals are made, in a consistent way, materially interested in the effects of their activity, it does not weaken the influence of non-economic factors; on the contrary, it favours their strengthening, especially as the system of incentives in a decentralized model is based on profitability, synthetically reflecting all aspects of economic activity.

Democratic centralism and the recognition of the wide role of economic incentives, are mutually dependent, since the initiative 'from below' can be reconciled with the priorities of general economic goals only if economic measures for affecting this initiative are employed as a matter of principle. By uniting these two aspects into a single whole, the decentralized model has a vital significance for the development of socialist self-government and hence in overcoming 'alienation'.

Both the conception of the decentralized model and, even more so, attempts made to convert it in part or in whole into real fact, are obviously today far from being complete. Nevertheless, it seems that the general direction for progress in this field has been correctly perceived—appropriate to the needs of the socialist system, particularly at the new stage of development into which the European socialist countries are now entering.

Index

Hagemejer, W., 70n.
Hayek, F. A., 29, 33–4, 39, 41
Hensel, K. Paul, 64
Hilferding, 20

Industrialization, rapid, 123–4

Jakubowicz, S., 138n.
Jelič, B., 123n., 186n.

Kalecki, M., 174n., 191n.
Kalinnikov, 47
Kantorovich, L., 126n., 167–8, 171, 178, 184n.
Kasevina, A., 97n.
Katz, A., 172n.
Kautsky, K., 20–1, 81
Khozraschot, 24, 43, 77–8, 130–1, 136, 168, 191n.
Khrushchev, Nikita, 73n.
Khudokornov, G., 99n.
Kogan, 50
Kondrashev, D., 79n.
Kondratiev, 47
Kornai, Janos, 70n., 82
Kritzman, Lev, 44, 48n.
Kronrod, J., 77n., 89n., 96
Kugelmann, 53
Kulikov, A., 97n.
Kurowski, Stefan, 64, 98
Kzhyshanovski, G., 45

Labour, 71–5, 90n., 91, 93–5, 103, 107, 109–10, 113–14, 127, 132, 170, 176
Landauer, C., 30n.
Lange, Oscar, 30, 35, 36–7, 39–41, 75, 135, 143
Introduction to Econometrics, 66
Political Economy, 2, 125, 141n.
(with F. Taylor), *On the Economic Theory of Socialism*, 28, 32–3
Lassenhous, H., 30n.
Lenin, V. I., 13n., 14, 18, 20, 22–4, 49, 92n.
Leontiev, A., 55n.
Lerner, Abba, 30, 37, 108, 132n.

'Statics and Dynamics in Socialist Economies', 32–3
Lewis, W. A., 81
Liberman, 86n.
Liebknecht, Wilhelm, 13n.
Lipiński, Edward, 16n., 102
Lipiński, Jan, 167n.

Marx, Karl, 13–15, 16n., 18, 20, 28, 88, 91, 93
Capital, 14–15, 17, 19, 99, 105, 116, 170
Critique of Political Economy, 124
letters, 53
Marxism, 3–5, 12, 61, 85, 88, 90, 100, 156, 167
Marxists, 12–13, 34, 40, 42, 60, 71, 94, 95, 97, 136
old guard, 44
Mendelson, 48n.
Minc, Hilary, 84n.
Mises, L. von, 28–9, 33–4, 39, 41, 46
Money, 21–2, 24–7, 45, 51, 71–80, 82, 89, 90n., 96, 130, 150
Morecka, Zofia, 72n.
Mosse, R., 75n.
Motilev, 48n., 52

New Economic Policy (NEP), 22–4, 43–7
Novozhilov, V., 8n.
Nussbaumer, Adolf, 179

Ostrovitianov, K., 90n., 94n., 97n.

Pajestka, J., 160n.
Pareto, V., 28–9
Pashukanis, 43, 48n., 52
People's democracies, 84–5
Pierson, N. G., 28
Pilič, Bogdan, 73n., 168n.
Pohorille, M., 160n., 165n., 183n.
Poland, 1, 34, 68n., 79n., 84n., 86–8, 160, 189
Economic Council, 154n., 174n.
economists' conferences, 90, 96

D0857537